A BUN IN THE OVEN

A Bun in the Oven

How the Food and Birth Movements
Resist Industrialization

Barbara Katz Rothman

NEW YORK UNIVERSITY PRESS

New York and London

NEW YORK UNIVERSITY PRESS
New York and London
www.nyupress.org

References to Internet websites (URLs) were accurate at the time of writing. Neither the author nor New York University Press is responsible for URLs that may have expired or changed since the manuscript was prepared.

ISBN: 978-1-4798-5530-8 (hardback)
ISBN: 978-1-4798-8230-4 (paperback)

For Library of Congress Cataloging-in-Publication data, please contact the Library of Congress.

New York University Press books are printed on acid-free paper, and their binding materials are chosen for strength and durability. We strive to use environmentally responsible suppliers and materials to the greatest extent possible in publishing our books.

Manufactured in the United States of America

10 9 8 7 6 5 4 3 2 1

Also available as an ebook

CONTENTS

ACKNOWLEDGMENTS

This book would not have happened without Jon Deutsch. Jon introduced me to food studies, listened to my early impressions of the relationship between the two movements, and handed me my book title and outline. He gave me a reading list, patiently read draft after draft, corrected my misunderstandings in the world of food. Anything I do understand about the food movement I owe to Jon; any ongoing misperceptions are my own.

Writing requires readers, people who will read drafts, point out errors or moments of confusion, badly organized thoughts, and all the rest. Ilene Kalish contributed greatly in her role of enthusiastic editor. I am particularly grateful to the following readers for their patience with draft after draft: Wendy Simonds, Holliday Tyson, Jacqueline Wolf for her attention to history, Scarlett Lindeman, and Keisha Goode. I have never published anything without the help of Eileen Moran's thoughtful, politically insightful reading, and thank her again for all of her time and help.

A number of people did various kinds of research assistance on this project, some more officially, some on an ad hoc basis, sending along articles and news stories, checking grocery shelves for an odd product, and more. I want to thank all, but most especially Erika Eitland (whose research assistance was another gift provided by Jonathan Deutsch), Lisa Pollich, Scarlett Lindeman, Daniel Colb Rothman, Leah Colb Rothman, Alexandrea Ravenelle, and Koby Oppenheim. I want to thank Marisa Tramontano for taking on "dissertation advisor role" when needed, and hope to return the favor.

Finally, Holliday Tyson led me out of a dark corner and into the sunlight, and made writing happen again in my life. My gratitude is boundless.

1

A Tale of Two Social Movements

This is a tale of two social movements.

There are people dedicated to improving the way we eat, and people dedicated to improving the way we birth. Both movements move back and forth between the intimately individual—the kitchen and the bedroom, the mouth and the womb—and the larger systems in which intimacy is housed, agribusiness and the biomedical industry. The people at work in these social movements seek change through individual education, but also, in larger ways, they are doing more. They are working on social systems, working with the checks and balances on medical and agricultural monopolies. They are seeking ways to change how the economy structures the "choices" that are available to individuals.

For both of these movements, one could say it is the best of times and it is the worst of times. It is the age of wisdom, it is the age of foolishness, it is the age of organic kale chips, it is the age of McDonald's, it is the epoch of belief, it is the epoch of incredulity, it is the moment of the unattended water birth, it is the moment of the elective cesarean section, it is the season of light, it is the season of darkness, it is the time of the rising of the star of the master chef, it is the time of ubiquitous processed corn, it is the spring of hope, it is the winter of despair.

I'm jealous. My movement, the one I've labored in for almost forty years, is the birth movement. The food movement, for all of the despair, incredulity, and foolishness, has had clear successes, while mine—sadly, not so much. The word "birthies" gets marked in red by my spell check, but "foodies" has made it into the vocabulary. And therein lies my problem. Basically from where I sit, the food movement is making strides on a dozen fronts: the need for a more natural, more organic, and tastier diet is acknowledged everywhere. Vegetable carts bring fresh fruits and vegetables to poor neighborhoods. High-end kitchen appliances are hot items even for people who mostly microwave. Exotic-food trucks ply the city streets. Anyone who reads the newspaper knows that school lunches need improving. People who don't really have the slightest interest in or knowledge of cooking watch cooking shows. Julia Child is some kind of a national heroine—played by Meryl Streep! Can you be more successful than that?

And my movement? The birth movement? Well, people might know there is one. They've probably heard of "home birth," which is some kind of progress from forty years ago. They cannot pronounce "midwifery," but they've heard of midwives. We got one movie out of it that maybe somebody heard of: *The Business of Being Born*. Thank you, Ricki Lake. I'm forever grateful, sure, but I'd way rather have Meryl Streep playing Ina May (oh, sorry, you probably never heard of her either—the midwives' Julia Child. Ina May Gaskin's book *Spiritual Midwifery*[1] didn't make the splash that Julia Child's TV show *The French Chef*[2] did, but it got some popular attention to the movement—more on that later).

I've been involved in the birth movement since 1973, starting with my first pregnancy, when I decided I wanted a home birth.[3] It was at a moment when home birth was pretty much unheard of in my world. Ordinary people went to doctors, who sent them into hospitals in labor and sent them home with babies a few days later. In seeking services and providers, I very clearly aligned myself with the outsiders. Outsiders are what make a social movement.

And food? When did I become part of a food movement? What constitutes being an outsider in the world of food? When I first baked bread? Bought a 1960s gourmet guide to New York? Went into Chinatown restaurants down dark strange alleys and pointed to the next table to order? Proposed a little study (which I never finished) on older women's memories of food and cooking in their lives? Or was it the moment when Jon Deutsch, then my colleague at the City University of New York, and an important figure in the world of food studies, called me, asked me about that unfinished work, and introduced me to the world of food studies? Most definitely it was when Jon and I introduced a food studies doctoral concentration into the CUNY Graduate Center—a PhD in food! Not food science, laboratory coats and agriculture, but a doctoral concentration in the social, political, and cultural relationships that make food what it is in our lives.

Trying to think through my own relationships to these two movements, I put on my sociological lens and start thinking about just what makes a social movement. Movements, people say, make waves, which is a good way of thinking about them. Picture a lovely, still body of water. Then picture a lone person splashing—a little ripply thing happens. But picture hundreds of people swimming along in a coordinated way, and the waves that can make. That's how I think of social movements, a few people splashing at the edges, more and more joining, and eventually big waves. Social movements make more than waves, though—they change things. Of course we think of the big social movements, like the French Revolution, the ones that gave us the very word. Grand, sweeping social movements make—or aim to make—enormous societal changes, redefining societies, moving from a dictatorship or monarchy to democracy; or redefining membership in society, like the civil rights, feminism, disability, and LGBT movements. Social movements push at the foundations of society, are collective political challenges to the powers that be.

Charles Dickens was writing his books—including *A Tale of Two Cities*[4] and *Great Expectations*[5]—in response to the great social movements of his time, the legacies of the Industrial Revolution, and the nascent workers' movements that it produced. His work exposed the horrible treatment of workers. We are in another era in which workers are very badly treated, and we see the rise of new workers' movements, including the work going on in the fast-food industry and in my own world of exploited adjunct labor in universities. The food and the birth movements, while they certainly include workers in those fields, are focused more on the consumption than the production end of industrialization. The first industrial revolutions remade the way we produce things; this one is remaking the way we produce ourselves, our lives as human beings. The worlds Americans think of as private and outside work, worlds of family and home, are increasingly usurped by industrial products and thinking. What are available to people in private spaces—the dinner table, the birthroom, the deathbed—are all being controlled more and more under industrial rubrics, with profit a core value. It was hard for workers to be taken seriously as political and moral actors; it is similarly hard for people as consumers to be taken seriously.

How can one even begin to organize consumers? There is the use of the boycott, a consumption strike, like the segregated bus boycotts of the civil rights movement; the Nestlé boycotts of the 1970s, responding to the company's aggressive marketing of infant formulas in countries where women could not afford not to breastfeed; or the lettuce and grape boycotts organized by United Farm Workers in the same years.[6] But boycotts are only one form of social action consumers take. It is harder to see the work of the food and birth movement as political— too often it is dismissed as elitist, consumerist choices only those with lots of choices could make.[7] But the food and the birth movements are filled with people who are working as consumers and as consumer advocates, working with committed providers to create an alternative to what industrialization offers, and to make that alternative widely available, available to all. That work, those attempts to deindustrialize the way we eat and the way we birth, are what I mean by these two movements.

Is it reasonable to even talk of our shifting relationship with food or with birth as a social movement? You can read a lot of textbooks on social movements and not see much on either of these. Jon and I have commiserated repeatedly about how our interests are seen as trivial within the academic and political worlds in which we move. If we want to study "access" issues, that's worthwhile—suffering and death, those are not trivial, and issues of food and birth can lead to either. Think starvation, malnourishment in impoverished countries or our inner cities; think of maternal mortality—though there we are encouraged to think of it only in impoverished places and not close to home. Think of infant mortality, a point of overlap for our two movements, as lack of access to good maternity care and to a good and healthy diet causes babies to die. The infant mortality rates across the United States, by race and by class, are as clear a map to our inequality as can be found.[8]

It is not only about access issues. Even for people who can get to a supermarket and generally meet nutritional needs, for people who can get to standard medical services and have obstetrical care provided, infant mortality rates still reflect our race and class disparities. For those people, and yes, for wealthy people too, for all people everywhere, food and birth involve life and death. The relationships are more complicated to study as you go up the racial and socioeconomic ladder. The obesity epidemic, type 2 diabetes, and high blood pressure in children, like the same conditions in women in pregnancy, along with the epidemic of cesareans, are all issues of safety, health, life, and death.

I do care about and study those things. I also want to go beyond that and look at the parts of birth and death that deal with life not as measured in years, but life as measured in joy and sorrow, in liveliness. Are the pleasures and joys people experience with birth or with food to be dismissed as trivial? I don't think so at all. Talk to people about their dinners or their births. You will hear stories of humanity, connectedness, social life, the sense of the body—stories about what life is about.

It is *so* easy to make fun of these movements, to see them as "first world problems," the concerns of middle-class white women. I want a movement of birthies, but know full well that "foodies" is itself a trivializing term, objectionable to many within the food movement.[9] Maybe I'm just being contrarian, but I am going to stick with those terms. They capture something I cannot otherwise express. I heard the word "birthies" long before what we now think of as a food movement. It was a kind of joking term we used for the hangers-on in the birth world, those of us who weren't midwives, weren't doing births as our work, but were somehow drawn to that world. My role as a researcher-scholar was anomalous. But there were others who were attending midwifery meetings who were not midwives. We joked we were "midwife groupies," roadies on this tour. We were drawn to birth, just as some of us are drawn to food. We're not chefs, we're not nutrition scientists, we're not making this our life's work. But we think about it, care about it, read about it, and, these days, watch videos about it.

"Activists" would probably be the more acceptable term for participants in a social movement, and for sure, there are both food and birth activists. In the birth world there were couples who handcuffed themselves together before going to the hospital so that the husband could not be put out of the delivery room. There are guerilla gardeners, people who break the law by trespassing to plant vegetables in city lots. There are people who work tirelessly on legislation, in food and in birth. But then there are the rest of us, those whose "activism" is mostly through consumption and networking, who think carefully about how we feed our friends and family, and how we give birth, and do some consciousness raising around that. It is best captured in "lifestyle" issues. Lots of people who don't think of themselves as political are drawn to the values and the art of food and birth. We want to make these better for ourselves and for everyone.

It's not all about organic kale chips and water births with yoga chants. When I find myself talking or writing in an impassioned way about birth, there is always someone around to dismiss it as a "white girl's problem," first world troubles that have no meaning for poor people, for people of color. The same thing happens in the food world: start talking critically about industrial farming and production, and someone pops up to tell you that the real problem is food insecurity, just getting enough food to eat. But there are risks and threats posed to our health and our lives by the way we in America manage birth and food, and as is always the case with risks, the people who are most vulnerable are the ones who are already "at risk."

Industrialized birth has caused enormous damage to poor women and specifically to women of color: just look at African American maternal and infant mortality statistics in the United States compared with the rest of the world.[10] And within the United States, the work done by midwives with "at risk" communities (read poor, Native American, African American, and some Latino communities) has demonstrated that another approach can and does bring down those death rates.[11] And this of course could not be more true in the world of food as well, where industrialized food has had its most striking health impacts for poor and African American people in particular, and the food movement, including work on the food stamps program and public school lunches, can save lives. Which children are showing up with early-onset diabetes, with high blood pressure in grade school? These, like infant mortality rates, reflect the race and class stratification of America. And if there are, as I will be arguing, social and emotional costs to the way that we manage birth and food in America, there too, who is going to be most hurt by those?

So what are these movements for, and what are they against? Why am I linking such seemingly disparate things?

Bear with me for a moment as I paint with a very broad brush now, details to be filled in later in this book: The course of the twentieth century saw birth and food swallowed up by science and industry. Food is produced by agribusiness; babies are born in industrialized "tertiary care" hospitals. Mass production was claimed to bring us better outcomes, better living through chemistry. Sometimes it worked—certainly in some ways it worked—but sometimes it failed us miserably. Ideas of cleanliness got twisted to mean sterile environments—while actual food production plants and actual hospitals remain sources of infection.

Science toyed with science fiction. Did we even need food—messy, unpredictable, variable cooking in our own little kitchens—at all? Or did we just need nourishment? Could we be fed like astronauts, little freeze-dried packages of nutrients? Good-bye oranges and squeezers, hello Tang! And did we need messy, painful, unpredictable, variable birth? Or could we knock women out and bring them to only when the baby was clean and wrapped? Schedule cesarean sections and let the women lie there like a car being worked on as someone else extracted the baby? Or can we skip it altogether, finally get that mechanical womb operating? Meanwhile, if food needs to be handled and babies to be birthed, can we just outsource it all, give it to the poorest of us to do? Enter the low-wage restaurant worker, enter India's surrogacy industry.

And through the course of that century, splashing at the edges constantly and occasionally coalescing into a social movement, were people who said no. People who said that you are what you eat, that what you eat and how you make it and how you serve it and how you come together to eat it are what makes us who we are. Food matters. Foodies. And there were people who said birth matters, that it is a crucial moment in not only bringing a baby into the world but in the making of a mother, the making of family. Birthies. The food people splashed harder, I guess, their issues resonated more widely—after all, everyone eats all the time, and only some of us birth and that only a few times in our lives. The food movement has had an impact and is shaping us a bit now. The birth people—well, we're still trying.

Part of what I am learning in looking at these two movements together is what makes a social movement work. How does it come to resonate? In sociology, we talk about that as framing a movement—how a social movement presents itself in terms of the values of the society it aims to change.[12] Because you don't really change from completely outside, not with the kind of social movements I'm talking about. This isn't armed revolution—this really is about changing people's hearts and minds.

Food and birth are part of a class of social movements that are meaning-seeking. They are responses to a deadening kind of society, the world C. Wright Mills described as an era of discontent, a time of unease.[13] Mills was a critic of "mass society," "mass culture," the increasingly proletarianized world of the mid-twentieth century. It's a world you can have fun with as you watch *Mad Men*, but there was a kind of deadening quality to the increasing homogenization of American culture. The new middle class of industrial society came from the rise of a world of fundamentally meaningless work, and thus the need to find meaning outside work.

Eli Zaretsky is a historian who wrote about this, brilliantly I think, in a little book published in the early 1970s, *Capitalism, the Family and Personal Life.*[14]

> The rise of industry separated most people (or families) from the ownership of productive property. As a result, "work" and "life" were separated; proletarianization split off the outer world of alienated labour from an inner world of personal feeling. . . . An ethic of personal fulfillment has become the property of the masses of people, though it has different meanings for men and for women, and for different strata of the proletariat. Much of this search for personal meaning takes place within the family and is one reason for the persistence of the family in spite of the decline of many of its earlier functions.[15]

People can and have made worldviews, religions, value systems out of their relationship to the land and the sea, out of their work as farmers, fishers, hunters. But as factory workers? Meaning-seeking moved from work to home.

With advanced industrialization, women, along with children, were no longer valued as workers; child labor became a social evil, and women's labor was marginalized to "housework":

> The housewife emerged, alongside the proletarian—the two characteristic laborers of developed capitalist society. While the man went out and did the meaningless but necessary work in the world of production, women—whether they too were on the assembly lines or not—were expected to take care of the home and family. Her tasks extended beyond the material labor of the family to include responsibility for the "human values" which the family was thought to preserve: love, personal happiness, domestic felicity.[16]

And, perhaps most powerfully, mass production transformed consumption into an art, a "civilizing" experience, the route of enculturation for generations of immigrants.[17] To shop like an American is to be an American.

Birth and food, once so profoundly part of women's world of production, ultimately came to be acts of consumption, all about intelligent, thoughtful, careful shopping, and making good choices.

Decisions about birth and about dinner feel so idiosyncratic, so personal, but they are framed inside a big machine, an industrialized, medicalized, and capitalist system. Let me take an example from another arena—fashion. Think for a moment of how fashion works. There's a point in the film *The Devil Wears Prada* in which a young woman who thinks (as I do of myself) that she's not "into" fashion, that she is separate from that world, that it has no meaning or influence on her life—and here comes Meryl Streep again. The young woman's disdain for fashion is deconstructed in a moment as Streep does a sweeping analysis of her sweater:

> This . . . "stuff"? I see, you think this has nothing to do with you. You go to your closet and you select out, oh I don't know, that lumpy blue sweater, for instance, because you're trying to tell the world that you take yourself too seriously to care about what you put on your back. But what you don't know is that that sweater is not just blue, it's not turquoise, it's not lapis, it's actually cerulean. You're also blithely unaware of the fact that in 2002, Oscar de la Renta did a collection of cerulean gowns. And then I think it was Yves St Laurent, wasn't it, who showed cerulean military jackets? . . . And then cerulean quickly showed up in the collections of 8 different designers. Then it filtered down through the department stores and then trickled on down into some tragic Casual Corner where you, no doubt, fished it out of some clearance bin. However, that blue represents millions of dollars and countless jobs and so it's sort of comical how you think that you've made a choice that exempts you from the fashion industry when, in fact, you're wearing the sweater that was selected for you by the people in this room. From a pile of stuff.[18]

Someone stands in a supermarket and grabs a jar of applesauce. There's a rice pudding recipe his great-grandma made that gets applesauce poured on top. He's not thinking about the history of apple farming in America, the narrowing of apple types that are farmed, the machines that were developed to peel and pit apples, the history of sugar and its place in the slave trade, the source of cinnamon, the way that applesauce became cheap enough so that his immigrant family could afford to buy it to dress up the pudding made out of the leftover rice. It's a personal choice, something special to his family. It's a bit of family tradition he wants to introduce to his children, is feeling like he's a good, modern dad, cooking with his kids, not just picking up ready-made dinner.

Someone is pregnant, thinking about the kind of birth she wants, looking at websites for obstetric practices. This one is all pinks and purples and looks like an ad for an upscale spa; this one shows photos of beautiful light-grain wood-finish floors and towers of technology; this one says it works with a doula trained in acupressure techniques; this one has a woman reading *Family Circle* magazine in a waiting room; this one has an earnest-looking couple leaning forward in conversation with a doctor behind a desk. She picks the one that feels most like her, like the kind of person she is, the kind of family she wants to be making. She isn't thinking about the development of obstetrics and how the doctors drove the midwives out, about how "prenatal care" got developed as a regular surveillance technique, about how obstetrics came to see the fetus as an entrapped patient. She's not even thinking about how each of those obstetrics practices has its own cesarean section rate. It's all so very personal.

In all of these arenas—birth, food, fashion, home design—we feel like we are making individual decisions and choices, reflecting who we are. These are all deeply personal, intimate choices about what will enter and change our bodies. But, to turn back to Mills and his presentation of the relationship between history and biography, or as second-wave feminists put it, the personal is political; these individual choices are made in social contexts.[19] Think hard about birth or about dinner, and you come to understand that the personal exists in the political, that biography occurs within history, that you are, however unique you feel, part of a big machine. Some of us want to make waves—not only seek out a good birth or a lovely dinner, but change the ways that births and dinners are served up. We are making waves against the machine.

When you just engage in personal resistance, try to find a better way for yourself, you're so very open to co-optation—in fashion, food, or birth. Social movements, of course, are always open to co-optation—it's the nature of the machine to steal people away, redirect rebellion. Even when we are feeling or trying to be rebellious, we are challenging society using the tools the society makes available. In the birth world, it was done with interior decorating, like fashion, yet another arena of personal meaning-making. I used to talk about it as hanging a plant on the IV pole. Attractive birth suites, wallpaper, a rocking chair. Over and over again I see them in hospital settings, one or two "birthing rooms," but no one actually using them—everybody risked out, moved out, sent off to the labor and delivery rooms, a third or more to the operating room and c-sections anyway. In the food world, it's about labels on industrial food products that show mamas in kitchens, for foods that were factory-made, the only mamas there working the lines or as underpaid, often immigrant, farm workers. The social movements raise the concerns and issues, and the industries—biomedical or food—respond with co-opting temptations.

There are good reasons why the food movement has had more success. People with some money can experiment, play with food. Every day brings new chances. They can go organic or vegan for a week or a year; try buying locally or growing their own vegetables. They can feel good about an organic, local, vegetarian dinner, but still take genuine pleasure in a rest stop hamburger on a road trip to the next city with a new set of options. It's harder, no matter how rich you are, to "play around" with birth—we get very few chances and, unlike dinner, much really does depend on each and every choice. And unlike dinner, we fear birth. We fear pain, we fear death, we confront our big fears with each and every birth. Ultimately, pain and death are there in our food choices too, but, well, not today. Sure, somebody dies of food poisoning, someone chokes to death on a chunk of food, but we don't look at dinner and worry about it. Diabetes or cancer or heart disease are real problems, but we are not going to die from this food choice at this moment.

But these are also good reasons why a birth movement can work: births are rare. You don't have to start all over again tomorrow morning. You have months to research your options, think carefully and choose your providers, commit yourself to a plan. And those people with options, people who are neither food-insecure and lucky to get enough food of whatever kind for dinner, nor limited to the local clinic that takes Medicaid, do tend to take pregnancy as, among other things, a big reading assignment, and—like dinner—ultimately another moment for informed consumption. There can be better births, and each better birth can be life-changing, life-affirming, in a way that no given meal can be.

Both of these movements face enormous economic forces. You have in both cases a system employing many where a little greening, naturalizing, humanizing doesn't threaten the system and in fact can create jobs and revenue. An obstetrician, plus an anesthetist, plus a nurse, plus a doula all working in a hospital with a redecorated birth suite are more expensive—and thus more lucrative in the economic system—than a home birth with a midwife. An organic/green line for a national food company works the same way. The alternative, to close the supermarket, grow food, barter, buy only directly from farms, threatens the industry. Co-option works. Clearly, we have our work cut out for us.

Why This Book?

This book started when I was introduced to food studies, and I started seeing parallels everywhere to the world of birth. I found in one week's Sunday newspaper a piece on hunting one's own meat, suggesting that hunting is the last bit of authenticity left in America; a piece on induced labor, showing a picture of a woman flat on her back being handed her baby; and a piece on Dream Dinners and similar companies, where people go and prepare, from prepared ingredients, dinners to take home and freeze. Underlying all three pieces, it seemed to me, was a concern with the place of people as embodied beings in contemporary society. In the world of food and the world of birth, issues of the natural, the authentic, and the importance of meaningful and personal experience get balanced against discussions of the sensible, the convenient, and the safe.

For forty years now, I have been studying birth in America, particularly the home-birth movement, the midwives who struggle to offer home-birth services, the women who seek out these births. And now that I have started to look at the world of food studies, I do really believe that people's search for meaning, for authenticity, in home cooking is part of the same larger fabric as the home-birth movement, that both express our uneasiness with consumer society. Within the family, within the personal sphere, within the bounds of our homes, we are trying to avoid being swamped with consumerism, to avoid bar coding everything. There's a sadness there, a deep-seated dissatisfaction with the marketplace as a way of life, and a longing for something better, more meaningful, that people are trying to express in places as seemingly disparate as the kitchen and the birthroom.

In the midwifery and home-birth movement, the struggle is to hold on to the meaning and place of birth in the context of family rather than medicine, to move birth out of the hospital as a big impersonal institution, and bring it home.[20] Birth is at the dramatic end, dinner at the mundane, but in both, I hear much the same concerns being expressed. As we find our lives taken over by huge institutions, industries, and media, we try to find a little place that's really and truly ours, where we can be ourselves. We search for something authentic, something meaningful in life.

Laura Shapiro, in her contemporary history of cooking, said that once we had so many alternatives, dinners out, premade foods to bring in, "it was never clear anymore whether making dinner was an honor or an obligation or even a necessity. And if dinner went, what was left?"[21] I have heard midwives say almost the same thing about giving birth. If you can just give birth with an epidural, not feeling it, or order up your cesarean like it was a tummy tuck, then what does it mean to have a baby? What about a world that offers us outsourced pregnancies to Indian surrogates, or the proverbial, much-worried-about babies out of machines? Who are we, they are asking, if we do not do anything ourselves, make anything ourselves?

Precisely because it is less fraught, talking to people about how they cook, what ingredients they use, what they do in the kitchen, can be informative, might shed some light on the larger issues of who we are in the world, how we negotiate our place. It's that interface between the body and the culture, seen in the kitchen rather than the birthroom, where the stakes are lower so maybe people are more creative. As the neurosurgeon hero of Ian McEwan's novel *Saturday* says, "In the kitchen, the consequences of failure are mild: disappointment, a wisp of disgrace, rarely voiced. No one actually dies."[22]

And it is true that the kitchen is a place where Americans are showing some resistance to consumer culture, to the fully commercialized, standardized world around us. In food and birth we see the same longings for less commodified and industrialized, more natural and authentic ways of doing things.[23] We go into the kitchen, take hold of something, and make something else out of it, using just our hands and some tools. In this, the most literal area of consumption, we become something more than consumers.

While each of us may or may not play in these two arenas—may give birth or be with someone giving birth a few times in our lives; may cook or may just order in a lot—some people make each of these movements central to their lives. Chefs, artisanal food makers—for these people, food is what they do, and they do it all the time. As midwives make birth central in their lives, birth is what they do and they too do it all the time, at 4:00 a.m. and weekends, on holidays and all year long. Midwives are the artisans of birth, and I begin this exploration of the two movements in the next chapter by explaining what midwives are, and what they are not.

A lot of Americans may know nothing about midwives, but we think we know all about home. "Home" feels like a self-evident fact of life, and yet that too has a history and a politics we need to think about if we're going to be talking about home birth or home cooking. Chapter 3 looks specifically at the home, what that means to contemporary Americans, and where those ideas have come from. It's not only birth and cooking we are trying to bring back home—home is central to our notion of family. Some of the same values I found in midwifery are there in the care of the dying, and Americans have been more receptive, at least "in theory," to moving death back into the home than they have for birth. If we think about what "home" means to people who are dying or caring for the dying, it will become a bit more clear what "home" means in the birth movement. The place of the artisan, the individualized care that people want, will be made more clear when we take the risk of death off the table: in hospice, death is what is happening, not what is being risked.

There is an even more fundamental question, though, than what we mean by home, and that is, Really, who are we? The "we" I am using now is the broadest—not we Americans, but we as human beings. We are mammals. Like other mammals we conceive babies in the bodies of the female of our species, carry them to some point of maturity, and push them out of our bodies at some point when they are still somewhat dependent. And like all mammals, we eat. We put something in our mouths, chew and digest, use what we can and eliminate the rest. Sometimes people take some pleasure in being like an animal, and sometimes we put a lot of effort and energy into distancing ourselves from that embodied physicality. Chapter 4 explores the ways we use ideas about what it means to be a woman or a man, about "culture" and about "science" and "taste," to distinguish ourselves from other mammals and sometimes from each other.

With that context established, chapters 5 through 8 explore the history of these two movements. I'm not much of an optimist, both in personality and in sociological training; I tend to be more focused on all that is wrong and troubling. But social movements are inherently hopeful things. People do get together to make the world a better place, and I look at how people working in food and in birth have fared. It's not a glorious success, but there is reason to hope. Social movements respond to the themes of their times, and I discuss what food and what birth, and the social movements surrounding them, looked like in an age of science, an age of consumer culture, and an age of counterculture.

Finally, in chapters 9 and 10 of the book, I ask, Where are we now? What are the current issues facing the food and the birth movements in this postindustrial and yet so very industrialized era? And finally, I ask how we can move forward in the birth movement to achieve what the folks in the food movement seem to have done.

2

Artisanal Workers

On Expertise and Craft

I've been a sociologist in the world of midwifery for a long time now. I go to midwifery meetings where I present talks, attend other people's talks, listen to informal chat, to serious conversations, to light banter. I've come to a kind of insider status, part of midwifery but not a midwife. I can talk the talk, but I cannot walk the walk. I have lots of what my mother calls "book learning," but no reality-based knowledge, no experience, and no hand skills. And those—the skills—are what make a midwife.

Midwives have been in an interesting position with regard to valuing their own skills. The emphasis many of us in the birth movement have put on the naturalness of birth itself, the awe-inspiring ability of a woman's body to successfully birth without intervention, without medical assistance, has made it hard for people to truly value midwifery skills. In the United States, when people talk about midwifery care, they often think of it primarily in terms of waiting—midwives permit more time, do not rush birth, do not rush women into cesarean sections when birth goes slowly. But midwives do far more than just wait. Midwives have skills of the hands, the kinds of craft skills that are increasingly being valued in our overly industrialized world. Everywhere we turn these days, we're hearing about artisanal this and handcrafted that, products and services being made the way your mother (or more likely your great-grandmother) may have done it. Think about how people are talking about food in recent years. Industrialized food is cheap, plentiful, and—at least in the short run—relatively safe. But people are yearning for something more than that, something authentic or traditional, food with warmth, love, and meaning in its production and presentation. And they are starting to think of safety in longer and broader terms: not just the immediate risks like food poisoning, but the long-term health risks to individuals and to the planet, the environment, of industrialized agriculture. They want a more natural, safer, sensually satisfying alternative to industrialized food.

And so it is with birth. In and out of hospitals, babies extracted vaginally or abdominally, mothers and babies bar coded with wristbands, surrounded by strangers—medicalized birth is a lot like industrialized food, and it does not have to be that way. Rather than settling for an industrialized hospital birth, midwifery offers an alternative, a handcrafted, individually made, and personally catered birth. Midwives can do that because they have the skills, the craft, to individualize the birth to the woman, to meet her physical, psychological, and familial needs. Whether it is knowing when a woman should be up and walking and when it will tire her out, when a partner needs encouragement to support the woman and when she needs some space from that partner, grasping immediately just what angle will help a stuck baby turn, or understanding which positions for that woman and that baby at that moment in second stage will help ease a baby out and avoid surgery—*those* are the skills that make a midwife.

In the American midwifery movement, there is much made of "instincts" and the "art" of midwifery. Maybe it reflects the particular moment when the new midwifery movement was born in North America, but they adopted a language of the natural, the instinctual, of "women's ways of knowing." I've never been entirely comfortable with that. I'm the one who heads to the back of the room—or better yet, out to the bar with a few like-minded folk—when talk of the goddess gets going, when anything overly "spiritual" gets flying. I'm more pragmatic. And in recent years, I've come to think that my pragmatism might be more useful to the movement. We need not be caught between hard, by-the-numbers science on the one hand, and soft womanly instinct on the other. We can, instead, look at skills and craftsmanship. In the world of food, people can talk about "natural" and "skill" in the same sentence, talk about natural ingredients and processes and skilled artisans making something beautiful. So it can be in the world of birth.

We need to think more about the learned skills, the mastery of skills, the true expertise of the craftsman, that comes to look like instinct. I am not offering this as an alternative to evidence-based, scientifically grounded practice. We know that in complex situations, randomized control trials are not going to give us universally applicable rules to follow. Science provides us a set of data, true hard knowledge about how things work, evidence that can inform practice. Science, in the world of food, can teach us much about how bread is made, the viscosity of an egg, the cellular life of wheat, the microscopic worlds of yeast. But a skilled baker does more than follow the scientifically developed recipe. The skilled baker feels the dough and knows that yes, this is the proportion of water to flour. But with this flour that was ground in this particular mill, from a strain of wheat that grew in this particular location at this particular time of year, and on this particular day in which it rained, the amount of water will have to be adjusted. If you know what you are doing, if you have expertise, you can feel that in your hands. Similarly, the midwife can understand all of the science and the evidence, and yet say that on this particular day, with this particular woman, her particular life story and her particular body, and this particular baby in the position it is, truly knowing and understanding all of what is going on, this is the moment for this particular bit of pressure. Or—in a nice point of overlap between midwifery and baking—a well-placed dab of olive oil may solve both problems.

We know that no amount of reading and learning the science will ever substitute for learning hands-on skills. One can understand everything there is to know about the making of a cello, the composition of the strings, the sound waves involved in each note—and still not be able to play the cello. One can understand everything about glass and heat—and still not be able to blow a vase from a molten lump of glass over a fire. Malcolm Gladwell famously claimed that it takes about ten thousand hours of practice to develop expertise.[1] That comes to about three hours a day for ten years. So too, I would suggest for midwifery care. Thousands of hours of practice go into making an expert midwife. Midwifery educators and preceptors know that. It is there in the work of how to teach those skills of the body, how to learn to see, feel, smell, hear, touch, and know. The elaborate internships, apprenticeships, placements, and residencies for midwifery students are ways that a safe learning space is provided. It's time the rest of the world came to understand that too: midwifery is an artisanal craft, not a supreme act of patience.

Midwives as Artisans

When my colleague at the City University of New York Jon Deutsch approached me some years back to join a group of food studies scholars, I was intrigued. I thought maybe there were lessons to be learned from home cooking to apply to home birth, maybe some useful comparisons could be made. At the first food studies meeting I went to, there was a panel of artisanal food makers—a brewer who was handcrafting beers, a cheese maker, and a baker who had resurrected a kind of wheat grain thought to be extinct, had it cloned, and grew and ground it again for the first time in a century. There was a brief self-congratulatory conversation, in which the food makers on the panel were celebrating their contributions, their uniqueness in the mass production society. "It's not like some company with a hundred employees," one said. "Ah, when you count the bottlers and all, I have a hundred employees," said the beer brewer. "It's not like we are using high-tech laboratories," the first offered again. "No," said the baker, "think about what we had to do to clone that wheat!" And the cheese maker agreed: "There is much laboratory science I need to use." A brief flurry of talk followed as they quickly sought some common ground: just what was it that made them all artisanal, all so unique?

I sat there and smiled to myself. I have heard such conversations over and over again at midwifery meetings. Among midwives, someone might have said, "It's not like I'm just working with strangers," and another would have said, "You know, sometimes at my hospital, the elevator door opens and out comes some sixteen-year-old kid in labor and crying, and even though I never saw her before, I am her midwife." "It's not like we are using high-technology interventions!" and another would say, "Well, with the HIV-positive women I am working with, I do often use those." And they too would have worked to find the common "midwifery" vision that they share, what it is that they bring as midwives that distinguishes them from obstetricians who "churn out" birth services. This discussion among the midwives, as among the food producers I heard at that conference, would have centered eventually on some "personal" quality. The midwives are not mass-producing births: each birth is focused on the individual woman, her needs, her life. The process is important, and not just the product. And so it was for the food makers—the making, not just the food, defines the art.

Midwives hold much the same position in the world of birth as do the makers of artisanal foods in the world of cooking.[2] Just about every human community has had midwives, just as almost all have people who know how to make certain foods. Consider the baker: each household could be making that product, doing that activity, at home, but most often one member of the community comes to specialize, to learn the particular skills of the trade. Similarly, each family could "catch" its own babies, but it gets complicated, and the body of sophisticated knowledge, the ways of handling problems, come to be located in a select few people. One big oven will suffice for the community, one mill for grinding, and a baker comes into being. Women who are called for births come to know more and more about birth, and then pass that knowledge on down to a next generation, and midwifery comes into being. That is why in many languages the term for that birth-attending woman is "wise woman," speaking directly to locating shared communal wisdom and skills in one member of the community.

Midwives and artisanal food makers both have a value system that disdains mass production and industrial style, whether they are talking about the ways birthing women are treated in hospitals or the ways foods are made. But both groups are concerned about being elitist, available only to a few wealthy or very knowledgeable people. In American midwifery, that value is often shorthanded as "going where the women are," that it is important to be practicing in hospitals if that's where ordinary women find themselves birthing. I was struck by the way the artisanal food makers faced roughly the same issue: how to make their fine, individualized products more available to more ordinary people. In the food world, it's there when chefs like Jamie Oliver try to bring cooking skills back to people without culinary training, and it's there in the work of those who are reforming the school lunches and even tackling the mess that is hospital food.

In both worlds, there are shared concerns about co-option, about losing the essence to people who market the ideology without following through. In birth, we see it in hospitals that offer lovely "home-like" birthing rooms, which they rarely use, that talk about "family-centered" births but have cesarean section rates of 30 percent, about four times what they were as recently as the 1970s.[3] In cooking, we see it in the use of the words "natural" or "organic," or just pictures of lovely grandmas in their kitchens or traditional food-making equipment, on the labels of industrial food products.

In both worlds, there is a very real concern with deskilling. In the world of birth, it happened first with breech births. By the 1970s, midwives in British hospitals had turned over the breech births to the doctors, and in short order, the surgeons responded to the problem with surgery. In contemporary US hospitals, a breech birth will almost automatically mean a cesarean section, and soon there won't be anyone around in the United States who even knows how to assist a woman with a vaginal breech birth. Twin births went the way of breeches, and almost always result in c-sections. And it continues: Will the availability of ultrasound, letting people see the position of the fetus, cost us the ability that midwives and obstetricians had to palpate the woman's belly and feel the position? Will the doptone, picking up the fetal heart tone and broadcasting it, lose us the ability to hold a stethoscope or old-fashioned Pinard, a little ear-to-belly tool, and hear heart tones directly? Will the endlessly beeping monitors lose us the skills to facilitate a labor, to ease pressure on a cord without rushing into surgery? I've heard, in those late-night conversations, midwives talk despairingly of women "not knowing how to give birth anymore," of having lost the idea of actually *giving* birth to the medical experience of *being* delivered. But it is the loss of midwifery skills we need to worry about, because it is midwives who teach the women how to birth.

In the food world, similar concerns are expressed, as both general and specialized knowledges are lost.[4] I don't think I even know anybody who knows how to pickle things. It is a skill that went first to small-craft workers, and then on to big industrial management. Now the crafts people are back—small-batch picklers show up at farmers' markets and shops, encouraging us to think about pickling as a craft, maybe an art. Some of us love that, think maybe we should try pickling something ourselves sometime. But often, in birth and in food, we face a larger world that says, So what? Who needs the skills to deliver a breech while we have the skills to do surgery? And who needs to know how to pickle a vegetable when they come that way from the supermarket?

With industrialization, birth, like bread baking, cheese making, and pickling, moved out of the community. And in our postindustrial society, some people have sought to re-create the traditional, the natural, the authentic. In birth, as perhaps in food, the focus in popular language is often on the "natural," but people who actually set out to learn the complex skills required for midwifery practice or artisanal food production see little that is natural there. In birth we speak of avoiding the "technological" or the "technocratic." In food, "industrial" is the object of derision. The artisanal food maker, like the midwife, tries to reclaim old skills and traditions, hone ancient arts. Midwives and artisanal food makers are facing much the same situation: they are the ones who represent these skills and arts, and find themselves in the awkward position of having to "sell" them to a community that comes to be called "consumers," while at the same time they are struggling to move beyond the values and limitations of the marketplace for meaning-making. They stand between a technical industrial world on the one hand and the everyday world of shared knowledge on the other. As cooking, like birth before it, moves into the mystification of specialized practice, they are the intermediaries between these worlds of meaning. Some people value them enormously. Some laugh at them derisively. They hold within themselves a set of skills that the society as a whole fears losing—but hesitates to actually use.

This is a good moment to rethink obstetric skills. Cesarean sections? Are those so very high-tech and hard to learn? In many other areas of surgery now, surgeons are offering laparoscopic and other truly high-tech surgeries, and comparing them to the relative barbarism of crude scalpel-based surgery. But cesarean sections can never be done laparoscopically, through the belly button! If we listen to what other surgeons have to say about the skills of obstetricians, perhaps we would be more comfortable talking about the truly advanced skills of midwifery. Faced with a difficult birth, the obstetricians now know only to take a scalpel and slice the woman open. Skilled midwives know how to ease that baby out, how to work with that woman and her particular body in its particular labor to safely bring that baby forth. These are the traditional skills we should be admiring. This is expertise.

I am writing this in a city that was just shut down by a hurricane. All of the bottom third of Manhattan is without power for days on end. And the reports, on the little transistor radio I turn to, speak with horror of the evacuation of hospitals—and take special care to tell us the number of laboring women and newborns. Those, midwives would know, are going to be fine. You don't actually need the hospital to give birth. The people recovering from cardiac surgery, the ones on life support while recovering from trauma—those people we need to worry about. Not healthy women giving birth. Yet those are the ones the reporters report, talking about all the amazing stories families will have about babies born during Hurricane Sandy who miraculously survive. And while we are without electricity, my refrigerator has been dead for days; it might actually be a good moment to know how to can and preserve food. Are these really lost skills, nonmedical births and nonindustrialized food?

There is movement to reclaim birth, just as there is to reclaim our food, and in birth, as in food, the purists are not winning. People certainly talk more knowledgeably about both midwives and "authentic," "traditional" food than they did twenty-five years ago. But in the United States, midwifery-attended, woman-centered home births are probably about as common in the world of birth as artisanal food is in the world of food. How many North Americans even know someone who has had a home birth? And how many don't know someone who has had a cesarean? What is called an epidemic of cesarean sections is as familiar—and arguably as bad for our collective health—as fast-food meals. In this context, people are still struggling, in both arenas, to find a path for themselves. Artisanal workers are leading the food movement, from elite food down to school lunch programs, educating the public about the value of their special skills, and so offering a fine role model for midwives to follow.

What is being valued is expertise, true traditional skills and knowledge, a shared, communal, cultural heritage embodied in the worker. We used to know how to make food that was healthy and natural, that was good for people, families, and the environment. And we used to know how to help women birth. We must not lose or allow those skills to be disvalued.

Recognizing and Valuing Expertise

What constitutes legitimate expertise that we can recognize in someone else, and what are the standards to which we hold expertise? Where do those standards come from? Our over-credentialized society? Is it about the right letters after a name? Or is it tone, the authoritative voice? In the movie *The Iron Lady*, former British prime minster Margaret Thatcher's handlers are shown teaching her how to modulate her tone, bring the feminine screech down to the masculine proclamation.[5] Clearly a lot of sounding authoritative is in the presentation of self, and the more you sound like an upper-class white man, the easier it is to sound authoritative.

Many of us, even when we know perfectly well what we are doing, get intimidated by the voice of authority. It happened to me a while back at a meeting of an experimental food collective. It was the pre-Christmas meeting, and someone had the delightful idea of having us break into groups and make eggnog. If you have only had eggnog from a container, you might not know this: Eggnog is all about beating eggs. Go look up some recipes—you separate and beat the eggs, then you can add milk or cream or both, nutmeg, whiskey or bourbon, but it's the separated beaten eggs, whipped to rich foam, that make eggnog. Each group was given a different tool to work with, representing increasingly sophisticated technologies: a set of bundled twigs, à la colonial days; a wire whisk; a rotary wheel hand mixer; an electric mixer; and some high-tech tool I didn't understand. I was in the whisk group, with two others. One I honestly forget, a young guy who kind of faded into the background. The other was a man who was a serious molecular chemist, whatever that is. I confess this here—I failed the chemistry Regents exam in high school and had to repeat the course. (Do not ask what happened in French, or NYU will take back my doctorate.) We got our eggs whipped, no problem. But then he, Dr. Chemistry-Hotshot, began mixing the ingredients together. Is there a cook reading this? Are you wincing? Not *folding*, not taking a spatula and gently folding ingredients over each other to preserve the air we'd just put in, but grabbing the whisk and *mixing*—stirring the whipped yolks and whites around, chasing down the lumps, making it smooth. And thin. Our eggnog was not rated the best, and it was not the fault of the whisk.

I'd like to blame it on the chemist, but really, what did he know? Let's blame it on me. I know how to fold egg whites in. I was just intimidated. A bit shocked at how he was screwing up and more shocked at how I was standing there watching, but still, intimidated. I am a home cook, competent, sometimes creative, but nothing special. I was in a room of chefs and chemists and who-knows-who-all. I had no confidence in myself.

Expertise does that to us, to most people some of the time, to some people most of the time. It renders us speechless on our own behalf, unsure of our own certainties.

Doctors have taken on the mantle of expertise like nobody else—they beat all the other experts at that game. I think it's because they combine the scientific voice with the parental, saying not only what "truths" are, but what you need to do about them. One hears grown people say things like, "My doctor said I should/shouldn't/can/can't . . . ," the way one hears children say, "My mother said I . . ." With about the same level of actual adherence, of course. Medicine too often silenced what we knew, told us what to do and how, and—abandoning everything our mothers knew, every certainty we had—we listened.

One of the ways science silenced us was with that voice, that educated upper-class white guy's voice, making us all answer back with our accents, our screechy, uneducated, uncredentialed voices. It's never just gender, or just ethnicity/race or just class: the story is in the interplay of all of them, as power flowed from those Dr. Hotshots at the top through their workers, their ladies, their assistants, their aides, finally silencing so many of us. All of us, with our ethnic diets, our old wives' tales, were left standing there like me with the spatula, whisked along into progress.

But Is It Safe?

When I first started looking at home birth a lifetime ago, the one question that always came up from everybody everywhere was, "But is it safe?" I understood that I had to deal with that question from family and friends around my own decision, but I quickly learned that in any setting, no matter how academic the discussion, whether I was presenting a paper on research methodologies I'd used for my dissertation, on theoretical contributions to the sociology of knowledge, no matter what, someone was going to stand up and ask me—really kind of accuse me, as if I hadn't thought of this—But is it safe? The question, I can assure you, predated our understanding of risk society. But now, in this era of risk, sometimes it does seem as if that is the only question. Safety—for the baby, always for the baby—is the only question anyone ever seems interested in. And sure, why not! Safety is important for babies; they are so very vulnerable.

Making a decision against the medical standard for birth, opting for home in a society that does not support home birth, is seen as a risk, an unnecessary, crazy risk. The data do not support that.

Home birth with skilled, experienced midwives is safe—as safe or safer than hospital births. When I say that, and I say it often at presentations and in conversations, I feel like the next thing I ought to say is, "And cows fly at night when you're not looking." To most people I meet, saying that home birth is as safe or safer than hospital birth is roughly that outrageous, that crazy-sounding. But, unlike the cow flying, it's true. I'll give you the data.

I'm going to focus here on midwife-attended, out-of-hospital births. Pretty much nobody anywhere is making claims that midwives in hospitals are any less safe than obstetricians in those same hospitals. The data there are pretty squarely on the side of the midwives for safety and better outcomes. So the real question is about the safety of home-birth practice compared to standard hospital management.

Home Birth Then . . .

The usual American version of the story of birth is that long ago there were no doctors and no science and birth was dangerous, and now there are lots of doctors using lots of science and because of that, birth is no longer dangerous. None of that is particularly true.

When people talk about safety in birth, they want to compare what they are doing in birth, how they are managing, to some baseline— and talk about "natural" birth as if there were such a thing. But birth is always and everywhere done by people who speak a language, share a culture, have ideas about women, bodies, babies, pain, work, noise, and blood, and that culture and those ideas shape how they "do" birth. "Natural" birth among one group of people might take place in a cluster of tents where everybody can hear everything; in another out in an isolated, basically soundproofed cave somewhere. In one place it might be among people who think menstrual blood is a horrid contaminate; in another among people who find sex during menstruation sexy. A thousand ideas and circumstances are going to inflect the way that birth is managed, and there is no "natural" for us to compare.

What might be useful, then, is to look at birth management in Western culture, with our loosely shared ideas about sex, gender, and the body, before the advent of modern medicine. So a quick trip back in time. Luckily for us, there were some literate women at the time, and some midwives who left us their records. We have two fairly detailed diaries. One is from Catharina Schrader, kept from 1693 to 1740.[6] She was a midwife, living and working in a community in the north of the Netherlands. The other diary is by Martha Ballard,[7] an American from Maine who kept a diary from 1785 to 1812. It's hardly random sampling, but this is what we have if we want a picture of birth before the doctors took over. Sometimes when we talk about bringing back the midwife, we are accused of wanting to go back to the past. That is not true: no midwife I ever met wants to eliminate cesarean sections. None of them want to get rid of antibiotics. They want the best of the tools of contemporary science and medicine available for when they are needed. But if we're forever being accused of going back, I'd like to at least understand what was happening back then. Without those tools that contemporary midwives have available, how did the earlier midwives manage? Just how scary is this past?

Let's start by looking at the scariest scenario of all, the death of the birthing woman, what we now call maternal mortality. Catharina Schrader left us a chronological report of her work as a midwife during a period of nearly a half century. She was an unusually experienced and well-respected midwife, called in on difficult cases. The background or expected maternal mortality rate is hard to measure. In at least six of those cases, she was called in when it was already too late, when they were lost causes. And she was the midwife of choice in complicated situations, so her record of maternal mortality can be expected to be higher than the background rate; but then again, since she was more skilled, maybe it should be lower. In other words, we have no way to get at a background, "natural" maternal mortality rate. Her rate of maternal mortality was something like 14 in 3,017 cases. Most of them were from infection, and the deaths occurred between three days and three weeks *after* the birth. In the three cases where the woman died in the first three days, the maternal death followed labors of three days and the death of the fetus, including two in which the fetal skull was perforated to get the dead baby out. In only one of the total of nine cases of infection had there been a "spontaneous" birth with a live-born baby.[8] And the other maternal death cases? A hemorrhage, after twins in two cases, and in another two cases, after a placenta previa (the placenta disengaged and was "previous" to the fetus). There was an unexplained death in a woman who had had four previous stillbirths. There was one maternal death where the woman might not even have been pregnant—she had heavy and constant abdominal pain but never got to term and never went into labor, so she might well have had something else going on, a tumor or a tubal pregnancy. Who knows? One woman died four days after a premature birth—she had a gangrenous leg.

Women died—but not in childbirth, not in the throes of giving birth. They died later. Infections, not birth, killed. Martha Ballard's experiences were similar: in almost a thousand births, she lost five mothers in the time after the birth, and none during the delivery.[9] That is not to say that there weren't some pretty awful situations. There were breeches and other problems of presentation, but she managed them. In Schrader's diary we learn that in a few cases, it went very badly—a dead fetus had to be removed with a "crochet," a hook to rupture the skull of the already-dead fetus and remove it. A couple of times she did that herself; a couple she called in a "man-midwife," an occupation just emerging. All told, in eighty-eight cases, or 3 percent of the total, she had to seriously intervene to get that baby out of that mother, use hand skills, versions (turning) or extractions to maneuver the baby out.

What do we make out of all this? There wasn't what our shared historical memory tells us there must have been—lots of women laboring endlessly, in agony, dying while birthing, languishing for lack of surgical help. That particular fear, the fear of dying in childbirth, while actually laboring and giving birth, has been with us for a very long time. In her book on the history of anesthesia and birth in America, Jacqueline H. Wolf calls the rate of actual maternal deaths "miniscule" in comparison to eighteenth- and nineteenth-century perceptions. Again, it's not that women didn't die—but they didn't die in childbirth. They died a week, two weeks, three weeks later; mostly of sepsis following major interventions. Our collective memory is all wrong—Wolf blames the misperception on the religious linking of birth pain with Eve's punishment, on a political response to dropping birth rates, on the intrinsic sadness and shock of maternal death and the way it thus sticks in the collective memory. Or maybe it's the not-unreasonable conflation of pain with death. As birth management made birth more and more painful and more and more isolated, it became more and more reasonable to think that as you reached transition, as the pain grew, well—at that rate, you'd die soon. More and more women came to think they'd been rescued from death in birth.

And what of neonatal deaths, deaths of babies at birth? The death of babies at or shortly after birth is far more common and apparently always has been. But it's even harder to figure out the numbers in this than in maternal death. In counting maternal deaths we all pretty much agree on what we're counting. It gets a bit confusing with a woman who may or may not actually have been pregnant, might have had some tumor or something else. And it complicates our data when someone with gangrene of the leg dies shortly after a premature birth—she counts as a maternal death, but it is not what most of us are thinking about when we talk about maternal mortality. But infant mortality? We'd have to agree on what is an infant or a neonate. How late a miscarriage is a stillbirth? How premature a baby do we count? How long does a baby have to live after birth before its death isn't a neonatal mortality? We now use measures of weight and gestational age to categorize the "products of a pregnancy" as an infant/neonate rather than a miscarriage. We've got international standards now on all of that, and still there are questions about just how records are kept. But trying to decode data from the early 1800s? It's pretty much a lost cause. Babies weren't weighed, and no one was counting gestational weeks. The obstetrician who reviewed Catharina Schrader's diaries found an overall newborn loss of 140 babies without mention of pregnancy duration, and an additional 27 Schrader mentioned as premature—that is an infant mortality rate comparable, he indicates, to that of the United States and Europe in 1945.[10] It's higher than our numbers now, but about what they were well after the move to medical births in hospitals.

Later data from the United States and the United Kingdom support that conclusion: In Washington, DC, as the percentage of births reported by midwives shrank from 50 percent in 1903 to 15 percent in 1912, infant mortality in the first day, first week, and first month of life all increased. New York's dwindling corps of midwives did significantly better than did New York doctors in preventing both stillborns and puerperal sepsis (postpartum infection). And in Newark a midwifery program in 1914–1916 achieved maternal mortality rates as low as 1.7 per thousand, while in Boston, in many ways a comparable city but where midwives were banned, the rates were 6.5 per thousand. Infant mortality rates in Newark were 8.5 per thousand, contrasted with 36.4 in Boston.[11] The situation was similar in England, where an analysis of the records of the Queen's Institute for Midwives for the years 1905–1925 found that the death rate rose in step with the proportion of cases to which midwives called the doctors.[12]

By the end of the Second World War, birth safety numbers had recovered from medicalization. Partly that has been the result of improved medical techniques and technologies, and partly by larger health and population shifts—eighth, ninth, tenth babies are at greater risk, and you hardly ever see those anymore. The dangerous conditions of early urbanization, like rickets and TB, are largely conquered. The infections that are always a problem in any institutionalized setting largely (though not completely) yielded to antibiotics. The women coming in are much lower-risk than women were in the nineteenth and early twentieth centuries. That is, not only were *practices* different but *populations* were different. It doesn't make sense to compare outcomes on thirty-two-year-olds having their eighth baby with thirty-two-year-olds having their first; doesn't make sense to compare birth outcomes in populations with rickets with those without; doesn't really make sense to compare women living with poor sanitation, no running water, with those living in contemporary suburbs. Again, always, it's not only about clinical care; it's also about public health.

And Home Birth Now

What hospitalizing birth and managing it medically have done is made it possible for it to be less painful and faster. No small accomplishments these, but each of those interlocking processes makes the other more important, and each makes the birth less safe. The things that provide pain relief slow labor down; the things that speed up labor make it more painful. Hospital management of birth balances those two, providing faster births at some risk, and making them less painful, also at some risk. So why are we even asking whether home birth can be as safe as hospital birth? Maybe the real question is how safe is birth anywhere ever, and what is done in different settings to make it safer or less safe.

To definitively assess the comparative safety of home and hospital birth, you'd need a matched sample of women randomly assigned to one or the other. That's not happening. So every study is comparing women who went out of their way to choose home birth with women who chose a hospital birth or, more likely, did not think about the choice at all and so ended up in hospital. You'd also want some way of selecting the providers and the places—not all hospitals are the same, not all providers are the same. Individual obstetricians have their own rates of cesarean section or any other intervention, for example, and those rates may vary considerably even within a single hospital. And in the United States, we have different standards in different places for birth attendants at home birth; some have midwives with certified experience and training, some not. And individual midwives have their own individual rates of interventions and transfers, just as the OBs do. Maybe most important, to do a comparative study, you'd also need some way of defining a home birth. Oddly, it's not just about where the baby was born. A woman who had every intention of having a hospital birth, and then had an extraordinarily rapid labor and found herself pushing a baby out onto the bathroom floor while dialing 911 shouldn't be called a home birth, while a woman who starts out at home, labors all day, finds herself stuck with a baby who is showing some heart-rate troubles and goes to a hospital to give birth, should be. A lot of the studies that say home birth isn't safe skip that part, and include as "home birth" all the women who gave birth at home accidentally as well as all the women who planned a home birth but transferred for problems.

So the study we want to see compares planned home births, wherever they ended up, with planned hospital births, for women who are in some way matched at least on the basic risk factors, and with providers who are also in some way not so much matched as judged competent in their settings. That is, we want the hospitals to be using accredited staff, which is usually a given, and we want the home-birth attendants to be equally well trained and certified. Given US and state-by state opposition to home birth and to midwives who do them, it can be hard to find the latter. Home-birth outcomes are not going to be as good as they could be if we accepted the idea of home birth, educated and supported the practitioners, and made backup services available to them when they requested them.

But even with all those provisos, every few years we get a study that compares "low-risk" women in home and in hospital births. Then we spend a few years arguing over the data, get a new study, argue that one—stir and repeat. The most current such study at this writing was published in the *British Medical Journal* in November 2011, and used UK data.[13] That has the advantage of consistency, since the midwives attending the home births were usually fully accredited, educated to the same standards as those in hospital. For quite a while, home birth was hardly welcomed or ordinary in the United Kingdom, but even with that, it was always far more so than in the United States, so transfers are integrated into the system, at least formally. (The new policy, in response to studies such as this one I am reporting, is changing that, and the United Kingdom is now encouraging home birth.) In an environment that accepts home birth, a midwife can transfer a woman into the hospital without having to try to hide that it was a home birth, without worrying about being arrested for practicing medicine without a license, or any of those issues we have in the United States, where midwives are unwelcome. On the other hand, because home birth has been rare in the United Kingdom, the authors note that not all of the midwives working at home were NHS midwives, and even those have "varying levels of experience of providing care in these settings." In other words, they may not really know all that well how to do home births.

The study involved over sixty-four thousand low-risk, full-term women, using hospitals, various kinds of birth centers, and homes. The findings: "Overall, there were no significant differences in the odds of the primary outcome for births planned in any of the non-obstetric unit settings compared with planned births in obstetric units," where primary outcome is a problem with the newborn, from a broken clavicle or humerus to a neonatal death. There were no maternal deaths. "For other maternal outcomes (third or fourth degree perineal trauma, maternal blood transfusion, and maternal admission to higher level care), there was no consistent relation with planned place of birth, although these adverse outcomes were generally lowest for planned births in freestanding midwifery units."

When they compared first-time births with later births, some differences did show up. There were considerably higher transfer rates for women who were having their first babies, a surprising 45 percent, compared to only 12 percent for women having second or later babies. This may tell us something about midwives' and systems' discomfort with home birth and an over-readiness to transfer. First labors are almost always longer. If you think of rates of transfer by hours of labor, forgetting for the moment about indications for transfer, you'd find more transfers in first births. That is, with that many more hours of labor, you'll find more transfers than you will in the almost-always shorter labors of women who have birthed before. There is also a nervousness about the "untried" woman—the midwives are less confident that she can do this, and it may well be in part a self-fulfilling prophecy. And women themselves, never having done this before, and with all the social pressure against home birth, may feel they are just trying it out at home, and if the baby doesn't come quickly and easily, they too want to move to the hospital.

The other differences were slight, but not to be ignored: There was a small increase in neonatal outcome problems for the first-time, home-birth mothers, though still quite rare, at a total of 36 of the 4,063 first-time mothers without complicating conditions at the start of labor, and an additional three problems with babies in the 425 first-time mothers who had complications (were no longer low-risk) and continued the home-birth plan.

"The odds of receiving individual interventions (augmentation, epidural or spinal analgesia, general anaesthesia, ventouse or forceps delivery, intrapartum caesarean section, episiotomy, active management of the third stage) were lower in all three non-obstetric unit settings, with the greatest reductions seen for planned home and freestanding midwifery unit births." Along with the better maternal outcomes, there were no differences, *none*, in any of those neonatal outcome measures for the "freestanding," out-of-hospital midwifery centers. Is that because of some safety resources that exist there that cannot be brought into homes? Or is it because the midwives are more organized and committed to out-of-hospital, non-obstetric birth? Because women feel safer in a birth center than they do at home? Really hard to know.

What we do know, based on these data, is that for women in second or later pregnancies (multiparas, or "multips"), there are no safety advantages to leaving home; and for first-timers ("primips"), there is a slight advantage in going to a freestanding, non-hospital birth center. On none of the outcome measures—maternal or neonatal—did obstetric units appear to improve things.

Maybe we're asking the wrong question. Maybe, instead of asking whether homes are safe places to give birth, we should be asking what made us think hospitals were?

3

No Place Like Home

On Place: The Meaning of Home

When I came to this issue of birth, I knew nothing of midwives. And cared less. What I wanted was a home birth—a phrase we didn't actually have then. What I wanted was to give birth in my bedroom.

Good thing I am a writer. I am sitting here forty years later and looking at the words I wrote then to justify, explain, and finally to plead for a home birth. My first publication was an article in *Ms. Magazine* about my home birth, and it includes the letter I wrote to the obstetrician to talk her into doing it. I had to call about sixty of them to find one who would talk about it; Marcia Storch was a strong feminist, had worked with the Jane Collective, a group of women working underground organizing illegal abortions in Chicago, and thought I had rights over my body. She also thought I was crazy to want a home birth, but her politics told her I had a right to be crazy. It was my body! So after several visits, I wrote to her, and now I sit here reading that letter, shocked by how little has really changed. I addressed issues of authority, comfort, and risk—and I will come back to each and every one of those as I write this book.

For here and now, though, let me focus on the issues of authority and comfort at home. Risk—and I argued it then and will argue it now—is everywhere. It is not located in the home and given up as you move to the hospital. But authority and comfort? I think those are located in the home and truly hard to move with you into the hospital. It is certainly what I was arguing to Marcia Storch:

This has something very basic to do with questions of control, power and authority. At home, I have it; in the hospital, it's handed over to the institution. I don't want this to come across in such a way that it is offensive to you, but the way I see it is that I am hiring you to do a service for me. . . . I have read arguments for home rather than hospital delivery that spoke about privacy. I think it's less a question of privacy and more a question of authority. At home, nobody's coming in the door that I did not choose to have come in. . . . if you wanted a whole damn roomful (of assistants)— okay. They would all be there because I personally hired them and I personally can tell any one of them to take a flying leap. . . . I'll do what you tell me to do, and see you as the "expert." But that's because I expect you to be making decisions on the basis of your medical expertise and not on the basis of "them's the rules" or what's most convenient in an institution that is simultaneously processing umpty-seven baby-making women.[1]

But I also wanted comfort, to be free to be myself:

In a hospital I am a patient. At home I am simply having a baby. You do not put someone in hospital gowns on hospital tables under hospital lights with little bracelets on so that you can always tell whose body it is whether they're socially present or not, and not create the image of patient. You cannot maintain a definition of self-as-healthy with all the external cues reading illness.[2]

I thought then, and I think now, that a woman can have authority to control her space and herself, and the comfort to let herself go and be fully herself, in her home in ways that she cannot in a hospital.

This idea of a home birth starts with an assumption that one has a home, that one has some authority in that home, and that it is a comfortable place. Quite the set of assumptions. There are two sets of obvious challenges: one is contemporary privilege; and the other is historical precedent. Just who is it that has authority and comfort in her home? And since when?

The "who" is, in America, classed, raced, and gendered. Homeless people do not have this. Battered and abused women do not have this. Poor people in seriously overcrowded space with inadequate infrastructure like heat and electricity and clean water, do not have this—though this one, when we turn to historical precedent, becomes questionable. What we consider adequate in the infrastructure of a home didn't exist for all the kings and queens, for the richest people on earth, until rather shockingly recently. And they managed to give birth. At home.

So just what is this thing called "home"? How did spaces get to be defined as our homes, what kind of space constitutes a home, and how did separate spaces within homes like kitchens and bedrooms develop? We talk about home birth and home cooking, and place them not only in something we know-it-when-we-see-it as a home, but even in particular rooms in that home. Think about the phrase left from illegal abortion days—not just "back-alley" abortions, the place where you procured the agreement to provide the abortion and the place you snuck through to get it, but the place the abortion was done: "kitchen-table" abortions. I had no thought of a kitchen-table birth! It is seemingly, seamlessly "natural" to think of the home birth as going on in the bedroom while people are cooking in the kitchen. But these spaces are never natural; nothing in human life is. It's a created concept, an idea as much as a reality.

Putting things "at home" is taking them away from the public sphere, from the institutional, industrial sphere, and putting them back in the family. And putting a thing in a particular room of that home is placing it within that family's structure as well as within the physical walls. But home is not the same as family. More and more of us—me too—live alone now. Maybe home is just, as my friend Eileen Moran says, the place your cat lives. That feels true to me, actually. It's the place where we put things we love, and if those things are no longer other people, perhaps they are our pets, or maybe just the collected treasures of our lives. It's a space, but it's also a feeling, that powerful, treasured feeling of being at home somewhere.

I needed to learn more about the history of home, what it has meant and what it has come to mean. I've spent so much time thinking and writing about where we who want home births do *not* want to birth, avoiding the hospital, but perhaps not enough thinking about what it is we are seeking to hold on to at home. One good place to start is with Witold Rybczynski's book *Home: A Short History of an Idea.*[3] First, think about the word: "This wonderful word, 'home,' which connotes a physical 'place' but also has the more abstract sense of a 'state of being,' has no equivalent in the Latin or Slavic European languages. German, Danish, Swedish, Icelandic, Dutch and English all have similar sounding word for 'home,' all derived from the Old Norse 'heima.'"[4] The concept is not universal; it arose socially.

Rybczynski acknowledges that you can't trace the evolution of something so amorphous as home, that there will be no identifiable moment of discovery or invention. But he does say that there is one place where the seventeenth-century domestic interior evolved to be exemplary of what we now mean by home, and that place was the Netherlands. For people who know the world of home birth, this would be a good moment to shout *Yes!* and pat each other on the back. The Netherlands is and has been the shining star of the home birth world, what I have called (only a bit ironically) "mecca for midwives," the place we turned to when we wanted to show this can work. While the United States had pretty much gotten rid of its midwives by the middle of the twentieth century, they continued as a strong, independent profession in the Netherlands. And while I was struggling to find a rationale for a home birth, the Dutch had more than a third of their babies at home. So yes, thank you, Dutch folks—if you invented home as I know it, it totally makes sense that you kept birth as I want it. Your cooking, though, well . . . we'll get to that soon.

Creating "home" happened, of course, in the larger context of the social and physical environment, and Rybczynski places it in the "golden age" of the seventeenth century, from the founding of the United Provinces of the Netherlands in 1609. They were a nation of townspeople. But they were building these towns on land that was often below sea level. (When I lived in the Netherlands on a Fulbright to study Dutch midwifery, at Dutch beaches I saw children building not sand castles, but sand canal systems.) It's expensive to build canals and the pilings on which you can build houses. The result was those extremely narrow houses, sharing walls. The lighter the house, the bigger the cost savings, so bricks rather than stone, and big windows made sense. The Dutch are the ones who developed those up-and-down or "sash" windows and the curtains to cover them. A house with light and air, a house we'd begin to recognize, starts to emerge.

The change was also in the household, who lives in that house. Unlike the British, the Dutch homes had no tenants; they preferred and could afford that, and they built separate establishments for businesses. Employees and apprentices no longer lived with the family, but had to provide their own lodgings. The Dutch system also discouraged servants through a series of special taxes. We begin to see the emergence of the "family home." And family changes too, as ideas about childhood changed. Philippe Aries, the best-known, most-cited historian of childhood, points to the way that having school rather than apprenticeship changed our ideas of childhood. I have argued with Aries's notion of an "invention" of childhood elsewhere, saying that it reflects men's but not women's experiences of what a child is. But his point sticks: it is how men viewed children that counted. Aries places the shift to more modern ideas of childhood later, Rybczynski notes: "This is precisely what happened in the Netherlands, where the family centered itself on the child and family life centered itself on the home, only in the Dutch home it occurred about a hundred years earlier than elsewhere."[5] He says that it was the "opinion of more than one contemporary visitor that the Dutch prized three things above all else: first their children, second their homes, and third their gardens."[6] "'Home' brought together the meanings of house and of household, of dwelling and of refuge, of ownership and of affection."[7]

So now we have the place: a self-contained unit where a family lives. How does it come to be a place where a woman can feel in control and comfortable? Let's stick with the Dutch for a moment longer.

Not only did even relatively well-off homes not have many servants, so unlike England and the rest of Europe, but what servants they did have were protected by strict Dutch law on contractual arrangements and on the civil rights of servants; servants dined with their masters at the same table, and housework was shared rather than delegated (This was not about democratization and human rights: these are the years of the slave trade.) Without large staffs of servants, even wealthy Dutch women did their own (and their family's) cleaning and cooking. "The feminization of the home in seventeenth-century Holland was one of the most important events in the evolution of the domestic interior."[8] Since Dutch women did their own cooking, "in the Dutch home the kitchen was the most important room."[9] So no, you won't get the elaborate French stocks that require days of preparation by staffs of workers. Stamppot, mashed potatoes with kale or something, is more like it. But a marble or copper sink, elaborately decorated chimneys, reservoirs with hot water, interior hand pumps in the kitchen, these were the "work amenities" that a mistress of the Dutch house could get. She had far more control over her work space than servants did.

And this "feminine achievement of domesticity"[10] is the concept that shaped the house that moved to England, that then came to what became the United States, that shapes where you are living right now. "Although English public buildings tended toward the Parisian, domestic architecture tended toward the Dutch. The small brick English country house, with its unpretentious charm, was in many ways a rural version of the Dutch row house."[11] And a model for every town house, suburban ranch, and, in some convoluted form, the floor plans for the high-rise apartments we live in too.

So about those floor plans: Over time, ideas of home grew to encompass more specific interior divisions, specified rooms for specified purposes. In England, by the nineteenth century, homes had developed a variety of common rooms. There was at least one public reception room and a formal dining room, for evenings.[12] Smaller rooms, called breakfast rooms, were used for other meals. In larger homes, other rooms like libraries and billiard rooms and studies were constructed. We can begin to see the split between the family room and the parlor, or living room: "The idea of providing two types of common rooms, one less formal than the other, was absent in French planning and was probably inherited from the Dutch."[13]

Kitchens became the distinctive site of authority for women, a work space they controlled. There is an odd tension between being trapped in the kitchen on the one hand, and owning it, controlling it, on the other. It's a tension we will see played out again and again over time and space as we look at women and cooking.

"Comfort" too is a word with a beginning, a concept recently named. The word grew out of its Latin root, *confortare*, to strengthen or console; by the sixteenth century it had the legal meaning of someone who aided or abetted a crime. It grew on to mean "tolerable" or "sufficient," ample if not luxurious. It was only in the eighteenth century that it came to mean the kind of contentment we think of as comfort today.[14] Comfort was meant to be undramatic and calming. It was to appear "natural," but, like the English garden or the English home, it was carefully contrived.[15] Alice Julier, in her study *Eating Together*, looked at how people play out friendship with food, and found that when she asked people to define "hospitality," "almost everyone said 'making guests comfortable.'"[16] When we have friends and loved ones as guests, we want them to feel at home.

In earlier times, before this newer floor plan, one enormous bed slept the household: all the children, the parents, the tenants, the apprentices, all piled into one big bed space. Individual beds in separate bedrooms for each person were not only about new sleeping arrangements, but the beginning of our idea that families are the place where you can be both part of this important collectivity and yet very much your own individual self. A bedroom is a place where you can be comfortable, a space to be relaxed, calmed: a place you can be yourself. It is an individual inner sanctum within the sanctuary of home.

Activities in the home were separated vertically; public below, private above. Everyone had his own bedroom. These bedrooms were not simply rooms for sleeping, however; children used their rooms for play, wives and daughters used their bedrooms for quiet work (sewing or writing) or for intimate tête-à-têtes with friends. The desire for a room of one's own was not simply a matter of personal privacy. It demonstrated the growing awareness of individuality—of a growing personal inner life—and the need to express this individuality in physical ways.[17]

Bedrooms were still social places, places where people visited. And so they were the places where people gave birth.[18] In these moments of intimacy, of weakness and fear, moments when we cannot fully "control ourselves," we want to be comfortable. We want to be free to be ourselves.

That is what I was asking for when I wanted to give birth in my bedroom: the authority to be comfortable.

And that is what I will be asking for when I am dying too, a place where I can have the authority to be comfortable, where I can have my needs met, reach out to part with those I love, be surrounded by people who love me. Like most people in America, I want to die at home, in my own bed.

Birth and Death

Can it possibly be right that almost every baby begins life in precisely the place almost every older person passionately wants not to end it? The hospital is a place no one wants to die. We accept it as absolutely necessary for some situations, but over and over again we hear that older people want *not* to go there to die. They want to be at home, with loved ones, not in an institution, and particularly not in that one, known to one and all as being cold, impersonal, unfeeling, too noisy to allow sleep, and—need I say it?—with bad food.

And yet we mostly do end up dying just there, hooked up to the machines we said we didn't want, tubes and wires our best connection to the world, diapers and catheters tended to by strangers, the colors of cleanliness on surfaces covered with germs, flimsy ugly drapes separating us from yet more suffering strangers. In we come and out we go, the gates to America marked "Emergency Room Entry" and "Hospital Parking Only."

Americans seem to like the idea of dying peacefully at home, or at least want what we now call hospice care, the plan that at the end, when medicine's over and done with its work, some lovely warm people can come in and ease the path out. Some hospice care is home based, and some—I'll talk about that soon—is in a specialized institution or wing of a hospital. It is home that people want, institutionalized hospice that they settle for. And yet. Average length of stay in American hospice is measured in days. Pretty much, when someone in your life is sent to hospice, make sure your black dress is ready because a funeral is on its way. Whether it is denial of death, family disagreements, or physician reticence, the upshot is we value hospice, but we just don't use it.

Even when people plan on dying at home, it all too often doesn't pan out that way. I was talking about this in a graduate seminar once, and a student shared this: her mother is a hospice nurse, doing administrative work and running programs. Every once in a while they get a call from a frantic family: Something's happening! Aunt Ellen is starting to breathe funny! Should they call 911? So if her mother's the only one around, off she goes, the nurse who hasn't done bedside nursing in years, sticking a stethoscope around her neck and sitting in the room. Aunt Ellen still breathes funny (for as long as she keeps breathing, usually not for long), but everybody else takes a deep breath and calms down. This is it. This is dying. This is what we knew we were here for, and—with someone "in charge" in the room—now we can do it, we can sit by Aunt Ellen as she dies.

It makes sense that for something as overwhelming as death we feel the need of some expert around. All around the world, someone serves that purpose: sometimes a priest or religious leader, but oftentimes, in many cultures, it is women who worked as midwives—the part of midwifery care we don't talk about so much in America now as we try to reinvent it to be all about normal, healthy women. But historically, in many places, it was indeed the midwife who came, just stepped in to get us through the liminal scary part, on to the other side, when the person is dead, the body washed and ready for its ultimate disposal, and the mourning rituals take over. While it doesn't have to be the midwife (and in a larger social system, it makes sense that there'd be more specialization, different people for different life transitions), there is a logic to it being the midwife who does this—death is a lot like birth, with the safety issues taken off the table. There's pain and fear and family, unaccustomed nudity, bodily fluids and messiness, and an unfathomable physical transformation occurring right before our eyes.

I think it's impossible to study and think about birth and not also think about death. For sure it's impossible at my age. But for as long as I can remember, the shadow of death has hung around the edges of the vision of birth. There is always the fear that death is going to come in and snatch someone, mother or child. But there is more to it than that. It's not just the fear of death-in-birth, but what we learn from how we birth and what that can teach us about how we can die. Or maybe the other way around. My Aunt Joan, the aunt I loved the most, respected the most, was a visiting nurse. She thought I was a bit crazy, I guess, on my home-birth decision, but then she listened to a radio program I did in the late 1970s, sat and listened to what people were looking for in a home birth, and drawing on her work experiences as well as her own family and life, said, Ah, now I see: it's like how we deal with dying, how much better it is to take care of things at home rather than in the hospital.

Over the years, I've done little projects comparing issues in birth to those of dying, as have a number of midwives I know.[19] I once did some interviews with midwives who've moved on to hospice care, and with one particularly memorable Dutch midwife who went on to become a funeral director. It's much the same job, they told me: there's one person in the center having a powerful physical transformation, and then all those people around—the loved ones, the less-loved, the tense, the teary, the hopeful, the terrified, the gracious, the bitchy—all needing to be managed to let the one in the center have what they need.

And, of course, as most of us have, I've gone down this path personally more than once. When my stepfather, Red, lay dying, I was very
conscious that I was channeling everything I'd learned from the midwives. Red said—and this is one of the greatest compliments I've ever
received or could hope to receive in my life—that I was good to have
around. I was easy, a peaceful, restful presence. It's a compliment because it was an accomplishment, a big one. I don't know that I have
ever felt more frantic in my life, outside of a few situations in which my
children were at risk. I was roiling, reeling, tumbling downhill quickly—
but that was all kept inside. My mother needed to relive and rehash the
things that happened to her the last time she went through this, with
the dying of my father. So at forty, I was learning things I was spared at
eight. In case it wasn't obvious to me, her grief and her stories made it
quite clear that this was "Losing Daddy, Take 2," and part of me just fell
back into being eight years old. I was, truly, a mess. But outwardly? I apparently succeeded. I was calm, easeful, at peace with the process, and
understanding of the overall theme of the symphony and the tonal variations that came my way. Sounds and sights and smells just washed over
me, nodding sagely, doing the small tasks that came my way, but mostly
just sitting, sitting, sitting calmly by his side. Like that ridiculous knit-
ting midwife the French obstetrician Odent likes to talk about—useless,
utterly totally useless and unskilled.[20] But peaceful and calm.

Since the ship of death is sailing where it is going anyway, and there's
not much anyone can do to fix it, well, we might just as well knit. A bit of
skill and knowledge might have come in handy now and again—couldn't
someone please have mentioned that morphine is constipating?—but
basically, this was going where it was going, and just easing Red along
was all that could be done. I found what I had learned from the midwives infinitely helpful. "There, there, there, you're doing just fine, there,
there, there." The midwife may be racing inside, accounting for a dozen
variables, measuring heart tones and thinking about the clock, and
worried about that little sound in the woman's breath—but outwardly?
Calm, peaceful, warm, and supportive.

What we mostly do now, how we live in America today, is we separate out each of these parts—the brain and the heart, if you will—and
hire people to fill them. We hire one person to do the technical stuff,
the thinking—in birth usually an obstetrician but sometimes a midwife

or a nurse-midwife; in death a physician of some stripe or one of his/ her nurse-delegates. That person keeps an eye on things, work that now can be done at a distance, easily monitored from down the hall, because the "things" are increasingly transformed into electronically transmitted data—rates and measures. We hire someone else to sit there by the actual bedside and be the warm, caring, calm presence. That person is called a doula, from the Greek for maidservant, and yes indeed, in birth and in death, it usually is a woman. Sometimes the word "doula" is borrowed and used for death, sometimes they are called hospice volunteers, sometimes they are (lower-paid) hospice workers. But it's not the obstetrician or the geriatrician or oncologist sitting there holding hands, wiping brows, being calm and peaceful—and it's often not the family either.

We do much the same in the mundane world of food, but it's harder or even impossible to track down and name the specific person with the skills. Who roasted that supermarket chicken, or harvested the basil for that jar of pesto? Some of those skills we really, truly do not want to know anything about: forget who roasted the chicken. Who killed it? Erika Eitland worked as a research assistant on parts of this book, and she tells me that as a child, walking through markets in India, she could see, hear, smell the chickens being killed and still somehow cope—but did not want to eat the one chicken she actually saw being killed.[21] American parents can tell you that one of the harder conversations you have to have with children, really harder than the "Where do babies come from?" one, is "Where do chickens come from?" Not eggs, not that question. But that drumstick—a chicken walked around on that? The chicken in the baby animals book and the drumstick on the table—oh no! The pork chop? The *hamburger*? They cut it and smashed it up? You expect your three-year-old, the one you teach to pet the cat gently, not hurt little kitty, to believe that? You're feeding her smashed-up dead cow?

So sometimes we are really, really happy that the skills happened elsewhere, not down the hall but far away in a factory of some sort somewhere. And sometimes we want some of those skills made totally apparent, almost flaunted. When we pay for an expensive restaurant meal, we want that chef out there working, are flattered when he pays attention to us. Many executive chefs express their frustration at being tethered to their restaurant kitchens.[22] Even if the other chefs and cooks have all the skills, can do all the food preparation and cooking work as well or better, restaurant guests want to see that big-name chef in the kitchen. In that, it's not unlike the "top specialist" doctor who delegates all the work to the more-than-able staff but must show up periodically to show the patient they are truly there and in charge.

At home, we like to step in and show off our kitchen skills and expertise at various moments, depending on our personal inclinations, the particular meal, time of day, work schedules, and who's coming for dinner. Sometimes all we do is "add the heart." We lovingly serve the dinner we actually reheat from plastic bags—plop something we bought into the microwave, put it on a nice dish, and maybe put some lemon wedges around the edges or something. Sometimes we make something ourselves. But where do you step in to that process? Take your basic as-American-as apple pie. Forget growing the apples. So you buy apples, peel, chunk, add (someone grew, harvested, processed) sugar, cinnamon. Then there's the matter of the piecrust. Let alone the little issues of harvesting wheat and grinding it, milking cows and getting butter— how many proudly homemade apple pies have I been served, and served myself, that were poured into premade piecrusts? There's a nice little distinction there too between the in-the-pan, edges pre-crinkled frozen crusts, and the packages you have to shape and drape over your own pan. How far back in the process do you have to go for this to be "homemade"? And that was just one dessert choice.

Still we care about family meals and home cooking. We buy parts, maybe lots of parts, maybe when you stop to think about it almost all of the parts almost all of the time; much of the time we bring home food that's largely premade, most of the skills and work already done. We make it our own by serving it with love. Then again, does it even matter who serves? Can we hire that out too, have the nanny put out the lunch? The sociologist Tamara Mose Brown studied the tensions between mothers and nannies over what food the children actually ate: upscale, mostly white families and their West Indian nannies looked at what each was feeding the children and thought, "Really? They'd feed that to a child?"[23] And the negotiations began, and continue.

For some fancy meals there will be a chef and a waitstaff, and some you will spend all day in the kitchen preparing yourself; sometimes the toddler will eat the veggies and fruits you sliced, and sometimes they'll eat the (other-) homemade rice and peas; some meals will be popped into the microwave or brought home and served right out of the paper bucket. That's the thing about food—it's mundane, it's over and over again each day, day after day after day, and we don't need one answer all the time, and most of the time it probably just doesn't matter.

But birth and death—they are *not* mundane for the people birthing and dying. Or for those of us who love them.

Did it matter to Red that it was me, not a random woman hired to sit there calmly, but *me*? That I was the kid for whom he'd gone looking all over midtown to find pumps that would fit my too-wide feet, so I could go to the prom feeling pretty? That I was the one who always wanted his gone-shabby work shirts to wear with jeans? Did it matter that I was probably wearing one of his shirts as I sat in the room where he lay dying? Did it matter that he'd been in my bedroom minutes after the births of my children, awkward about my breast exposed for the first time in front of him, bloody messy rags at our feet? Or could it have been just any warm body, anyone hired to sit there and be calm? Obviously it matters to me; you can hear that as you read this. Did it matter to him? I want to think so.

What is lost when we hire doulas to be the warm presence? What is lost more generally when we outsource ourselves, as the sociologist Arlie Russell Hochschild calls it in her book *The Outsourced Self: Intimate Life in Market Times*? Because that is exactly what we are doing, *outsourcing* ourselves, hiring people to do what we used to think of as being the heart, doing the intimate caring. Hochschild started her book with her own search for care for an elderly dying aunt, and moved on to the vast world of outsourced selves, from surrogacy to hospice care, with dog walking, party planning, eHarmony matchmaking, and love coaches along the way. According to Hochschild,

> Even more than *what* we wish, the market alters *how* we wish. Wallet in hand, we focus in the market on the thing we buy. In the realm of services this is an experience—the perfect wedding, the delicious "traditional" meal, the well-raised child, even the well-gestated baby. What escapes us is the *process* of getting there—the appreciation we attach to the small details of it. . . . Riveting our attention on the destination, we detach ourselves from the many small—potentially meaningful—steps

in our journey. Confining our sense of achievement to results, to the moment of purchase, so to speak, we unwittingly lose the pleasures of accomplishment, the joy of connecting to others, and even, in the process, our faith in ourselves.[24]

That's the truth, the meaning I'm looking for in home birth and home cooking, and, yes, in dying at home too—there are, even at a death, pleasures to be had, if only the pleasures of accomplishment. We can take pride in having done what needed to be done. There is in birth and in death most assuredly the joy of connecting and yes, the faith in ourselves. Does birthing at home make us stronger, more confident people somehow? It's one of the most powerful lessons I learned in my years of studying midwives—it's not just the miracle of the baby, but the miracle of the mother, the transformation of a woman into a mother that so engages midwives. I once tossed off a sentence about that, and it found its way around the Internet world. As one of my students recently said to me, stumbling across it yet again, "You're a meme!" What I said, resonating so widely in the world of birth, is that "Midwives know that birth is not only about making babies. Birth is about making mothers—strong, competent, capable mothers who trust themselves and know their inner strength." Interestingly, most of the time the sentence shows up without the prefatory, "Midwives know that." But it is a truth, one that midwives know and teach us, and that is a strength one needs as a mother, as someone about to set off on raising a child, taking on the great human responsibility of another's life. It's a strength a family needs, a strength that sometimes comes when people work together on a birth, or on a death, learn to trust each other as well as themselves. By not outsourcing this one, by doing it ourselves, we learn something about ourselves, and maybe, in the process, find our faith in ourselves and in each other.

Home birth is not the answer to capitalism, industrialization, humanity's inhumanity; is not the answer to outsourcing, the turning of people and life and everything into disposable industrial commodities. But it is a *response* to it, a claim that in this one place we are going to respect each other's work, value the work we and each other do, value our relationships, value life itself.

I know I'm romanticizing. I hear in my head the specific cynical voices of friends and colleagues. But I am writing this book because I am trying to see where we can find meaning in American life, in our commercialized, industrialized world. Perhaps too the foodies are romantics, and they're accomplishing something good in the world with that romanticism, making (small) inroads that are improving our health, our social connections, our markets.

Many of us know now that there is something wrong with the way we are dying, just as many know there is something wrong with the way that we are eating. It's all far too industrialized. With food, we've got that movement going to put the self and the heart back in, to personalize, to make meaning there. And we've got an ongoing critique of the "American way of death," as Jessica Mitford called it, though she was looking more at funeral than hospice care.[25] She actually went on to write *The American Way of Birth*, one of the early writers to call our attention to those similarities. Big books about death and dying appear regularly; magazine articles about the horrible dying of this or that parent, friend, or loved one are pretty much media staples. But some "mommy wars" articles aside, birth is mostly ignored, something Jon, new to birth as a movement, pointed out to me the other day. From the early food fanatics like Graham to now, sex was linked to food as a social movement, but they just glide right over birth. Is it because of gender? I'm not sure. Jill Lepore did a wonderful book, *The Mansion of Happiness: A History of Life and Death*, with an acute awareness of gender, and yet somehow skipped from the discovery of the ovum and the development of the fetus to breast-milk pumping.[26] And I was maybe the only person surprised by that.

The reason, sad to say, is that the industrialization of birth was successful, in its own terms: birth is relatively cheap and efficient in its factory form. While quite clearly the United States is not doing as well as most of the places one would think of for comparison in infant and maternal mortality rates, the fact is that the survival rates are pretty high. People expect mothers and babies to come through it alive. And it is certainly efficient. Labors have gotten shorter and shorter over time, hospital stays dropped down to the "drive-through delivery" level, and the costs seem manageable. Not so for death—as labors got shorter, dying got longer. Ira Rosofsky titled his book on elder care *Nasty, Brutish and LONG*, and long it is.[27] Used to be, people got old, "took poorly," and died. Not now. Now each and every part is separately repaired as often as it can be, each death dragged out. Nursing home or the oddly named "long-term care" facilities take us in that limbo between living our lives and dying our deaths. Dying is powerfully expensive, with an enormous percentage of our "health care" money spent in the last months of living/dying. And still, at the end, you die.

People see those deaths in ways they don't see the births—you visit Grandma in the nursing home, leave thinking, "God no, never, I don't want ever to be like that." You walk away from the hospital bed where Grandpa's laid out, laboring his last breaths, and think, "Spare me that!" Most Americans do see sad, troubling, unpleasant bits of the long dying process, even if they never see anyone actually die. But births? Birth is short—someone goes in, comes out the next day, with a baby. You don't see any of it—only on television and in the movies, the screaming woman rescued by the doctors—before the one you're doing yourself.

For all these reasons, people do want home deaths, in far greater numbers than they call for home birth, want the dying brought out of the factory and into the home, personalized care replacing institutional care, individualized decision making replacing bureaucratic. But while the vast majority of Americans want to die at home, only 20 or 30 percent actually do so. Some, like the occasional home birth, slip out between the cracks, happen suddenly, unplanned, unforeseen. Some manage the hospice care, the lovely death with the family standing around. But 70 or 80 percent die in hospitals and nursing homes, half of those in intensive care units, the deepest circle of the inferno, entirely tethered to the hospital machinery, in and out of consciousness. The "death movement," like the food movement, has been more successful in raising consciousness, in getting people to talk and to think, than in actually changing the way we behave.

Sometimes the word "family" gets substituted for home—a family-centered birth or death, a family meal. When we do that, I think we are switching the focus from the arena of production (home cooking) to the arena of consumption (family meals). Men's family was the world of consumption, the castle; women's family the world of production, cleaning that castle, making the meals. Contrast "family man" with "homemaker."[28] But women (elite women anyway, women who can afford it) are living like men—consuming family and home life as much or more than producing it.

And that, I think, is a powerful lesson in American life. Life seems to be switching from production to consumption. And it's all outsourced. Instead of a home birth surrounded by family, we can have a doula sitting by a woman's bed in a hospital; instead of a family gathered around a deathbed, we can have a nursing home and hired companions; and instead of home cooking, we can pick up a bucket of chicken and gather round the table. At its most serious and revolutionary end, that is what the food movement is challenging—it's not just the authenticity of your taco that the foodies care about, but the badly paid, exploited labor, the industrial farming practices that get the food produced at its most basic level.

For years, when I'd say birth was important, people told me I was making too much of it; it's only one day, after all. And now I'm starting to think that may actually be worth thinking about. If we want to change our relationship with food, if we want to make the process of growing, harvesting, preparing, and cooking our food more sustainable, with less economic and social injustice built into it, we're going to have to change the way we live. And if we're going to give each other good deaths, it's going to take years out of our lives. Caring for a dying loved one is long and unpredictable, and drags out over months. It's come to seem optional: a friend's brother said he's "not good at the bedside thing," and left his father's deathbed to the care of others, completely accepting and normalizing the idea of this care as a market choice. Arlie Russell Hochschild had to outsource it herself, eventually—she, like the rest of us, couldn't drop everything and go take care of her aunt for months and months, maybe years. But birth? Can we really not pull ourselves together for a day? Not quite a scheduled day, but close—within a couple of weeks of a given date, notice given months ahead of time—can we not just drop everything and do this one right? Must we outsource it, and thus lose "the pleasures of accomplishment, the joy of connecting to others, and even, in the process, our faith in ourselves"?[29]

4

Living the Embodied Life

How did we get here, where people fundamentally cannot feed themselves or others, or give birth or help others give birth, without an entire industrial army behind them? I hate that obnoxious phrase my undergrads like to use "Through all of human history," this or that was true—but you know, on this one, I find myself saying that. It is a truth. Through all of human history people knew how to feed themselves and how to give birth. And now we don't. What happened?

Birth and food have, of course, very different histories and occur within different sets of constraints. In vague generalities one could talk about how birthing and cooking were women's work that men took over, applied a scientific lens to, and moved to the realm of industrial capitalism. And while that's true enough, that level of generality does not really capture the experience of moving birth into factory-like hospital settings, separating the act of giving birth from home, the place where babies were mostly conceived and mostly raised; nor does it capture taking most of what we thought of as cooking out into factories, and leaving us "food preparation"—mixing, heating, nuking, and serving—to be done at home. But mostly what that kind of a "men take over women's work" history does is blind us to how active women were in dumping that work and that labor, how much women as consumers not only accepted but fought hard for the convenience the scientific model promised. And then fought just as hard against all of it. The coalitions, the bargaining with devils corporate and other, the mommy wars of mother-outmothering-mother, the hard work we all put into all of it—we have to remember that.

Mostly when I tell the story of the history of obstetrics and midwifery, it is that sad-but-standard tale of rich white men running over women, and especially poor women of color. In the United States, well into the twentieth century, "of color" included the Italians, Irish, and Jews, all the immigrants who didn't come off the *Mayflower* or from the select European countries. But in the United States, *all* the women lost their mid-wives and *all* the midwives lost their women, from the elite on down. Sometimes the midwives were rather casually thrown away in the name of progress, and sometimes they were wrenched away, but it is a tale of loss. I've written this story a bunch of times, and approach it now again with a deep sigh and a heavy heart. But this time, I'm going to be rethinking it, telling the story of women's loss and attempted recapture of birth in social-movement terms. Because while there are victims in this story, there are also women who were fighters, who pushed hard to get what they wanted, who traveled far, argued, wrestled, and won. They were not always, history now tells us, pushing for the right things, making good choices. But they were trying to think their way through a series of tough situations, trying to make birth work for them.

The same is true of food. Getting out of the kitchen was a battle cry of 1970s feminism. But how did we get in there in the first place? How did food production get to be so splintered and so gendered? One of the games I played in school was "The Farmer in the Dell," a "choosing" game to establish grammar-school hierarchies. And the first thing that the farmer chooses is a wife. How did the farmer get to be a man? It is neither inevitable nor universal that growing and harvesting food came to be men's work, and getting it to the table women's. Cooking came to be splintered into gendered worlds of daily dinners and mundane cook-ing for women, and fancy restaurants and the occasional barbecue for men. And now we have seen a social movement for men and women to reclaim cooking, but beyond that, to go back to the land and farm, hunt, tend the flock. Birth, on the other hand, was always women's work. Birth is gendered, and as long as there is gender, birth will be staying gendered. It's going to take a lot of work in the transgender movement before we need a gender-neutral term for a birthing woman. We are not yet close to that point where pregnancy is not automatically understood to be a condition of women. And for all of human history, women at-tended other women in birth. Not all women gave birth, and not all women attended births, but it was a woman's world. But what does that tell us about birth and the way women feel about it? If we've learned one thing from contemporary feminism and the arguments around it, it is that there is not one kind of woman, some abstract "womanhood" speaking with one voice.

We certainly do not speak in a single voice about birth. We can't even agree about what it feels like. Jacqueline H. Wolf introduces her book on the history of anesthesia and birth in America with a section called "'Terrible Torture' or 'The Nicest Sensation I've Ever Had'?"[1] Women speak, she points out, in language of hyperbole—agony or orgasm, hellfires or transporting joys. And me—guilty as charged. That was me she was quoting, finding pushing the first baby out to be "the strangest, and in some ways the nicest sensation I've ever had." So when we look at the history of birth we're going to find women on all sides, as patients and as providers, as midwives and as obstetricians, pushing for and pushing against every technology and every practice you can imagine, and some you couldn't have dreamt up in your worst nightmares or wildest fantasies.

And when we talk about food, it will be much the same. There were and are women pushing to get out of the kitchen and women clawing their way back in; women applying the rules of industrialization to the kitchen and women fighting it; women demeaning other women for their food practices as mothers; women rescuing Old World recipes; and women in the food laboratories.

Women's Ways of Knowing?

I really, really do not want to get stuck in talk about "women's ways of knowing," as if women were somehow essentially different in our brains and thinking than men. It doesn't ring true to me. I'm not an intuitive type; I am as rational and organized a thinker as any man I know, and probably more so than the men I know best. But whether that dichotomy puts me in the right box or not, my bigger concern is dichotomizing itself: thinking that there is an either/or in our ways of knowing and being in the world, dividing us into types, and then gendering or racializing or in whatever way politicizing the types—that is a bad way to go, a dangerous and pointless path to step out on. But enough smart people in both the food world and the birth world have felt compelled to make that contrast that I have to at least think about it, try to understand what that means and where it is coming from.

In the birth world it's obvious enough where a focus on "women's ways of knowing" would come from. The birthing woman is engaged in a bodily process that blurs lines between conscious, knowingly controlled actions and instinctual or spontaneous actions. Unrestrained, when a woman starts to push the baby out, she moves herself around to a good position to push, or to what at least feels for the moment like a good position. Look at the woman rolling herself around, bending over, squatting, wriggling herself till it feels okay, and then look at a woman being strapped flat on her back into stirrups, and it starts to make some sense to talk about women's ways of knowing and contrast them with the men who invented those delivery tables. Look more carefully, though, and you may see the woman who's never before given birth, never seen a birth other than on a screen, looking frantically to the woman OB or women nurses attending her to tell her what is happening now, why she suddenly feels new, weird sensations, and what she should do next. Giving birth is enough of a natural or spontaneous activity that left all alone, locked in a stuck elevator or trapped in a cave, a woman who has never seen a birth will still probably manage to push a live baby out of herself. And giving birth is enough of a social activity that she may well not feel as if that is true.

If it is hard to talk about what is instinctual in giving birth, it is all the harder to talk about instinct in attending a birth. I think there is no logic or value in talking about womanly arts and women's ways of knowing and women's instincts when we are talking about midwifery care. And yet the world of midwifery is filled with that language, blurring the line between the instinctual in giving birth and in attending birth. In the world of natural or alternative birth and midwifery, or what is often called, borrowing from the Dutch, "physiologic birth," there is much made of putting the birthing woman in touch with her own body, her own instincts. And that makes sense—this is a process of the body, and working with rather than against it is very much in the woman's own interests. If you've ever taught a baby how to blow its nose, helped someone with a middle-of-the-night leg cramp flex against it, helped someone stop their hiccups by any of your favorite tricks, you've done a kind of midwifery. You are there, caring, able to see and to say and to show: here's your body overwhelming you with what "it" is doing; here's how to work with your body and get it to feel "under control" again.

Where do you get the knowledge to do that kind of care of another person? Some comes from living in a body of your own. You've had stuffy noses enough times to recognize it in the baby, and you've figured out this great way of clearing the passage, so you can teach it. Giving birth isn't quite like that. No one has done it enough times to recognize from their own experiences all the variations in what that other woman is feeling. Labors are just too varied, and personal experience too limited, for personal experience to be all that helpful. So one kind of knowledge comes from having attended a lot of births, or at least having been taught by people who collectively have attended a lot of births. When you see this, you can be taught, this is what is probably happening, and this is what will probably help. And if that doesn't work, try this, then this, and then this. And if none of that is working, call in someone who has seen yet more births.

There's another kind of knowledge that comes from knowing the particular person very well. What it means when one person says they are scared, or it hurts more than they can take, is different from what it means when another person says it. And what helps—silence, encouragement, touching, hands off, pressure, a cool breeze, a warm blanket, light, dark, music, a joke—that varies too from one person to the next.

Neither of these kinds of knowledge—experience across a range of bodies-in-labor, experience with this particular person and her body—lends itself to tight rubrics. They require a certain amount of flexibility, of moment-to-moment responsiveness. I think this is what people really mean when they talk about women's ways of knowing and instincts: a constant attentiveness to small variation.

What, then, do we mean by that other way of knowing, the one assigned to men in this typology? It is the knowledge of standardization, of rubrics, of randomized controlled trials for everything, of systems of management into which you slide the person or problem. Maybe it is just about industrialization.

And what does any of this have to do with food? If the difference isn't between women's ways of knowing and men's, but between local, individualized, specific ways of knowing, attentiveness to small variation, and standardized, industrial practices, the parallels emerge. Some in the food world also use the idea of women's ways contrasted with men's. Vandana Shiva, no stranger to "men's ways of knowing," with a doctorate in philosophy on hidden variables and locality in quantum theory, talks about women's ways of agriculture.[2] She is not essentializing this, not claiming some inherent intuitive knowledge women have. But she does show how the knowledge, skills, and values of agriculture developed by women over millennia are being lost, and what the consequences are:

> The worldwide destruction of the feminine knowledge of agriculture evolved over four to five thousand years, by a handful of white male scientists in less than two decades has not merely violated women as experts but, since their expertise is modeled on nature's system of renewability, has gone hand in hand with the ecological destruction of nature's processes and the economic destruction of poor people in rural areas.[3]

While so many argue that science, education, and Westernization will free women and girls, give them power over their lives and their bodies, Shiva is making a different claim. In a way, but with infinitely higher stakes, this echoes the contrasts between schools of feminist thought discussed earlier, the Betty Friedan versus Julia Child issue: Should we free women from their traditional roles, or should we value those traditional skills? Not that it has to be quite that either/or, but this does help to clarify the issues. Women's work as food providers, Shiva argues, is invisibilized, disvalued, and discounted. The switch from women's ways of agriculture, as she calls traditional techniques of food growing, to our contemporary industrial agriculture is particularly important because of the loss of biodiversity. The dominant agricultural paradigm is monoculture—row upon row, field upon field, of the exact same crop, mass-produced. In contrast, she cites studies showing that in Nigerian home gardens women plant 18–57 different species; in sub-Saharan Africa as many as 120 different plants; in Thailand, 230 species in home gardens. "Women are the biodiversity experts of the world."[4]

It's not so much a way of knowing, this traditional way of farming women have, but a way of working, a kind of grounded theory. You start with what you have. You grow what grows, work with what works. In contrast, modern agriculture starts with a plan: you buy land, you buy seeds, you plan out the field and hire the workers. It ought to work magnificently. Sometimes it does. And sometimes, not so much: it risks spectacular crop failures, extraordinary vulnerability to being wiped out by a single shift in the environment, be it via weather or virus. It's the same in the kitchen. This grounded approach is like the example of peaches I give later—you could start with some peaches, see what you could do with them. Or you could start with the idea of a peach-flavored product, and start commissioning and sourcing the ingredients.

Shiva wants to go past the gender ideology, to a third concept that she calls transgender. "In this non-gender based philosophy the feminine principle is not exclusively embodied in women but is the principle of activity and creativity in nature, women and men."[5] Every remaining chapter of *Staying Alive: Women, Ecology, and Development*, though, is "women and"—women and nature, forest, food chain, waters. Like those who look at midwifery, however much she presents it as beyond gender, about ways of working and knowing, it is so hard not to somehow see it as all about gender.

This relationship between industrialization, standardization, and the loss of biodiversity, gendered or not, is not just a problem for produce in India or Africa. Take Canada. In *The Industrial Diet*, Anthony Winson talks about the dramatic reduction in varietal bounty.[6] He gives the example of apples—as American as it gets. He shows a chart that provides only a partial list of varieties of apples grown in Nova Scotia in 1916: over 130 are named, including charmers like Salome, Sutton Beauty, Late Strawberry, Ingram, Jacob Sweet, and Wealthy. He says that there were perhaps two thousand known apple varieties in 1916; one Cornell University apple researcher says there were over six thousand on record. That was 1916. And now? Two-thirds of total apple production in Canada is in just three varieties—McIntosh, Red Delicious, and Spartan.[7]

So what is being lost? Nutritional variation, for one thing. Antioxidants and phytochemicals and a lot of other things vary between apples, or as Winson says, "Not just any apple a day keeps the doctor away."[8] What might be in any given variety of apple that fights tumors, helps the immune system, keeps our bodies going? So maybe they should be figuring out which is the "best" apple and growing just that one? But experience teaches us that whatever is the magic ingredient in apples this week, there is probably some other thing that is going to show up next week. Maybe it's the variety itself, as Winson argues, that is so helpful—eating a dozen varied apples or so over the course of a month might get you all kinds of good things, and it may be the variety itself that enables a healthy body. Taste too—maybe there are one or two or three kinds of apples that we can agree taste best, and we can grow only those. But that variety, in taste too, has its own value. Biting into an apple is a little bit more interesting than biting into a name-brand potato chip. You know what you're getting but actually, not really. There is a bit of variation there, even within standardized McIntosh apples. How much more delightful to have yet more variety.

But neither taste nor nutrition is key in the mass marketing of apples. Put as simply as possible, these are the demands of apples for a global trade—be hard, be pretty, store well.[9] Variety isn't worth as much on the open trade market as predictability. When you open up a global market in apples, when the purchasers aren't the consumers but the supermarket chain distributors, when you are ordering apples not one or two at a time, not in five-pound bags for a family, but by the ton, what you want is consistency of product. That is a very, very different thing than someone wandering a field in her community picking some apples to munch on and give her kids.

I'm taking the example of apples because I'd never think of apple growing as part of women's ways of knowing. In American lore, those farmers were men, there wasn't Susie Appleseed but Johnny Appleseed. Everything I can picture about apples and orchards in every child's book, it is men's work, women making pies in the kitchen out of the bushels the men haul in.[10]

In Winson's discussion of loss of diversity, apples are one small example. He points to the even more dramatic loss of diversity in potatoes, as the one used for fast-food french fries has overwhelmed all other kinds grown. It's true globally, but there is variation: I remember my shock at a German open-air market a decade or so ago. There were dozens of types of potatoes, whole stands devoted only to potatoes. I had no idea there were so many types. Now more and more varieties are showing up at greenmarkets here. But in big supermarkets, in the standard food distribution chain, the only variety that is left in most vegetables and fruits is color—apples come in green and red and yellow, as do peppers. Red, pale, and brownish skins distinguish potatoes. Onions come in white, red, and yellow. As my supermarket upscales, I start seeing a few more choices, Vidalia onions, fingerling potatoes, purple potatoes, a half dozen or more different kinds of apples. Thank you, foodies! Of course whatever variety I see in produce is nothing, truly *nothing* to compare to the "variety" in that cereal aisle.

These are very much "rich world" problems, concerns at the level of taste and the joy of food. If the stores carry only a few types of onions, we can go off to specialty markets and explore expensive variations. We can have lovely things grown locally and delivered to our local farmers' market or shipped into fancy specialty stores. It's not the same as the consequences for poor people when variety is off the table.

And there, of course, is a key lesson here: for rich people, that lack of diversity isn't going to mean much. Rich people will be protected from crop failure. If one kind of apple or tomato or onion or potato goes, no problem, in short order they'll replace it with another for us. The farmers who depended on that crop, that's another story. And if we're not getting enough nutrients out of that apple, well . . . we get enough variety. It's not without health consequences for the wealthy of the world, but obesity is different from starvation; our kind of malnutrition has longer-range consequences, consequences we won't live to see in our children and grandchildren. Not so the malnutrition of missing nutrients, of not enough food. Our kids' and grandkids' arteries are clogging, insulin-production systems are overstressed, but we won't live to see most of the consequences of that. We're not watching our hungry children starve.

In sum, I don't think we're looking at "men's ways" or "women's ways" of knowing in birth or in food, but the distinction between industrialized and not industrialized. Are we looking at mass manufacturing and processing, or artisanal craft? Partly the answer lies in asking, What's it for? Or more accurately: In whose interest? Whose interests does this serve? What are you growing that apple or cooking that meal *for*? Or actually for whom? If you are growing it for your kids, that's one thing. If you are growing it for your friends and neighbors, that's something else. And if you are growing or producing it for the corporate purchasers of millions of boxes, why, that is something else again.

And when you are setting up a birthroom, ask the same question. Who are you setting it up for? Yourself or your sister or your lover? For the use of the women in your small community? Japanese midwives set up the birthroom in their own home, bring the women to them. Or are you developing this as the standard model for a health and hospitals corporation to set up all over the country, export all over the world? If the point is not care and comfort and nurturance, but—as it has to be in industrial capitalist systems, where all the incentive lies—profit and predictability, why would that work any better with birth? Industrial birth is managed no more in the interests of birthing women and babies than industrial food is managed in the interests of its consumers. Industries run in their own interests—in for-profit systems like the United States, profit is a part of it, obviously a very large part of it; and in state-run systems, cost saving is going to be largely determinative. But it is not only about the money; it is also about control and predictability, the systems of processing the units through industrial production. Industrially processed food stops being food, and in a way, industrially processed birth stops being birth. Yes, something that sustains and nourishes gets produced in the food industry, and babies get removed from pregnant women in the birth industry. But something—process, relationships, joy, pleasure, taste, and some elements of safety, particularly long-term safety—is too often sacrificed.

The food movement is doing a good job of making people aware of these problems, from the loss of biodiversity on a planetary level to the consequences of an industrial diet on our waistlines. I want a birth movement that can address the industrialization of birth as the food movement has done for the industrialization of food.

Nature and Culture

In 1974, the same year that I was choosing my home birth, the anthropologist Sherry B. Ortner asked—and in her asking answered brilliantly—"Is Female to Male as Nature is to Culture?"[11] She came to this question in addressing a fundamental problem in the newly emerging feminist anthropology: Wherever they looked, no matter how far and wide they sailed off, in society after society, men were judged superior, and women were devalued, subordinate to men. You could just say, duh, men are superior, and the universality of that finding proves it. But the science doesn't support that idea, and the oddity in the cultural findings is that what makes men "superior" is different in different places. There is something going on, she argued, that is culturally universal that is not biologically explained. The problem becomes "What could there be in the generalized structure and conditions of existence, common to every culture, that would lead every culture to place a lower value upon women?"

Ortner said we have to connect it to the other cultural universal, the distinction between the body, the physical world, or what we call "nature," and our transcendence of nature with our minds and our culture itself. We are embodied physical beings; but we feel like more. We have our minds, our culture:

> Every culture, or, generically, "culture," is engaged in the process of generating and sustaining systems of meaningful forms (symbols, artifacts, etc.) by means of which humanity transcends the givens of natural existence, bends them to its purposes, controls them in its interest. We may thus broadly equate culture with the notion of human consciousness, or with the products of human consciousness (i.e., systems of thought and technology), by means of which humanity attempts to assert control over nature.[12]

Women, Ortner argues, are identified with, become a symbol of, that nature which the culture is bent on overcoming. Women, culture after culture declares, are more rooted in the body, or, as Simone de Beauvoir put it, women's "animality is more manifest."[13] That difference gets explained by menstruation and pregnancy—though really, why bleeding a few days a month entirely trumps our shared pissing and shitting every day, I am personally not sure.

Ortner made the connections to cooking, building on Lévi-Strauss's idea that transforming the raw into the cooked represents the transition from nature to culture. Since women do the cooking in most places, that would seem to make women aligned with culture. But like everything, it's complicated. Women do the daily cooking, the domestic cooking, but Ortner argues that when a society develops its cooking into an art, then men take over; the haute cuisine, whether European or Asian, is the province of men, and lower-order cooking is women's project. It seems to me that this goes beyond cooking. What Ortner is saying about women representing the "body" and men the "culture" rings true, but we also have the idea of women as the civilizing force, that boys will be boys, and men are wild, that women and girls tame and control. In other arenas of life besides cooking, women perform lower-level conversions from nature to culture, while men do the higher-order ones. Women teach babies to walk and talk; men do choreography and write symphonies. Women teach little children the alphabet; men are the scholars. All of academic feminism has worked on opening up those higher-level transformations to women.

Ortner was focusing on gender, but if you think about all of the groups of people that are devalued, peoples judged inferior, this connection to nature rather than culture comes to the fore: we do it racially, we do it with disabilities. The normal, whole, full people rise above their bodies. Those with "spoiled identities," as Goffman put it, are plunked back into their bodies, into their physicality, their "nature." At some moments we seem to almost praise that physicality, like when we look at our environmental disasters and climate change, and admire those primitive people, so close to nature, unlike "us" with our "civilization." But no, we are not about to give up that civilization and embrace primitive life. And so we can admire primitive women who can squat in a field and birth their babies, but we are so far beyond that. We can appreciate the paleo diet, but Google "paleo diet recipes" and you find red meat grilled with balsamic vinegar and Dijon mustard.

In food and in birth, we are working to overcome the body, nature, with culture. But what does that mean? How can we ever do that? One way we do it culturally is by silencing things: some of our bodily functions are to be done only in private. What more embarrassing thing can happen than to soil yourself in public with excrement, urine, or menstrual blood? Go look at how much space is taken up in stores with products to prevent that from ever happening. And yes, we eat in public, but how much time and effort are taken up with "civilizing" practices around that? The careful placing of assorted forks and napkins for fancy meals, sure, but even for hurried, gobbled snacks, we teach children basic table manners. Many years ago, back when help wanted ads for men and women were listed separately in the *New York Times*, the only job I could get was teaching children who were then called "retarded." I remember this little kid with Down syndrome. He was a bit fat, somewhat clumsy. I spent so much time teaching him to chew with his mouth closed, to pick his food up without appearing to grab and "paw" at it. It was so obvious even to my young self that if he didn't have good table manners, he was going to look like an animal. Maybe some nerdy kid could get away with an occasional bit of juice slobbering down his chin, but not Andy. I didn't have the vocabulary for it at the time, but clearly what I was seeing was that this child needed to learn to manage his body to align himself with culture rather than nature, to show he was more human than beast. Does it signify something different when a skinny little blonde kid is a sloppy eater than when a big black kid is? When a white woman throws herself growling into her labor and when a black woman does? One of my professors, early on when I was doing my dissertation on the home-birth movement, told me I had no idea what a joy it was for a controlled, professional woman to just let herself scream out in the delivery room. But did her education, age, and most of all her whiteness free her to do that? Who can go squat in their backyard and birth under the moon and declare it a beautiful, freeing moment, and who needs to prove she's above all that?

Science and Taste

And how can we control the body, rise above it in our physicality, as we eat and as we birth? In the American context, our culture gives us two lenses, science and taste, with which to view our bodies, and thus two sets of tools to work with. Science is about rationalizing, organizing, systematizing knowledge. We manage birth and food scientifically. Taste is our sensibility, our feelings about things. I am thinking about taste both in its literal meaning in the world of food, the sensations evoked on our palate, and in its broader meaning: "tasteful," cultured, a more refined and lovely thing. Through the lens of science, the body is a knowable but difficult-to-maintain biosystem. If we think about food, about feeding that body, a lot of what we are doing all the time seems, through the scientific lens, to be pretty absurd. Why on earth am I starting my morning sipping coffee, eating blueberries and yogurt? If I need protein, carbohydrates, caffeine, and vitamins, why don't I just take them? There are pills and protein drinks that would provide far more carefully measured doses. And if the new data say that we aren't absorbing the vitamins in those pills, well, go back to the lab and find a better pill! There is something just silly about picking blueberries off bushes, milking cows, adding bacteria to the milk and culturing it, growing coffee beans, roasting them, shipping all this stuff all over the place for me to have breakfast. Surely scientific nutrition could do better?

On the other hand, or through the other lens, there is taste—the sensually alive body, the joys of each bit of what we do with food, maybe growing a blueberry bush, or (because that's the part I don't like) buying the blueberries and rolling little ones on my tongue, biting in and feeling the slight tang and variation between berries, enjoying the coffee-making ritual, holding the favorite mug as I face the new day. And how much more it all means if that coffee is handed to me by someone who loves me, brings it to me made "just the way you like it," to help my day start right.

Through one lens we go off to the least-embodied science, and through the other we go to the most embodied of experiences, to the tastes, sensuality, sociability, and feelings of food.

And so it is with birth. The science lens suggests that we carefully select among all those sperm for the good ones, pick out only the finest of the eggs, test and screen and judge for the best of the lot and only then bring them together, with thoughtful scientific management. Then grow it safely, perhaps in a carefully monitored woman, maybe someday in a totally controlled laboratory environment. Wherever it has grown, the moment of harvesting and the method should be the safest, which for most people seems to mean the most controlled: careful scalpels extracting the endangered fetus from the uterus without the long and often unpredictable vaginal passage. Ah, science: the baby in vitro, the baby in a laboratory-controlled environment. The other lens, the idea of taste, of values, of sensation, suggests that we should conceive our babies in deep love, in commitment and in passion both, grow them under our hearts with the most tender of feelings, bring them into the world in loving ways, cradling the mother and the baby in tender care and soft blankets.

At the one end the disembodied science, managing the body as a project; at the other the body and the relationship and the community all welcoming the baby, in deeply sensed, socially shared, and physically experienced ways. We want USDA-inspected blueberries, and we want fetal scans just to check that the baby's okay. And yet do we trust the USDA? The makers of the scans? Do we trust the industrial power that brings us our food or our babies? Why would we? How do we find our way through, think our way through the omnipresent risks weaving through every food and birth decision?

There are a million stops on that road between growing a blueberry and milking a cow and all that on the one hand, and the pills on the other; and a plastic container of Light n' Lively blueberry yogurt (with its listed nutrients and ingredients, not to mention unlisted trace plastics) sits pretty firmly in the ordinary middle now. With food, we've gotten used to the idea that there are a million stops on the road. And we've come to feel that craziness lies at the extremes—the purist who won't eat anything they haven't grown or at least known the person who grew it, the person whose food is watched over diligently if not lovingly at each and every step; and at the other, the person who eats nothing but junk food, whose idea of a home-cooked meal is something in a plastic tray that goes into the microwave.

But it's just now sneaking up on us how industrialized birth has become, how far along the path we've moved. There are fewer stops and less charted territory, but it is comparable; the one trip can teach us something about the other. In both areas, we are going to see a shifting tide between science and taste as consumer values, as first one and then the other ascends. In the first part of the twentieth century the quest for science dominates what people are looking for; in the second half, the shift is toward taste. Those are the first two phases of the birth and food movements we look at. The third phase, the counterculture moment, sees the turn against both bourgeois science and bourgeois taste—a shift to something "natural," "authentic," the countercuisine, counterculture moment of post-sixties America.

This is the history we bring to our current century. We live now in what has been called "risk society," and in food and in birth, the language of risk rings loud. With every food choice and every birth choice, with each and every option, we are confronted with the risks we face. We no longer trust science or taste. Science asks us to be more controlled, more exacting. Taste asks us to be more natural, more authentic. We live with the fear that science has the potential to take it all over—and nature has the potential to take it all away.

5

Two Movements in Three Phases

An Introduction

The next three chapters of this book will provide the contemporary history of birth and food, what happened throughout the twentieth century that has brought us to this moment.

But on the birth side of the story, we have to go back a little further than with the food story. The big changes in birth began in the eighteenth century, and to understand what is happening today, it helps to start with the background story about the way men entered the birthroom and eventually took it over, in what's called the "displacement of the midwife."[1] The earliest industrialization of food in Western history could perhaps be traced back to the single windmill grinding the flour and making the bread for a town, but that miller-baker really was like the community midwife. That was the person in whom a community invested its knowledge, its skills, and its resources. We don't each have to do our own grinding, we don't each have to have ovens—and remember those were wood-fired ovens—capable of the steady temperatures breads need. And so ultimately, we don't each know how to bake our own bread. That is the kind of centralization of knowledge and skills that created midwifery. We still see some remnants of community differences, in local breads from specific European towns or regions. The local knowledge of midwifery seems to be harder to find, homogenized by medical takeover and then reconstructed in a more global, literate world. Traces of indigenous practice emerge and are treasured, but in the United States the distinction between, say, Irish and Italian midwifery practices in tenement immigrant communities are not maintained in communal life the way the differences between Irish breads and Italian breads are maintained.

So our birth history will go back earlier and across the ocean, to set the context, beginning with a few pages on the end of midwifery. Then we'll move to the United States, where I will discuss birth and food in three phases of social movements.

Phase One is the introduction of science as a way of understanding and managing life itself, everything from procreation to nutrition, sex and elimination included. Phase One saw the beginnings of packaged, processed food, food as a commodity, food as a brand. And Phase One saw the kitchen turned from hearth to home laboratory, a place that the new, organized, scientific woman could manage. Birth too moved to a kind of science-temple, out of the bedroom and into the hospital. Along with the first-wave feminist movement, women worked to get anesthesia for childbirth. The introduction of anesthesia was an extraordinarily successful movement. Along with anesthesia came the physicians, who at first objected on the basis of safety concerns—ether and chloroform, the anesthesia available, made birth more dangerous for both mothers and babies—but quickly bought in and used anesthesia as a way to solidify professional control over birth.

Phase Two brings us to post–World War II America, a place where people did indeed worry, in the words of the World War I song, about how you were going to keep them down on the farm once they'd seen Paris. Taste returned to culture. People came back from their European experiences awakened to a new world in the Old World, a world where food was regional and seasonal, where SPAM and Gold Medal white flour and canned vegetables, let alone Jell-O, did not dominate the table. Phase Two of the birth movement largely overlapped the era of the feminine mystique, between waves of the women's movements. And here too a vision of France danced in our heads: following "Lamaze," women moved to get anesthesia back out again. That second phase, the natural childbirth movement, was pretty much a failure at making birth "natural" or less medicated. Perhaps because it wasn't connected to larger feminist politics, it didn't confront the power relations within the birthroom, but focused on the behavior and treatment of the birthing woman herself. What it did succeed at is making birth a project, like cooking with Julia Child, something a woman could do, engaging her husband, and do with some style. You could birth in good taste.

The third phase is where I and my generation of baby boomer, hippie, second-wave feminists came in: Counterculture everything! Countercuisine[2] and home birth—all on the Farm! Herd those goats, cook that tofu, and having a baby's a trip, man! (I'm allowed to make fun of this—these are my own people.) We opened up that kitchen, got rid of the white tiles and went for exposed brick and grow-your-own herbs.[3] We brought back the midwife, in Birkenstocks. We had our babies in our own beds (or rocking chairs or on the floor, maybe chanting, maybe being massaged). We had some successes: brown bread! Breast milk if not breastfeeding. People know what a midwife is! But the cesarean section rate went from around 7 percent to upwards of 35 percent on our watch.

This is the history we need to understand to make some sense of our current, extraordinarily bifurcated era: an epidemic of obesity, a McDonald's on every corner; and arugula, organic artisanal pickles, and sixteen kinds of granola in every supermarket. And in the birth world— unattended home births, like as not underwater, on the one hand; cesarean sections scheduled for mutual convenience between the obstetrician and the birthing woman on the other. And whatever you choose—and it is *all* about choice!—you will be reminded by family, friends, and subway ads about the risks you are taking.

It is indeed the age of wisdom and the age of foolishness, the epoch of belief and the epoch of incredulity, the spring of hope and winter of despair all at once, and anyone's call which is which.

The End of the Midwife as We Knew Her

The first part of the history of birth is about who's in charge, and the answer is not the birthing woman. We're not talking here about any given birth, when maybe, in ideal circumstances, that birthing woman is running the show, making the decisions, controlling her birth. That idea of self-control as desirable and respectful is a fairly contemporary ideal, and more on that later, but it's imaginable for a particular birth. A woman can, under some circumstances, run her own birth. But when we talk about the history of childbirth, we're talking about social management, social definitions, ideas about what birth is, how people should do it, who should be there, and who should be in charge. And the answer, up until very recently, has been what we now call midwives, women who are experienced at birth, women who have learned from other midwives what needs to be done and how to do it. Every culture in the history of the world has had its midwives; wherever there have been women, there have been midwives. It makes sense. Watch a cat give birth, then try to bend yourself that way, so you can really reach, let alone lick, your own crotch. Now imagine doing it with a pregnant belly. Between the large heads of our species and the upright stance and consequently shaped pelvis, we're just not well-built to birth alone.

The recorded history of midwifery goes back as far as any recorded history. The wife of Pericles and the mother of Socrates were midwives, and in Exodus, Moses's midwives, Shifrah and Puah, were rewarded by God for not following Pharaoh's orders to kill the boy babies of the Hebrews. But two important things happened in the modern history of midwifery: midwives lost autonomy, control of their work, to doctors; and doctors and midwives allocated patients according to notions of appropriate "territory." The two problems are interrelated. Doctors carved out as their territory pathological or abnormal births. They then went on to define all births as either inherently or at least potentially pathological and abnormal, so that there was no room for the midwife. Obstetricians like to say that a birth is normal only in retrospect, and—making clear that they really don't trust birth or women's bodies—that nature makes a bad obstetrician. Even today, midwifery care in the United States is seen as suitable only for "low-risk" births, while more and more births are being defined as "high-risk."

Midwives came over with the Pilgrims, and indeed the native peoples had their midwives before that. What is different about the United States, compared to other countries, is that it was almost unique in the world in largely abolishing midwifery before reinventing it in a new form, as a branch of nursing. There are continuing midwifery traditions all over the world, sometimes with more power and sometimes with less, and their independence and their relationship to medical practice directly reflect the history of imperialism and colonization. The history of midwifery reflects world history: America won World War II and Japanese midwives lost status and power as Americans restructured Japanese hospitals; East and West Germany went separate ways in birth practices; countries colonized by the Dutch show a different midwifery than those colonized by the British. But in the United States there was a pretty successful attempt to simply abolish midwifery.

The beginning of the end of American midwifery goes back before the establishment of the United States, and has its roots in British and European history. The earliest sign of encroachment on midwifery came from the development of the barber-surgeons guilds. In England, for example, under the guild system that developed in the thirteenth century, the right to use surgical instruments belonged officially only to the surgeon. Thus, when giving birth was absolutely impossible, the midwife called in the barber-surgeon to perform an embryotomy (crushing the fetal skull, dismembering it in utero, and removing it piecemeal) or to remove the baby by cesarean section after the death of the mother. The genuine challenge to midwives came with the development of forceps in the seventeenth century, bringing men into live births. Interest in abnormal cases increased throughout the seventeenth and especially the eighteenth centuries, which may have been due to rapid urbanization and the resultant increase in pelvic deformities caused by rickets. It was not within the technology of the barber-surgeon to deliver a live baby from a live mother.

The change came in the early seventeenth century, when the Huguenot barber-surgeon Peter Chamberlen developed the obstetrical forceps, an instrument that enabled its user to extract the fetus without necessarily destroying it first. The Chamberlen family kept the forceps secret for three generations, for their own financial gain, and only let it be known that they possessed some way of preventing the piecemeal extraction of an impacted fetus. The right to use instruments resided exclusively with men, and when the Chamberlens finally sold their design (or the design leaked out), it was for the use of the barber-surgeons, and not generally available to midwives. This is the power of guilds, or monopolies, and we are still facing those problems in birth and in food. Patents are used now to accomplish what the Chamberlens accomplished with big cloaks, gilded boxes, and blindfolds for the birthing women—hiding their tools and keeping them solely for their own economic gain. You wanted the tool, you had to hire the Chamberlens. The physicians and surgeons did not have the opportunity to observe and learn the rudiments of normal birth, and were therefore at a decided disadvantage in handling difficult births. And unlike in the pre-forceps days, when a barber-surgeon was called in only if all hope of a live birth was gone, midwives were increasingly encouraged and instructed to call in the barber-surgeon whenever birth became difficult.

The midwives of the time expressed their concerns. Sarah Stone, an eighteenth-century midwife and author of *The Complete Practice of Midwifery*, alleged that more mothers and children had died at the hands of raw recruits just out of their apprenticeship to the barber-surgeons than through the worst ignorance and stupidity of the midwife.[4] The noted midwife Elizabeth Nihell, author of *A Treatise on the Art of the Midwife*, in 1760 questioned the value of instrumentation as a result of her training in France at the Hôtel-Dieu, where midwives practiced without male supervision or intervention.[5] Instruments were, in her opinion, rarely if ever necessary. The forceps of that time were of a primitive design, originally not even curved to fit the birth canal. They were what is now called "high" or "mid" forceps rather than the "outlet forceps" that became more commonly used in modern times; and they were not sterilized. A journalist of the time, Philip Thicknesse, agreed with Elizabeth Nihell that the growing popularity of the man-midwife, the barber-surgeon, and his instruments was not because of his superior skills but because of the power of men to convince women of the dangers of childbirth and the incompetence of the midwives. The men were aided by the growing prestige of male birth attendants as a symbol of higher social status, possibly because of their higher fees. Nihell complained that not only did the men use their instruments unnecessarily, resulting in maternal and infant mortality and morbidity, puerperal fever, and extraordinary birth injuries, but they were so adept at concealing errors with "a cloud of hard words and scientific jargon" that the injured patient herself was convinced that she could not thank him enough for the mischief he had done.[6] "Meddlesome midwifery," as it was called at the time, was the forerunner of what later became known as "interventionist obstetrics."

Spurred on by the development of basic anatomical knowledge and increased understanding of the processes of reproduction, surgeons of the eighteenth century began to develop formal training programs in midwifery. While a French woman, Louise Bourgeois, had written a textbook back in the seventeenth century and was part of a larger movement to educate and certify midwives, the British situation was different. Women midwives were systematically excluded from such programs. Women were not trained because men believed women to be inherently incompetent. Sure, some men surgeons did try to provide training for the midwives, sharing with them the advances made in medical knowledge. Even these attempts failed in the face of opposition from within medicine, supported by the prevailing beliefs about women's inabilities to perform in a professional capacity. The result was a widening disparity between midwives and surgeons.

We cannot assume that midwives would have been incompetent to use these technologies. Rather, their basic experience with normal birth probably made them eminently more capable than the inexperienced men. It's usually said that the first cesarean section recorded in which both mother and child survived was performed by an illiterate Irish midwife, Mary Dunally.[7] For some reason, whenever you read about her, the fact that she was illiterate and that the home had a dirt floor seems to come up. It's not like there was a training manual she could have read, a book of instructions waiting somewhere with a sterilized tile floor. She understood the body, understood the position of the baby, and presumably knew how to sew. As a (woman) surgeon once reassured me, "My father was a tailor. I grew up doing Vogue Patterns—of course I can do this!"

But there was no test-comparison of skills. It was a battle of power in which men won, women lost. As physicians gained near-complete ascendancy, the midwife was redefined from being a competitor of the physician-surgeon to being, in her new role, his assistant. Midwives lost autonomy over their work throughout most of Europe and in England, to a greater or lesser degree losing control over their own licensing, training requirements, and the restrictions under which they functioned. Once physicians came to be *socially defined* as having expertise in the management of difficult or abnormal birth, midwifery effectively lost control over even normal birth. And it is a "social definition," not a simple fact of acquiring greater expertise. The iatrogenic, or doctor-caused, illness resulting from the new obstetrics outweighed its benefits, particularly for normal and healthy pregnancies. The rise of obstetrics in the United Kingdom, in Europe, and in cities throughout the United States killed a lot of mothers and babies.

But once the surgeon or physician is deemed necessary "in case something goes wrong," then the midwife becomes dependent on the physician and his goodwill for her "backup" services. If a midwife decides a particular woman needs medical assistance—a cesarean section, a drug only doctors have the right to prescribe—she needs the physician to accept her transfer or call for request. When physicians want to compete with midwives for clients, all they have to do is withhold these backup services, that is, refuse to come to the aid of a midwife who calls for medical assistance. This is a pattern that began in the earliest days of the barber-surgeon and continues right through to today.

Even when physicians are not in competition with midwives, but really need midwives to handle the cases that they, the physicians, wish to avoid—such as the rural poor or the tediously normal births—physicians still control the stage by setting the standards for training and regulating which instruments and procedures they may use, and for which they must call on their backup doctors. While these decisions are ostensibly made to bring about the best possible health care for mother and child, by preventing "unqualified" persons from providing particular services, that is certainly not the way it always works out. When midwives in the most isolated areas of the world learn how to do cesarean sections, they save the lives of mothers and babies. A wonderful documentary, *Birth of a Surgeon*, shows midwives in Mozambique providing necessary surgeries.[8] But there is great opposition to teaching "unqualified" people— non-physicians—how to do surgery. And again, this is a problem that repeats itself over and over in different eras. In a work written in 1736 as a question-and-answer session between a surgeon and a midwife, tellingly titled *The Midwife Rightly Instructed*, the surgeon refuses to tell the midwife how to deal with a hemorrhage. The surgeon warns the midwife not to aspire beyond the capacities of a woman, and says, "I never designed, Lucina, to make you a Doctoress, but to tell you how to practice as a Midwife."[9] There is almost no way for a doctor to be called in quickly enough to save a hemorrhaging woman, even assuming he knew how to do it. Was it a safety concern that had the unqualified midwife stand by while the woman lay there bleeding till someone got on a horse, found the doctor, and brought him back? That even now requires a woman to be transported for eight hours on a makeshift stretcher dragged by a bicycle over unpaved roads to the nearest hospital?

Safety is not the driving concern. Monopolies and guilds are. This was the relationship between midwives and doctors that framed what came to happen in the United States.

6

Phase One

Scientific Society

The monopoly that medicine has over the management of our bodies is so entirely complete that hardly anyone even questions it anymore. We don't ask whether "medicine" should be in charge of this or that bodily function, but rather which kind of medicine—which specialist? There is some competition, some sense of "alternative" medicine, but just calling it "alternative" clarifies where the standard lies.

Yet the American story of birth isn't just about professional monopolies or guilds, as important as those are. The American story is less about physician control, and more about the move to hospitals, the removal of birth from the lives and the spaces of women and families, and into the world of institutional management.[1] It is less about the control of one individual (the birthing woman) by another individual (the physician or, for that matter, the midwife) and more about the institutional control and management of all of them.

In that way, birth and food are a lot alike: they became institutionalized, industrialized. As did pretty much everything else in America. Prisons, schools, child care, disease, dinner (and maybe especially breakfast), transportation, housing, clothing production—you name it. It all came under the rational, systematic gaze of science.

Scientizing

Sociologists talk a lot about medicalization, and when you're in the birth world, medicalization is everywhere. Things that used to be in the realm of the lay world become subject to medical definition, what we call diagnosis. That moment of diagnosis can be enormously satisfying personally in a world that recognizes only medical knowledge about the body as legitimate knowledge. After days or maybe months or sometimes years of trying to understand what is happening in a body, there's that moment of diagnostic acknowledgment. A diagnosis proves there's something wrong—look at that X-ray, sonogram, lab test, MRI, whatever. It's not all in my head, or if it is, look there at the neurology report! With that diagnosis comes analysis and ultimately control.[2]

Medicalization runs all through our lives and is completely dominant in the world of birth. When we switch our attention to food, we see a mix beyond medicine. There absolutely is a medical element: "My doctor won't let me eat that." "Pediatrician-approved!" But there's something going on beyond the specifically medical, and if we look, a larger move toward "scientization" comes into focus. Scientization sounds like one of those words I sometimes make up, but no, I looked this one up, and "scientize" means to treat with a scientific approach, first used in 1890, fittingly enough, and thoughtfully criticized as recently as 2012 in the *New Atlantis: A Journal of Technology and Science*,[3] where Austin L. Hughes critiques the way science has taken over from philosophy: "Central to scientism is the grabbing of nearly the entire territory of what were once considered questions that properly belong to philosophy." I am more concerned here with the ways science has taken over from embodied ways of knowing, from lived experience, from things we used to call craft, or taste, or judgment.

The year 1890 was a good time to start using the term, because it was around then that we needed it. Life was increasingly coming under the scientific gaze, for good and for ill. Americans developed a world in which science became the only legitimate form of knowledge, where the scientific method became the accepted way to test facts. How do you know something? And how are you allowed to know something? You know it when you know it. You can explain it to others, to outsiders, when you can know it scientifically, when you can prove it. One of my kids once turned to me while the weather report was on and said, "How does he know that? Does he feel it in his bones or is he just guessing?" I laughed (hope you just did too), but think about it: she offered embodied knowledge as authoritative. I started explaining, sort of, as best I could, something about the science of weather forecasting. And yeah, actually, they are kind of guessing.

Knowing something "in your bones" is a way of knowing that we acknowledge in the arts. If I'm facing a blank page armed with ink, crayon, musical notations, or paint, it's reasonable to say that I've got just the right word, tone, note, shade in this piece of art, I can feel it. But prove it? How could you? Making a violin and picking exactly the right bit of wood? We can show you later how it sounds, but that is very different from being able to develop the formula to prove it. Years ago there were nurses who worked in newborn nurseries who noticed that the yellowed, jaundiced babies did better if they were near the window. Fortunately a medical scientist, with the legitimate right to know that, researched it, and we have phototherapy. It is particularly fortunate, because when was the last time you saw a window in the intensive treatment areas of a hospital?

What people see, feel, know may be interesting, may warrant further study, but it proves nothing. Science proves things. My son Daniel once showed me this fabulous thing they did in first grade. It took quite some setup time: baking soda, vinegar, clean glasses along the kitchen counter, and then wow! Exciting little explosions of foam. "Yes, Daniel," I said, "that is way cool. What makes it happen?" He looked hard at me, cocked his head, then threw up his arms and announced, "Science!" in much the same tone he'd heard other performers announce, "Magic!" Science works to legitimate knowledge in our world.

But once you know it, can prove it, have moved your knowledge into the realm of science, then what? Schopenhauer famously said, "All truth passes through three stages: first it is ridiculed; second it is violently opposed; third it is accepted as being self-evident."[4] In the nineteenth century, during his lifetime, science was growing to dominance. By the early twentieth century, we had the words "science" and "scientists," and science as knowing had become self-evident. Science became the way we have knowledge.

Once the knowledge is taken for granted, what can we do with it? We can use it for a legitimate basis of action: Why are you doing that? Because it's scientifically shown to be the way to do things. And then, given the world we live in, it's going to go two ways in short order: we're going to try to use the science to do it "better," which might mean standardizing so that everyone does it the "right" way, the science-based way; and we're going to find someone capitalizing on it. This is, after all, a capitalist system, and figuring out how to turn things to profit is how we do things.

Take something that is *not* (yet) scientized. Like teaching a baby to walk. What would the steps (as it were) be to scientific control? You'd have people studying how it is being done "naturally," observing people doing whatever it is that people customarily do. Then you'd come up with "best practices." Just let your mind play with this for a minute. Picture babies becoming toddlers, those transitional weeks, what the babies do; what the parents and other surrounding adults do. Grasping things? The lowered finger-grabs we offer them? The "cruising" from table to chair to person and back down to crawl? Just picture it in your head.

If we got this figured out, how babies and their families do it, and what the most successful "techniques" are for helping them do it, what would happen then? I'd venture to guess that pretty quickly we'd be looking for the early-to-walk techniques, and pushing to lower age-at-first-step by offering some training in those techniques. And I'd imagine that in short order there would be a pile of books and videos and YouTubes teaching us these tricks. I would be really, *really* surprised if pretty quickly there weren't a bunch of objects being sold to promote early walking with best walking practices: maybe firm artificial finger grabs; or fancy cruise-spaces with stable objects along a winding path to toys; or maybe some early-walker rug. Some life arenas have been more resistant than others to scientizing, as to medicalizing. It's hard to think of anything that has totally resisted—there are, after all, early-intervention programs for slow walkers, the coming-and-going of various baby-walker products, "tummy time" playthings to encourage the move to crawling, and more.

Is there anything not scientized? I want to say intimacy, the deeply personal in our relationships, that somehow intimacy has been kept intimate—but I know how commercialized intimacy is, made so very clear with sexual intimacy. Think about how much the sold images of bodies-in-sex shape the lived experience of bodies-in-sex. The level of commercialization made use of some scientization, some level of medicalization. And while individual acts of sex are not particularly medically scrutinized, the selling of appropriate levels of sexual interest, from Viagra to the recent creation of categories of low desire as a treatable medical problem,[5] speaks dramatically of how scientized and medicalized sex has come to be.

The Scientific Kitchen

The only memory of food I have from home economics in elementary school is something called succotash—an exotic recipe, made by combining one can of creamed corn with one can of lima beans. I knew creamed corn, we had that, but those canned lima beans, now that was pushing my family's boundaries into the unfamiliar. That was the 1950s. They also tried to teach us to sew a full apron, something I was about as likely to use as, oh, a creamed corn and lima bean recipe. It's hard to underestimate how totally deadening those courses were. I laughed in recognition when I read Laura Shapiro's history of her own seventh-grade encounter with home economics, in the form of carrot-and-raisin salad:

> I have only made carrot-and-raisin salad once, the day it was taught to me in seventh grade, but the memory of those bright orange shreds specked with raisins and clotted with mayonnaise has been unaccountably hard to shake. It's easy to understand why the recipe appealed to the teacher—carrots made it nutritious, raisins made it sweet, and the mayonnaise made it a salad—but I can't explain why a combination I never hoped to eat again was able to lodge itself so firmly in to the apparatus of my adolescence. . . . Eerily enough, this course, which purported to be about the real world, had nothing whatever to do with anything that happened in my home or that I had ever seen happen anywhere else. . . . Who on earth wore pink cotton "hostess aprons" or worse yet, had to sew them? . . . The sheer emptiness at the core of home economics was stunning if not within the reach of consciousness just then.[6]

Look at one of those home ec classes and it's not hard to envision consciousness raising and a feminist movement—we may never have actually burnt a bra, but we sure did get rid of those aprons!

The harder thing to understand is that those courses were themselves the product of a social movement, a feminist movement, a social movement by women and for women. Home economics grew out of an early food movement, with roots back in the late nineteenth century. Gas stoves and electric lights and eventually electric refrigerators were entering our homes. Canals and then railroads were bringing grain and meat across the country. Canning developed into a major industry. Industry is really the right word here—the sociologist Anthony Winson calls the period from the 1870s to 1949 "the first industrial dietary regime." He uses the term "dietary regime" to call our attention to the fact that diets are ultimately social and political projects and focuses on the way that industrial capitalism reshaped the world of food along with so much else.[7] Industrialization brought us the standardized American diet, losing regional and seasonal variation.

Wheat flour was one of the first foods to become a commodity. Shortly after the Civil War, transportation made it economically feasible to switch to the hard wheat that grew in the prairies. A new milling technique, rolling mills, produced the white flour Americans tend to think of as regular flour, rather than the specialty stone-ground, whole-wheat product. "By further refining the flour and thereby eliminating the more perishable parts of the grain, and the wheat germ in particular, milling companies ensured that flour would have enhanced storage qualities, making it possible to service a larger market area."[8] Without the germ and the bran, the wheat loses many essential nutrients. We can see the beginnings of nutritionally degraded grain food, processed to make it easy to store, easy to use, and more and more nutritionally worthless to eat.

It wasn't just food—the turn of the twentieth century brought us an urbanized, industrialized world Americans can begin to recognize. In the first years of the twentieth century, subway tunnels were drilled, and cars were starting to come off assembly lines. By the late 1910s a majority of the US population had left the farms and moved to cities. People alive today lived—some still do—in homes that were built in those first years of the twentieth century, as electricity was first coming in. We have cooked in kitchens built then and modernized over and over again. And some of us were taught how to cook in those kitchens by home ec teachers who were themselves babies at the turn of the century.

Ellen Richards is credited as the founder of "domestic science," which eventually morphed into home economics. She was a Vassar graduate and the first woman to enter the Massachusetts Institute of Technology—in 1870 MIT had to admit her as a "special student," because they had no women. In the active years of her career, through 1910, the culinary historian Laura Shapiro tells us, domesticity expanded into an objective body of knowledge that had to be actively pursued; it was no longer to be treated as a God-given expertise insensibly commanded by all women. The most popular way to refer to this approach was to call it "scientific." Indeed one of the most impressive ways to describe anything in the latter half of the nineteenth century was to call it scientific, and terms like "scientific motherhood," "scientific charity," and "scientific cookery" were in constant use whenever women analyzed their modern responsibilities. By scientific they meant rational, objective, and methodical—traits that gave the term a definite air of maleness.[9]

We think of science as male, accept that dichotomy between the life of the mind, the scientific rational way of knowing, and women's "intuitive" knowledge. But scientific knowing was new to men too. It took over their world first, but in the greater scheme of things, it was but a moment between the scientific rational organization of men's work world and that of women's. "The woman who boils potatoes year after year, with no thought of the how or why, is a drudge," Ellen Richards explained in 1890, "but the cook who can compute the calories of heat which a potato of given weight will yield, is no drudge."[10] And the woman who knows which potato to boil and which to bake, how to season and best bring out flavors in that boiled potato? Those are lovely skills to have in our mothers and our cooks—but not valued as science nor as art in the world of home economics.

The Boston Cooking School, the home of scientific cookery, was founded in 1879. There, in the reformist heart of America, they set out to create not so much a new kind of meal as a new kind of woman, an educated, intellectual, scientific worker in domestic cooking. "These newly educated cooks pursued the science of food, not the sensuality and worked to establish a cuisine that would be nobler, somehow, than the act of eating."[11] The more I read about the Boston Cooking School and Fannie Farmer, who joined it and brought it to prominence, and all the cooking schools that followed the scientific approach, the more I realize that white seems to have been the major contribution of scientific cooking to the American table. Basic white sauce, made with butter, flour, and milk, with no flavoring, was used "not to enhance but to blanket food. . . . There was virtually no cooked food that at one time or another was not hidden, purified, enriched or ennobled with white sauce—among scientific cooks it became the most popular solution to the discomfiting problem of undressed food."[12] White china, white cloths, white napkins, boiled chicken, whipped potatoes, boiled cod . . . I am reminded of a bizarre dinner I fooled around with a few years ago— the black meal. Black rice, Chinese black chicken, black kale. I did it as a joke. These folks were not kidding.

"The kitchen itself was becoming whiter by the turn of the century. Announcing as it did a pure and germ-free environment, whiteness became the prevailing aesthetic in kitchens and bathrooms, where walls and fixtures could be painted to display the outward sign of inner sanitation."[13] Women cooking in those kitchens were to stay clean and "dainty." Daintiness was a big deal, a sign of delicate femininity. Bring on those aprons! And they did—out of those cooking schools and off to conquer the world: "Once lodged in the public-school system, in fact, domestic science was lodged in American life. Cooking-school graduates found plentiful job opportunities in the public schools, and they planted the ideals of scientific cookery wherever they settled."[14] As Laura Shapiro and I, with our unfinished aprons and untasted foods, can attest.

A Bite to Get Us Started: Breakfast Is Served

Between the industrialization of our diet, the growth of food-as-commodity on the one hand, and scientific cookery on the other, taste was pretty well killed. Food products were grown from the start with an eye toward shipping rather than taste, and those industrial needs continued to dominate at each stage of the process. Food was sold— and bought, always important to remember that consumers were actors in this—for its convenience, its nutrition, its scientific provenance and management, not particularly its taste. Eventually taste came in as yet another marketing tool—the "salt, sugar, fat" trilogy explored in Michael Moss's 2013 book, *Salt, Sugar, Fat: How the Food Giants Hooked Us.*[15] But I am jumping a bit ahead of the story.

Once the process is completed, the obvious, self-evident nature of the scientizing blinds us to the process itself. Are you surprised at a recipe that calls for a level tablespoon of this, a half cup of that? Those scientific recipes are brought to you by Fannie Farmer, and now seem like the only way you could write a recipe out. But for much of our diet, the recipe is irrelevant: we are not cooking or even combining, we are opening food.

Take breakfast—one small yet peculiarly noteworthy piece of the food world. I guess we've all heard the story that Graham crackers, best known in my world for the crust for my mother's My-T-Fine chocolate pudding pie, were invented as a health food, an attempt to have a more whole-grain flour. And we've all heard that Kellogg was some kind of health nut, and that the Kellogg brothers, Dr. John Harvey and Will, invented cornflakes, a new way of processing corn.[16] Now that very word "processing" is so much more associated with the problem than the solution, but the Kelloggs were working on making healthy foods to serve to the patients at a sanitarium (think nursing home/convalescence place/upscale health spa) they ran in Battle Creek, Michigan. There was a split between the two brothers: one held a "scientific approach" to what we now would call health food. The other zeroed in on the market and the business issues. John Harvey was making his reputation and career on the health food end; Will went for the mainstream consumer product. Health reformers and nineteenth-century medical professionals had zeroed in on breakfast, seeing it as an important meal itself, and as an unnecessary source of fat and grease—butter and lard being, at that time, quite cheap. Graham himself had little effect on breakfast, but others used his flour, with various re-baking techniques, to make Granula, the foremother of granola. Kellogg's Corn Flakes were an alternative: crumblier, easy to eat, simple enough for a child to assemble. When I was growing up, cereal boxes were proudly placed on the lowest pantry shelf in our house, so we children could reach them.

That ease of preparation and the child-friendliness of cereals, along with the medical voice-of-authority endorsement, had extraordinary traction in the course of the mid-twentieth century.[17] Advertising grew and grew, maybe largely on the back of those cereal boxes. "Breakfast cereal entrepreneurs such as CW Post and the Kellogg brothers used the emerging technologies of mass marketing to create nationally branded products in the early decades of the 20th century."[18] Cereal seems to be one of the first products advertised directly to children. Pass through the sugar rationing of the Second World War into the sugar-drenched 1950s, and of course Frosted Flakes, Sugar Pops, and Trix practically invent themselves. Kellogg brought out Sugar Pops in 1950, Frosted Flakes in

1952, and General Mills introduced Trix, a full 46 percent sugar, in 1954.[19] Breakfast cereals are served in nine out of ten American households, are the third most popular product sold at supermarkets, and somehow went from a health food to being "now considered major contributors to excess sugar in the American diet, especially in the diets of children."[20]

I spent a day or two reading about all this and then, in the normal course of the day, went out to replenish my groceries, including my supply of low-fat granola at the supermarket. I just stood there, gaping at that whole long aisle, as long as any other single-item aisle in the whole store, entirely devoted to breakfast cereal, as if I'd never seen it before. And I guess I really never have. When I was a kid, and when I had kids, I just walked through and grabbed the Cheerios and Rice Krispies. I bought those special six-packs of mini-boxes of sugar flakes and captain chocolate or whatever nonsense for children's treats for family vacation time. And somewhere in the 1980s, when the health food co-op opened in my neighborhood, I switched to granola for myself. But really, what the hell? Breakfast cereal? As a special order of food? Where *did* that come from? How does choosing which healthy ready-to-eat cereal come to seem like the ordinary choice? Where did the assumption of health in the box of cereal come from? And now I know.

That's scientific food for you—processed, corporatized, international. And convenient! Open a box, plop it into a bowl, pour on some milk, and breakfast is served.

Childbirth Movement, Phase One

When digestion came under a scientific, medical gaze, some pretty strange things happened. Consider "fletcherizing" one's food: chewing and chewing and chewing until it pretty much disappeared. That's a bit of science at the table that popped up and comes back now and again. More significantly, there's science at the macro end, nutrition scientists responsible for creating various food pyramids, and nutrition scientists responsible for creating the fast-food menus. There are scientists working on making food safe and scientists working on making it cheap. There are scientists working on functional foods: chips or gums to fight cavities, boost your immune system, help your digestion or improve your sleep; there are some working on making it pleasurable to make your life sweeter and nicer, and some working on making it pleasurable to increase sales.

And so it is with birth: "science" and "scientists" are found at every end, measuring, controlling, testing, trying, evaluating, and inventing new tools for every aspect and every moment of birth.

At the turn of the twentieth century, when science was gaining its ascendency in our lives, Americans were living in a powerfully hierarchical world. We were well within living memory of slavery: the people who were children under slavery were only in their forties. We were in a time in which the poor were getting poorer and the rich were getting richer, the Carnegies and Rockefellers and other American nobility establishing their place. And women's suffrage had yet to be won.

Science was men's science, and those men were elite men. We talk as if science was pure knowledge, but we know that the production of knowledge is always framed by the social position of the people doing the producing. How elite people see the world shapes the science that they can imagine. Women were largely excluded from the growth of scientific thinking. The same way that a woman had to go to MIT and get accredited so she could run a school to teach women how to measure the calories in a potato so that they could be fine, educated, scientific women—that is the same way a woman had to claw her way into medical school so that she could strap another woman to a table, lock her legs in the air, and pull her baby out of her. The woman who made a wonderful family meal, like the woman who helped another woman give birth, was just old-fashioned, out-of-touch, and not part of the modern, forward-thinking world.

Birth, to state the obvious, is something that happens only in/to/by women's bodies. And gender, the very nature of what it means to be a woman, is culturally framed. The science of gender and the science of birth are very much the product of the race/class/gender system in which they were produced. In the United States, by the middle of the nineteenth century, as Jacqueline Wolf points out in her history of anesthesia in America, "being a woman and being weak and unhealthy seemed to go hand in hand."[21] This was of course true for only some women—white women for sure, and within whiteness, for urban middle- and upper-class women, the women of the new capitalism. With growing industrialization and urbanization, the United States was just starting to become what it is today, and family as we understand it was just rolling into being. Poor women, farm women, slave women—that's a different story. Their physical strength was assumed. But the wives of wealthy men, like the bound-foot wives of the wealthy Chinese, were there for adornment, for a conspicuous display of wealth. The idea of strength as masculine and crude, and weakness as feminine and refined casts a long shadow: women's sports teams are still dealing with it.

If genteel women are weak, how do they give birth? How do they find the strength to open up and push a baby out? They felt they couldn't. They needed help, demanded it, sought it, found it in doctors who could "spare" them the birth. Enter anesthesia. One could argue that the use of routine obstetrical anesthesia was the fruit of the first women's health, patient-advocacy movement. To be sure, it wasn't always the woman herself who could take this active role in getting help. Wolf says that it was the wife of Henry Wadsworth Longfellow who became the first woman in the United States to inhale anesthesia while giving birth—and it was Longfellow who searched for and found the physician, a dental specialist, who agreed to dispense the ether. Fanny Longfellow felt herself "proud to be the pioneer to less suffering for poor weak woman-kind."[22] Her strength was in her weakness; her weakness her strength. Elite women, in their weakness, learned to be strong to get help, and doctors quickly learned that providing ether or chloroform was a way to entice patients, build a practice, make a living.

It's unclear, knowing what we know now about labor, birth, and the way that ether and then chloroform were used, that they actually did much to achieve less suffering. They were used only at the very end of the labor, as the baby was emerging—a moment some women find lovely, and not as painful as the hours of labor that preceded it. A very important point that Wolf makes is that not only is labor different for different women, but it is also different in its different parts. Early labor drags on, hurts, aches, drags on some more, hurts, aches some more. Then it drags on. Late labor, "transition," hurts like holy hell, to speak hyperbolically again. And then pushing the baby out, that's pretty over-whelming, but not usually all that painful. This varies, I know that. But that's the pattern. The end is not the hard part, but it sure looks and sounds like it is. Women's faces are contorted, flushed, beaded with perspiration, "animalistic," working hard, pushing, totally caught up in the moment. Childbirth educators, back in the day, sometimes played a soundtrack of a late-stage labor, the woman starting to push. It was hard not to blush listening—"Oh oh! Oh! Oh God! Oh! OH! ohohohohohho, grrrrrrrrrrrrrrrrowl, aaaaaaah. Deep breath." The language of orgasm, birth, and torture are remarkably similar—a lot of calling on gods you may or may not believe in, much guttural sound, some rising open-throated noises, and then—for birth and orgasm in distinction from torture—long sighs.

> By the end of the nineteenth century, rendering women unconscious or semi-conscious at the moment of birth, and usually only at the moment of birth, was a common practice in homes and hospitals alike. What phy-sicians saw and heard—women forced during second-stage labor to bear down and emit involuntary groans because of the powerful force of the uterine muscle pushing the fetus from the birth canal—as opposed to what mothers felt came to dictate the traditional timing of the adminis-tration of obstetric anesthesia.[23]

Anesthesia at the end spared women—and their doctors—the loud-est, "grossest," most "primitive" parts, but not the most painful ones. What it did was spare observers the sight of women in that space. And eventually, with its widespread use, how were women or doctors to know that the part you were missing wasn't the part that hurt the most? As the doctors replaced the midwives, in homes and increasingly in hos-pitals, the nature of birth changed. No longer a social event, with the sisters and neighbors of the birthing woman keeping her company, birth became a medical event, a clinical service. Women's job was to lie still, keep quiet, and let the man do the work. Pretty much what was expected of wives too.

Eventually—a fascinating tale for which I suggest you read Wolf's book—the use of anesthesia grew to cover earlier labor, with more, and more dangerous, techniques, making women semiconscious, delirious, and ultimately amnesiac. Women pushed for more and more pain relief, welcomed "twilight sleep," and saw the medicalization of birth as part and parcel of the new Progressive Era. And then the trickle-down began.

By the nineteenth and early twentieth centuries, midwives and physi-cians in the United States were in direct competition for patients, and not only for their fees. Newer, more clinically oriented medical training demanded "teaching material," so that even immigrant and poor women were desired as patients. The only midwives that were spared were those in geographically undesirable places. African American midwives continued to practice in the deep, rural South long enough so that the new midwifery movement of the 1970s could rediscover them, rename them from the disparaging "Grannies" to the honorific "Grand Midwives." But in the urban areas, doctors used everything in their power to stop the midwives from practicing. They advertised, using racist pictures of "drunken, dirty" Irish midwives and hooked-nose, witch-like Jewish midwives. They played on immigrant women's desire to "become American," linking the midwives with "old country" ways of doing things. The displacement of the midwife can be better understood in terms of this competition than as an ideological struggle or as "scientific advancement." Physicians, unlike the unorganized, disenfranchised midwives, had access to the power of the state through their professional associations. They were thus able to draw women in with their advertising, but also to control licensing legislation, in state after state restricting the midwives' sphere of activity and imposing legal sanctions against them.[24]

And where were the resisters? Where were the feminists? This was a moment, familiar to us, I suppose, where feminism fractured along class and race lines. Wolf says that there was indeed a call to action, and women were major players in the

> flurry of reform now known as the Progressive Era, from roughly the 1890s through World War I, when reformers worked to mitigate the social problems generated by rapid industrialization and urbanization. Given the perceived link between the debilitating effects of "civilization" and middle- and upper-class women's increased difficulties giving birth, many women viewed the twilight sleep movement as a logical addition to the many other efforts aimed at alleviating the problems inherent in urban living.[25]

And so, in the spirit of sisterhood, called on to fight "not only for yourselves, but fight for your sister-mothers, your sex, the cradle of the human race,"[26] the feminists joined forces with their brothers in the medical profession and sold their midwives down the river.

What did the medical takeover of birth mean for women and babies? Medicine would have us believe that it meant above all a safer birth. The profession of medicine claims that the decline in maternal and infant mortality that we experienced in the twentieth century was a result not so much of women's hard-won control over their own fertility, or even of better nutrition and sanitation, but rather of medical management. Medical expansion into the area of childbirth began, however, before the development of any of what are now considered to be the contributions of modern obstetrics: before asepsis, surgical technique, antibiotics, anesthesia. At the time when physicians were taking over control of childbirth in the United States, the noninterventionist, supportive techniques of the midwife were safer for both the birthing woman and her baby, a point we will come back to when we discuss safety issues.

In sum, during the course of the late nineteenth through the early twentieth centuries, medicine gained virtually complete control of childbirth in the United States, beginning with the middle class and moving on to the poor and immigrant population. Midwifery almost ceased to exist in this country, and for the first time in history, an entire society of women was attended in childbirth by men.

The Scientifically Managed Birth

What did this medically attended birth look like, feel like, to the women who experienced it?

The standards for obstetrical intervention that gained acceptance in the 1920s and 1930s remained in place through the 1970s. These practices can be traced back to a 1920 article in the *American Journal of Obstetrics and Gynecology*, "The Prophylactic Forceps Operation," by Joseph B. DeLee of Chicago. DeLee's procedure for a routine, normal birth required sedating the woman through labor, and giving ether for the descent of the fetus. The baby was to be removed from the unconscious mother by forceps. An incision through the skin and muscle of the perineum, called an episiotomy, was to be done before the forceps were applied. Removal of the placenta was also to be obstetrically managed rather than spontaneous. Ergot or a derivative was to be injected to cause the uterus to clamp down and prevent postpartum hemorrhage.[27]

It's worth noting a distinction between the DeLee as represented in that infamous article and the actual man. Jackie Wolf, the historian whose work I quoted earlier, read an early draft of this chapter and called this to my attention:

> I know he's become the evil father of modern obstetrics due to his 1920 AJOG article. But DeLee lived in turn-of-the-century, everything-was-class-based Chicago. He birthed Maxwell St. babies as well as Prairie Ave. babies. And he used the outlandish sums that he charged the Pullmans and the Ogdens and the McCormicks and the Schaffners on Prairie Ave (he charged upwards of $1500 to attend some of their births in the 1920s, I've seen the arguments he had with husbands over the bills) in order to fund the Maxwell Street Dispensary so he could birth babies for free on Maxwell St. His dispensary had the lowest maternal mortality of *any* clinic in the U.S. *and* Europe and the women who went to the dispensary were the poorest (talk about "at risk") in the city. And his medical practices were different in the two places. No interventions for poor women, fabulous outcomes. Some interventions for wealthy women to justify his prices. He knew the game he was playing. And he ended his life by defining "good obstetric treatment" very simply: as prenatal care, treatment of complications before mother or baby were endangered; asepsis ("sterile technique"); and the presence of a skilled physician who never attempts to "streamline" birth. I think there is evidence that he ultimately regretted what he had wrought.[28]

This is a particularly important distinction, not just to be fair to DeLee, but because it's a problem we are still dealing with: wealthy women can get what they want. Then what they want becomes what is on offer. Wealthy women wanted to turn birth over to their doctors. That worked for the doctors and they made it their own. Eventually it became all that was on offer.

So why were DeLee's procedures, rather than allowing the mother to push the baby out spontaneously, so widely accepted by the 1930s? On one level, we can answer this in terms of the needs of the still developing profession of obstetrics: the need for teaching material; the need to justify both the costs and the prestige of obstetrics by providing a special service that midwives and general practitioners had not provided; the need to routinize patients in a centralized facility. Consider, however, the medical rationale, the reasons doctors themselves gave. They thought that what they were doing was a reasonable response to the demands of labor. Just how did they understand labor, and what is this medical model of birth?

The use of forceps was to spare the baby's head, DeLee having famously compared labor to a baby's head being crushed in a door. The episiotomy was done to prevent tearing of the perineum, something that is almost inevitable with the use of forceps. Even without forceps use, however, US physicians were finding tearing to be a problem, most likely owing to the use of the American-style delivery table, which required the supine position, with legs in stirrups.[29] The clean cut of the episiotomy was held to be easier to repair than the jagged tear. DeLee further claimed that the stretching and tearing of the perineum resulted in such gynecological conditions as prolapsed uteri, tears in the vaginal wall, and sagging perineums. It wasn't until 1976 that an empirical study was done to determine the long-term effectiveness of episiotomies, and the results indicated that episiotomies caused rather than prevented these conditions.[30] Episiotomies have been the most widely performed surgical procedure on women, and every few years another study comes forth showing that they do not work. Most intriguingly, perhaps, DeLee claimed that the episiotomy would restore "virginal conditions," making the mother "better than new." All through the 1970s obstetricians were heard to assure husbands, who were just then starting to routinely attend births, that they were sewing the woman up "good and tight." The forerunner of our modern "cosmetic surgery" business for vaginas?

For the baby, according to DeLee's article and his many followers, the labor was a dangerous, crushing threat, responsible for such conditions as epilepsy, cerebral palsy, "imbecility," and "idiocy," as well as being a direct cause of death. For the mother, birth was compared to falling on a pitchfork, driving the handle through her perineum. Using these analogies, DeLee was able to conclude that labor itself was abnormal: in both cases, the cause of the damage, the fall on the pitchfork and the crushing of the door, is pathogenic, that is, disease-producing, and anything pathogenic is pathological or abnormal.[31]

The implication of the DeLee approach to birth for the mother is that she experienced the birth as an entirely medical event, not unlike any other surgical procedure. At the beginning of labor she was brought to the hospital and turned over to the hospital staff. The sedation of the 1930s, 1940s, and 1950s was "twilight sleep," a combination of morphine for pain relief in early labor, and then scopolamine, believed to be an amnesiac. A woman under twilight sleep can feel and respond to pain; the claim is only that she will not remember what happened. Women in twilight sleep therefore had to be restrained, or their uncontrolled thrashing could cause severe injuries, as the drugs left them in pain and disoriented. Obstetrical nursing texts offered warning pictures of women with battered faces and chipped teeth who were improperly restrained and threw themselves out of bed.

The birth itself was not part of the mother's conscious experience, because she was made totally unconscious for the delivery. Such women required careful watching as they recovered from anesthesia. They were in no way competent to hold or even see their babies; it might be quite some time before they were told the birth was over.[32] The babies themselves were born drugged, and required careful medical attention. That drugged, seemingly comatose newborn was the source of the popular imagery of the doctor slapping the bottom of the dangling newborn, attempting to bring it around enough to breathe. It was several hours, or even days, before the mother and baby were "introduced."

That essentially the same management existed through to the 1970s in US obstetrical services was documented by Nancy Stoller Shaw in her observations of maternity care in Boston hospitals.[33] Shaw reported that obstetrics residents went by the book, and the book (the "Procedures and Policies" book of the hospital) said,

> The use of premedication for labor and anesthesia for delivery are an integral part of the philosophy of this hospital. . . . It is the conviction of this institution that the use of adequate medication for labor and anesthesia for delivery serve the welfare of the mother and baby best, not only when difficulties develop suddenly, or unexpectedly, but also in uncomplicated situations.[34]

And with regard to the interventionist management of labor and delivery, Shaw wrote,

The Maternity Division staff strongly believes in an activist controlling approach to labor designed to make it as short as possible. Synthetic labor stimulants (oxytoxics) are injected into the woman, especially the primipara, to stimulate labor. . . . In addition, during the expulsive stage of labor (delivery) the obstetrician is expected to *routinely* use episiotomy and low forceps delivery to minimize damage to maternal soft parts, to diminish the need for subsequent gynecologic surgery, and to *shorten the duration of pressure on the fetal head.*[35]

Shaw's observations led her to conclude, "These patients become totally alienated from their birth experience. They are treated like lumps of flesh from which a baby is pulled."[36]

But women are most assuredly not lumps of flesh: we are also political actors, people who take control over our lives and our circumstances. While some women were working hard, pushing doctors in the development of twilight sleep so that they could avoid feeling birth and have so-called painless labors, other women were fighting this turn of events. When the DeLee approach developed in the 1920s and 1930s became dominant throughout the United States by the 1950s, a countervoice was raised, calling for a return to a more "natural" childbirth.

7

Phase Two

Consumer Society

Refuge and Resistance

I invited the members of my yearlong doctoral seminar on writing for publication to my house for a chili party. I stocked up on beer, which is one of the basic food groups of graduate school. I bought chips, cut up veggies, made some guacamole, and a lot of brown rice, put out salsas and the cheeses and the grater, and made three kinds of chili—red bean with ground turkey; black bean with potatoes and corn (the house specialty); and white bean, pretty much a failure. But it was pretty.[1]

It was fun—fun to spend a few hours cooking, fun to take out the huge collection of clear glass bowls that serve chicken soup with kneidlach for Passover and transform into pasta or stew or chili bowls for big buffet parties. Fun to have the kind of kitchen that can produce food for ten or twenty or even more people without a stretch.

Whenever people cook, we do have the audience in mind. Whether it's an end-of-class meal prepared for graduate students, a birthday party for a child, a Thanksgiving dinner, or a neighborhood potluck, what we serve is a statement. Food is a medium through which people communicate, what Annie Hauck-Lawson calls "the food voice."[2] Food, as we prepare and present it, is a home-based language. Some of it is presented to the outside world as dinners served, dishes brought. And some of it is far more private. A view of the kitchen can give as intimate a glimpse into someone's life as the medicine cabinet or the bedside table. There is both a public and a private world of the kitchen. People think about the kitchen they want to have, the foods they feel they ought to eat or be feeding their family, and the way their kitchen really does look and the foods they really do cook. There's truth in both: as in any language, we're communicating on more than one level, saying more than one thing at a time. Food expresses class and status, ethnicity, "taste" in all its mean-

4

4

ings, values, and beliefs. The vocabulary of food—what we purchase, what we do to it, and how we present it—is one of the ways we talk to each other within the family, and one of the ways we present both ourselves and our families to the outside world.

The world of science and industrialization brought us easy, convenient, prepared and packaged food. But here we are, a century later, and we are still messing around with cooking, still—maybe even more—obsessed with the creative consumption of homemade food. Who taught us to speak that language of food as not just having but *expressing* taste?

Food is obviously about consumption and about industrialization, but it is also about reclaiming from a massified, industrialized, commodified world a little tiny private space. The kitchen is a site of resistance, a place where people refuse consumerism even as they play it out, where they refuse industrialization, even as they play that out too. The kitchen, so thoroughly disclaimed, the place women wanted to escape from, is also a place to escape *to*, a place that can be—that for many of us is—*comfortable*. There's a tension here, between all of these meanings and uses of food and cooking and the kitchen. Dinner is a chore, a creation, a responsibility, an opportunity, a peaceful moment, a harried time.

The tension is between consumption and production, between falling neatly into line as a market segment and being our own true selves—even imagining what that might be. It's the tension teenagers display so openly and almost pathetically: dressed proudly "weird," "different"—and virtually in one uniform or another. I think a lot of us—Americans, women especially, mothers maybe most of all—feel that tension in our lives. The kitchen is one of the places people resolve it; they walk into the kitchen and get creative, playful, accept and resist both what tradition has to offer and what the market has to offer. It's about food, but clearly so much more.

Because I think the kitchen is a place where we are showing some resistance to consumer culture, to the fully commercialized, standardized world around us, I can see that even when we are doing something as slight as combining two jars of sauce to make the one our family likes, or adding extra cocoa to the cake mix, we are claiming a little space for ourselves.

We've all seen enough almost-new ice cream makers, bread machines, juicers, garlic presses, and other kitchen tools sitting at yard sales to know that some kind of active fantasy life is governing those purchases. There was a moment there when someone thought she was the kind of person who'd be freezing her own ice cream, probably out of organically grown berries from her backyard, or crushing garlic from the strings she had hanging in the newly painted kitchen—till they were covered with dust and shriveled.

If it were all about the fantasies that just don't play out, this would be depressing. But I don't think it's that at all. I think there is something wonderful going on there. What I love about the midwives and those of us who have home births, in our grand gestures of empowerment and demystification, I find there in the kitchen too.

But where did we learn to think of food and cooking as this outlet for creativity? When did putting together packaged, processed, semi-prepared ingredients we bought in a store become an act of creativity? How and when did consumption become a kind of creative production?

Creative Consumption

That feeling, so deeply personal, of creating, of *meaningfully* creating something in my own kitchen—that was a feeling sold to Americans with just as much energy, intelligence, and advertising dollars as any box of cereal. Dinner was "reinvented," as Laura Shapiro says, in 1950s America.[3] You've probably heard the more-or-less apocryphal story of the cake mix. It was possible, the story goes, to have a mix in a box to which one just added water, put it in a pan, and poof, a cake. Women rejected it, the story goes, until the mix was adjusted to require eggs to be added too. Then, with some real ingredient pulled out of one's fridge and beaten into the powder in the box, it felt like baking a cake, and the mixes sold. That one might not be quite true, but the story actually has some meaning. If cooking is too fast, too easy, it's not really cooking at all. I haven't made you a birthday cake if I snip the strings on the bakery box and transfer it to a plate. How can I say I made it if I only spent a few more minutes pouring powder into a bowl and stirring? How much do I have to do to have made your cake?

One answer would be in terms of time, how many minutes or hours it will take me to "make" this food. But there's another, better answer, one that worked. Laura Shapiro credits it to Ernest Dichter (the "mad man," to use today's word for it) at the Institute for Motivational Research and his work analyzing "today's lady consumers."[4] Dichter is the one who taught manufacturers to add "creativeness" to the selling of packaged food. Shapiro says Dichter spelled it out in the form of a dialectic:

THESIS: "I'm a housewife."
ANTITHESIS: "I hate drudgery."
SYNTHESIS: "I'm creative."[5]

"Creativity," then, was a solution brought to us by the packaged food industry itself. "Above all, creativity was the fairy dust that would transform opening boxes into real cooking."[6]

The post–World War II years, the fifties and early sixties, weren't known for creativity; the joy of creativity was largely gone from most people's lives most of the time. It was an era of conformity, of the development of a corporate style for middle-class people, heading off to work in cubicles, returning to suburbs. Malvina Reynolds captured it in the song "Little Boxes"—the houses, the people in them, the children who go to university where they're all put in little boxes and they all look just the same. "There's a green one and a pink one, / And a blue one and a yellow one, / And they're all made out of ticky tacky / And they all look just the same."[7]

And yet people do create, do want to create. Birth is of course the quintessential creative act: parents stare at the newborn, in awe of their creation. Ask most people about playing music or painting or sculpting or any creative acts, and you get, "Who's got the time?" And it's true, really—creativity is a luxury. But not in the kitchen. People actually do make something, take things and transform them into something else. It's ironic and charming to me that in this most literal area of consumption, we have one of our few outlets for production. Obviously it involves enormous amounts of consumption; maybe all the production, the creativity, for most people boils down to just combining two different brands of barbecue sauce to get the flavor they want, but still. It seems to me that in the ordinary course of a day, the time in the kitchen is the one time for most people that they are making something.

I talked to some people about home cooking and what it means to them, and creativity came up regularly.[8] One person spoke about the accomplishments of producing: "You know, it's like you're taking your time out and you have the time and the energy. At the end you see: Wow, I made this. It's gratifying." Another spoke even more pointedly about creativity: "I can't paint, I can't sing. I can cook. . . . It's creative. You can do whatever you want with it." People cannot very well just have more children for the sheer joy of creating them, but they can, and do, cook meals they do not even want. One woman talked about cooking as a way of relieving stress: "During finals week, I will cook like two to three meals a day and not eat it myself and just give it to people 'cause I need to zone out, which includes baking and roasting and just weird things that I don't even eat. Why I would roast a chicken if I'm vegetarian, I do not know. But finals week, it will be roasted and it will be given to my parents." She created for the pure joy of creating.

The "fairy dust" of creativity allowed women to be creative while stuck in that world of "drudgery." In suburban tract houses, mothering the baby boomers, cooking was an outlet for some creativity; it was the part of housework women liked the most.[9] Making it too easy, too convenient, would kill it, suck the juices out of it. Creativity got you past the ticky-tacky.

There was space there for personal meaning, for personal story making. But there was also space there for a classed, raced story: all of us buying pretty much the same processed foods, but putting them together in our own/communal ways. There was space too for an elite. You could go beyond doctoring up a canned, boxed, packaged meal, which meant combining things your own way, your family's way—you could "glamorize."[10] "Anybody who could splash sherry over the peas or set fire to the dessert could glamorize, and soon, it seemed, everybody did. Glamorizing food was a lot like doctoring it up, but the aim wasn't merely to be creative, it was to achieve an unmistakable impression of luxury and sophistication."[11]

The French Connection

And what did luxury at the table mean to Americans? It meant haute cuisine, a French take on food. Or to be really accurate, an American take on a French take on food. *Those* people, Americans think, know how to live. *Those* people are living in their bodies in ways that we are not. They know from sensuality, pleasure, physical joy. In the American psyche, the French are to the British as our id is to our superego. When we are dissatisfied with how we are managing things of the body, we turn to the more sophisticated, glamorous, sensually embodied French. It's true in food and it is true in sexuality and it is true in birth, but more on that later.

There was a reaction to the overly scientized, overly industrialized world of American food, growing in the postwar years, but starting early on. James Beard had his first book contract in 1940, for a book called *Hors d'Oeuvre and Canapés*. Beard, who we think of as a kind of father of American cooking, started with that French title. But his mission wasn't about spreading French techniques, it was "to defend the pleasures of real cooking and fresh ingredients against the assault of the Jell-O-mold people and the domestic scientists."[12] French food is, in American-speak, the opposite of industrial food.

For Americans, French food defines fancy, or glamorous, as haute cuisine. The first two food magazines in the United States have French names: *Gourmet* (from the French for wine tasters, *groumets*, and de-fined as a *connoisseur* in eating and drinking) started in 1941. And *Bon Appetit*? That magazine started in 1951.[13] It is, it would seem, hard to talk about elegant or fancy or cultured food in American English without invoking French.

The most famous of the French restaurants to define American fancy food grew out of the 1939 World's Fair. Henri Soulé opened Restaurant Francais and made quite a hit, and then opened Le Pavillon (named for its World's Fair French Pavillon roots) in 1941 in New York, rather satis-fyingly within a block of Madison Avenue. As David Kamp points out,

> That a restaurant such as Le Pavillon could storm out of the gates during wartime, with a full reservation book and adoring press write-ups, while rationing was still in effect and the Depression still cast a pall over the economy, speaks volumes about the esteem in which educated Americans held French culture and French cuisine. Among the upper classes, Fran-cophilia had held sway for some time, and it was de rigueur for society mothers to hire French governesses for their children. . . . World War II and the decade that followed it represented a high water mark in Franco-American goodwill. The returning GIs who fought in France became be-sotted with the country they were liberating.[14]

Not only the haute cuisine, but the bistros, the cafés, all the lovely places to eat, all the bakeries, patisseries, boulangeries, a strong dollar and a weak franc, the arrival of jet travel—the stage is set for French cooking in America.

And we all know who walked out onto that stage: Julia Child. Her first show went on the air in 1963, and truly, the rest is history.

A Bite to Get Us Started: Meatloaf

Meatloaf started showing up in cookbooks late in the nineteenth century. In the Depression years it became popular, a way to stretch the meat. There are of course lots of historical variations; chopping up meat and blending it into things is not new. There are Dutch meatballs with just as lovely a history as an "ethnic food" as the Italian ones Americans know. Really all over the world you find some variation on this, from the filling in a Chinese dumpling to gefilte fish. Anyone with a bit of leftover meat and a few people to serve is bound to think of chopping it up to divide more evenly. But if you've ever faced meat scraps armed only with a chopping bowl and a chopper, you wouldn't be thinking of it as a convenience food, a quick way to put dinner together, which is how most of us now think of meatloaf. The invention of the mechanical meat grinder made that altogether easier. It clamped to the table and you turned a crank, and meat fed in the top came out the side, evenly ground. I had one of those, finally gave it away when I moved to a smaller place. When did I ever use it? Ground meat is readily available in packages in every supermarket. With the thriving meat industry of the early twentieth century, with the availability of refrigeration and packaging, ground or chopped meat changed. It wasn't a way to use up scraps of meat in the home kitchen, but a way to use up industrial scraps, the bits that did not fit into the roast, the tougher chunks. Issues of adulteration, fears of contamination aside, ground or chopped meat is enormously convenient for all, producers, home cooks, and consumers. It is, after all, the basis of the hamburger, our quintessential fast food.

Meatloaf began to show up in cookbooks in that early scientizing age as a way to use leftover roasts and hams, to have them show up on the dinner table the next day made new. And not surprisingly, food companies suggested ways to doctor it up—a can of Campbell's tomato soup, a bit of Post Toasties.

It was in the 1950s, though, that meatloaf came into its own, became the staple and comfort food Americans now know it to be. It went from being just a way of using up odd bits of meat to a product on its own. Meatloaf was perfect for the job: packaged chopped meat was available in the growing supermarkets or from the still-extant butchers, and it was relatively inexpensive. It was a packed, pure form of meat, protein by the pound. It was "wholesome" and easy, that epitome of science and convenience we were looking for in our kitchens. Eventually even choice cuts came to be used for meatloaf, upscaled to "ground sirloin." The cheapest cuts could also be dressed up, made unique and creative, a bit of taste added to the convenience. The *Betty Crocker's Picture Cook Book* of 1950 introduced the "festive" meatloaf baked in a ring—not a loaf at all, but somehow far more elegant.[15] And the options are almost endless. Given chopped meat and ovens, nothing could be more convenient; but given that formless glop in the bowl, nothing could lend itself more to individualizing, to making one's own. Taste enters anew: no end of products to mix in, spices off the 1950s spice rack on the kitchen wall, ready-made sauces or mashed potatoes (homemade or out of the newly available premade boxed mix) slathered on top, hard-boiled eggs (a Jewish and German specialty, Wikipedia tells me!) hidden within, baked in loaves or rings or individual treats. Not chunks of meat left from other purposes, not bits of leftover dinner, but a new meal, homemade, saying lovin' from the oven.

That's the mix (as it were) that was brought to birth: do not question the science. Do not question the industry. But make it your own.

Childbirth Movement, Phase Two: Consumer Society

At that same 1939–1940 World's Fair where Soulé was establishing what would become Le Pavillon and creating Americans' ideas about what elegant people's food should be, the Maternity Center Association was offering its ideas about what pregnancy ought to be. And as Soulé was shifting our thinking away from the "science" of home economics courses, the MCA was shifting our thinking about pregnancy. It too was moving from science to something we could call taste, ideas about taste-ful, modern ways to have babies. Fear had dominated that science age of food—fear that we weren't getting the right nutrients, that our food was contaminated. And fear had dominated the science age of birth—fear that our babies would die, that mothers would die. Those fears were actively sold to get people to buy into the products of science, to become consumers of industrial food and of medicalized birth. In the 1930s, pregnancy reformers produced "powerful imagery of childbearing as scary and dangerous with the aim of validating and amplifying existing pregnancy anxieties. By instilling fear in the hearts and minds of expect-ant women and men, experts and reformers hoped to push prospective parents into practicing medically supervised prenatal care."[16]

That scare tactic had been extraordinarily successful. For middle-class women, and increasingly for all women outside the rural southern Black communities, birth had moved into hospitals and under medical control. But the times, they were a-changing. Sophisticated consumers began to want something more than what mass production was offering them. Ideas about pregnancy itself were changing, being incorporated into the romantic marriage, the nuclear family with its ever-in-love, best-friends spouses. While birth had gone from the world of women to the world of medicine, pregnancy was moving from the world of women to the world of couples. And those men were about to enter the birthroom.

For its 1939 exhibit at the World's Fair in New York, the Maternity Center Association switched from fear to a new message, "projecting happiness, sunshine, cheerfulness." Pregnant women were to be happy, enjoying their pregnancies and their coming motherhood. But so too were men to be enjoying this, and the new MCA literature began includ-ing fathers, "assuring husbands that they 'will find that preparing for the baby is one of the happiest times in your lives.'"[17] The 1940s and onward, Ziv Eisenberg notes in his history of the making of modern pregnancy in America, were "marked by a movement toward a new cultural under-standing of pregnancy as safe and 'happy.'"[18]

By the 1950s, once we had come through World War II and had the energy to think about such things, pregnancy became something to share, to celebrate, to buy things for, and finally even to laugh about. The boomers were coming, and pregnancy was everywhere. The Victorian practice of holding a tea party for expectant mothers grew into the baby shower, the umbrella-wielding Victorian woman providing the symbol. And in 1952 we had our first shared, celebrity pregnancy, precursor to all the baby bumps to come: Lucille Ball, of *I Love Lucy*, shared her real-life pregnancy with viewers. It was somewhat controversial—"disgusting," wrote some in letters to newspapers, offensive to show a pregnancy.

Scholars and popular writers who examined Lucy's pregnancy have mostly focused on the December 8 episode's title, "Lucy Is Enceinte," and offered the same narrative: in the early 1950s, the word "pregnant" was not part of polite discourse. Fearing to offend viewers, CBS prohibited Lucy's production members from using the term and forced them to change the title to "enceinte." To make sure that the pregnancy episodes had met contemporary decency standards, a committee consisting of a Catholic priest, a rabbi, and a Protestant minister approved all the scripts and oversaw the production.[19]

Whatever caution censors did or did not show, it's worth noting that when they went to find a "nicer" or less "disgusting" way to talk about pregnancy, they went straight to French. *Naturellement! Enceinte* is just French for "pregnant." But more refined, you know? By the second episode, the word "pregnant" was okay, and the trials of pregnancy were explored a bit: "Pregnant Women Are Unpredictable" was the title. The series then had an episode in which Lucy hired an English tutor so she and Ricky and neighbors Fred and Ethel would be ready to raise the baby properly; took a sculpture course with the same thing in mind; had Fred help her throw a party for Ricky so he won't feel left out; and finally we have the episode in which, with much slapstick nonsense, they all fly around the apartment trying to get the early-laboring Lucy to the hospital.

What would happen to the woman when she got to the hospital would not make for good TV fare. Lucille Ball herself was actually having her second baby, and had had a cesarean for the first. But Lucy Ricardo, her character on the show, was having her first baby, and had no reason to be expecting surgery. Just a standard American birth. Doctors had taken over birth, women of the upper classes had gotten what they thought they wanted, but it failed them. Their weakness had left the world of gentility and moved into a new vulnerability. Medicine had them strapped on gurneys, transported in hospital gowns across hallways, alone and frightened in labor rooms, exposed and strapped into place in delivery rooms. Lucy would get to that hospital, be stripped, changed into a hospital gown, given an enema, have her pubic hair shaved off, and be strapped into a labor bed. Ricky would be picturesquely pacing in the hallway. Oooh, la la.

Dick-Read: Childbirth without Fear

There were instances of American women rejecting one or another aspect of modern obstetrics long before any "movement" began. Margaret Mead, for example, writes in her autobiography, *Blackberry Winter* (1978), of her attempts to re-create for herself in a US hospital the kind of natural, unmedicated birth she had seen so often in the South Seas.[20] The first major thrust of the childbirth movement, however, was the publication in Britain of *Natural Childbirth* by Grantly Dick-Read in 1933; notably, the US edition was released in 1944. Dick-Read was an English obstetrician, and so his work must be understood in the light of a different cultural experience surrounding birth. English midwifery survived the growth of obstetrics, and English obstetricians, quite possibly balanced by the existence of midwifery and relatively uninterfered-with births, never became as interventionist as US obstetricians.

Dick-Read developed his concept of "natural childbirth" as a result of a home-birth experience. He attended a woman in labor in a home he described as a leaky, one-room hovel lit by a candle in a beer bottle. As the baby's head was crowning he offered the mother a chloroform mask, which she rejected. She went on to have a calm, peaceful, and quiet birth. When Dick-Read asked her later why she had refused medication, she gave an answer that became a classic statement of the natural childbirth philosophy: "It didn't hurt. It wasn't meant to, was it, doctor?"[21]

In the years that followed, Dick-Read decided that no, it was not "meant to hurt," and developed a theory of natural childbirth:

> Civilization and culture have brought influences to bear upon the minds of women which have introduced justifiable fears and anxieties concerning labor. The more cultured the races of the earth have become, so much the more dogmatic have they been in pronouncing childbirth to be a painful and dangerous ordeal. This fear and anticipation have given rise

to natural protective tensions in the body and such tensions are not of the mind only, for the mechanisms of protective actions by the body include muscle tension. Unfortunately, the natural tension produced by fear influences those muscles which close the womb and prevent the child from being driven out during childbirth. Therefore, fear inhibits: that is to say, gives rise to resistance at the outlet of the womb, when in the normal state those muscles should be relaxed and free from tension. Such resistance and tension give rise to real pain because the uterus is supplied with organs which record pain set up by excessive tension. Therefore fear, pain and tension are the three evils which are not normal to the natural design, but which have been introduced in the course of civilization by the ignorance of those who have been concerned with attendance at childbirth. If pain, fear and tension go hand in hand, then it must be necessary to relieve tension and to overcome fear in order to eliminate pain.[22]

In a nutshell: "If fear can be eliminated, pain will cease."[23]

Dick-Read's is a fairly sophisticated statement of psychosomatic relationships, and notably one that does not "blame the victim." Unlike many other statements by physicians that held the "weakness" or "delicacy" of "civilized" women to blame for pain in childbirth, Dick-Read places responsibility with birth attendants for the "evils" of fear, pain, and tension. The pain, he acknowledged, was real, but it was not necessary.

For Dick-Read, motherhood was a woman's "ultimate purpose in life,"[24] her crowning achievement. He saw the laboring woman as drawing closer to God as she worked to bring forth her baby—and Dick-Read definitely viewed labor as work, "hard work." This is hardly what most of us in the United States think of as modern feminism, but it was a kind of woman-centered approach, a spiritual focus on motherhood and a respect for the work laboring women do. It is a far cry from the dominant medical approach, which saw the laboring woman as essentially no different from someone in the hospital for gallbladder surgery.

Dick-Read's philosophy had some appeal among educated white women in the United States as well as in Great Britain, women who could be "natural" without being seen as "primitive" or "animalistic," and it is its Americanization that concerns us here. *Childbirth without Fear: The Principles and Practices of Natural Childbirth* was published in

the United States in 1944, one generation after DeLee's article had introduced the full-blown American birth. In 1947 the Maternity Center Association invited Dick-Read to the United States for a lecture tour. While
Dick-Read's book and method appealed to many American women, for
a number of good reasons, the Americanization of Dick-Read was, in
practice, something of a disaster.

Dick-Read called attention to the context, the actual setting, in which
birth takes place; he did not speak only of its psychological meaning
for the individual woman. Having a "good attitude" was not enough.
Dick-Read taught women relaxation techniques now familiar to many
of us: how to find and then release muscle tension throughout the body
by unwrinkling the brow, letting loose the hunched shoulders, and un-
clenching the fists. He taught those techniques before labor, but then
reaffirmed that teaching throughout labor. He stated, "No greater curse
can fall upon a young woman whose first labor has commenced than
the crime of enforced loneliness." He related his own fear during a war-
time battle in which he "learned the meaning of loneliness."[25] He said
that women needed *continual* comfort and emotional support during
labor.

Women in the United States who attempted to follow Dick-Read's
advice did so under hostile conditions. They were confined to labor
beds, they shared labor rooms with women who were under scopolamine, and their screams, combined with the repeated offering of pain-
relief medication by the hospital staff, reinforced the very fear of birth
that Dick-Read set out to remove. But it's more than that. Sophisticated,
often college-educated, the women of the "feminine mystique" who
were exploring their kitchen creativity with Bisquick, wall-mounted
thirty matching-bottle spice sets, and ground beef, were not much in
the mood for learning deep truths about womanhood from someone in
a one-room, candle-in-beer-bottle hovel. Natural, or "primitive," births
did not have much appeal, nor did the spiritual call reach this audience.
Dick-Read did not speak to American women.

Lamaze

Marjorie Karmel was an American woman of some apparent means,
married to Alex (she never does mention what he does for work) and

living "comfortably," as they say, in Paris. It was the mid-1950s, and Karmel was pregnant. "Wonderful!" Alex said—and "What do we do next?" "I haven't any idea," she answered. "I suppose you ought to see a doctor," he suggested vaguely.[26] And thus began her journey to birth, as they like to say now.

Karmel wasn't coming at this with an agenda, with a birth plan, with any real ideas about birth. Someone at a party in the United States, while she was back in the country for a visit, handed her Dick-Read's book, and she took it reluctantly, but ended up staying up all night reading it on the ship back to France. Alex read it too.

> The one thing we found we could not share was Dr. Read's profoundly mystical view of the spirituality of motherhood. I wanted to have a baby very much, but I did not feel I could get rhapsodic about giving birth. I doubted that I could waft myself through the experience without the assistance of an anesthetist. But I was thankful for the knowledge that would enable me to approach the experience in a rational manner.[27]

Dick-Read's natural childbirth wasn't for her, but someone introduced her to a Dr. Lamaze, a physician who had trained in what was called the "psychoprophylactic technique," an approach to childbirth based on Pavlovian conditioning. Pavlov is the Russian scientist who showed that if you rang a bell when feeding a dog, eventually it would salivate at just the sound of the bell. Uterine contractions—like the bell—were held to be stimuli to which alternative responses could be learned. Most women had learned pain and fear responses; it was believed that with training, these responses could be unlearned, or deconditioned, and replaced with such responses as breathing techniques and abdominal "effleurage," or stroking. It is the Lamaze technique that introduced the rhythmic "puffing and panting" that characterizes, maybe caricatures, the portrayal of birth in popular media. It was held that concentration on these techniques—techniques based on the methods used by midwives—would inhibit cerebral-cortex response to other potentially painful stimuli. In contrast to Dick-Read's evocation of God and the spiritual, this approach was couched in the language of science. The method was developed in the Soviet Union, and in 1951 was established there as the official method of childbirth.

In that same year, 1951, Fernand Lamaze and another French obstetrician, Pierre Vellay, traveled to Russia and observed obstetrical practices. After making some relatively minor changes, Lamaze introduced the method in Paris. In 1956 he published a book on the method, *Painless Childbirth*,[28] and Pope Pius sanctioned its use.

This was an approach that appealed to Karmel, and she hired Lamaze as her obstetrician. She always refers to it as the "Pavlov" method, and she makes it clear that it isn't about "natural" birth but about a science of pain management that would work in conjunction with obstetric care. She gets annoyed when people talk about it as natural or as just getting past fear. At a party back in the States, after her first birth in France, a "tactful old lady" waits until they're alone to speak (bet you a dollar I'm older than that old lady was). She clarifies that Karmel had had no drugs, then says, "That's the way it is over there. . . . Backward. Haven't made any scientific advancement. Not living in the modern world. That's the way it used to be. Now in America they can . . ."[29] Karmel interrupts, assures her she wanted it that way, but cannot convince the old lady that she had a painless birth without drugs: "In her mind there were only two possibilities—pain or drugs." For Karmel, this is a third way: the Pavlovian method is a series of scientific techniques, exercises she carefully learned and patiently explains. She writes about Mme Cohen, who taught her all the exercises and then stayed with her to work them through in labor. She titles a chapter "Six Easy Lessons," and compares it to "all the ads for dance studios or language records—'Learn to Whatever in Six Easy Lessons.'"[30] Birth, like dance or language—or like cooking—could be mastered by an intelligent, thoughtful woman.

She had her baby in a French hospital as unlike what American hospitals of that moment were like as you can imagine. She was given some tea and encouraged to go for a walk in the gardens of the hospital while she was in labor. She wore her own clothes, and the baby was dressed in the clothes she was told to bring with her. There was only one room for labor and delivery, and the baby was placed in his cot by her side when he was born. She never actually mentions that baby again. Did she breastfeed him? Hold him in those first hours? We don't know. The book she wrote was about birth, not motherhood. She came to write the book because when she found herself back in the United States and pregnant with her next child, Dr. Lamaze was gone and she was alone with Alex in America.

She translated Mme Cohen's lessons, how to relax selected muscle groups while tensing others, how to respond to stimuli with careful breathing, how to do different kinds of breathing, and how to gently stroke or massage the belly. That massage technique, to be done by the woman or by someone with her, never did get translated: it's called *effleurage* in her book, and when I checked with Google translate, apparently the English word for *effleurage* is "effleurage." That French phrase adds a nice touch, *n'est-ce pas*?

She had that second baby, in an American hospital, and in 1959 she published *Thank You, Dr. Lamaze: A Mother's Experience in Painless Childbirth*. In 1960 Karmel, along with a physiotherapist, Elizabeth Bing, and a physician, Benjamin Segal, founded ASPO, the American Society for Psychoprophylaxis in Obstetrics.[31] Bing went on to develop "Lamaze" for years, for decades to come; Karmel died of cancer in 1964, just thirty-four years old

ASPO, as Bing and Karmel developed it, unlike the Dick-Read approach, was specifically geared to the American hospital and the American way of birth. Catch the vaguely medicalized name—it hardly sounds like a challenge to medicalization. They're talking about obstetrics, not birth, and a method, psychoprophylaxis, that sounds like doctor-speak of the 1950s. The only challenge ASPO offered to the status quo concerned the use of anesthesia. ASPO substituted psychological for pharmacological control of pain. While the difference between consciousness and unconsciousness may be all the difference in the world for the mother, from the point of view of the institution, that single factor is relatively minor. The original ASPO training course, written by Bing and Karmel and published in 1961, stated, "In all cases the woman should be encouraged to respect her own doctor's word as final. . . . It is most important to stress that her job and his are completely separate. He is responsible for her physical well-being and that of her baby. She is responsible for controlling herself and her behavior."[32] Basically, be a good girl. This certainly poses no threat to the control of birth by obstetricians As Vellay himself, the other French developer of the method, wrote in 1966, "We have always maintained the *Painless Childbirth belongs above all to the obstetrician.* They can estimate and understand better than anyone else the very special behavior of the pregnant woman."[33]

Even on the question of pain medication, the doctor's rather than the woman's perceptions were to be valued and trusted: "If your doctor himself suggests medication, you should accept it willingly—even if you don't feel the need for it—as he undoubtedly has very good reasons for his decision."[34] Note that this was written long before obstetricians were familiar with the technique, and so could not possibly be accurate in their judgment of the need for pain relief—if in fact one person can *ever* judge another's pain.

The physical trappings and procedures surrounding the American birth were written into the original course, including the perineal shaves (back in the day when women did not wax our labia), enemas, delivery tables (although women were taught to request politely that only leg and not hand restraints be used), episiotomies, and all. ASPO accepted the medical model's separation of childbirth from the rest of the maternity experience, stating in this first manual that rooming-in (mother and baby not being separated) and breastfeeding are "entirely separate questions" from the Lamaze method.

ASPO managed to successfully meet both the demands of women for a nicer, more refined birth and the demands of obstetricians for "good medical management." The issue became resolved over *consciousness.* The title of the first book published by an American obstetrician supporting the Lamaze method makes the point: *Awake and Aware: Participation in Childbirth through Psychoprophylaxis.*[35] Control came to mean simply control over one's behavior (notably pain response). At first glance, the Lamaze method may appear to center on the woman's autonomy, but that confuses consciousness and pain control with power. Women, especially the middle-class educated women of the 1960s and 1970s who used the method and made it so popular, may have felt that it met some of their desire for control over their bodies. But this was a deceptive thing, a false consciousness. The method succeeded where Dick-Read had failed because it was the only practical method designed to deal with the hospital situation.

Lamaze courses were designed as six weekly sessions, evening courses for six or seven pregnant "couples," husbands and wives. Husband participation was considered advantageous but not initially considered necessary for the use of the method. "Enforced loneliness" was not considered an insurmountable handicap, though for many women the real battle they fought was to bring a husband or someone into the labor room with them, and not the right to breathe in rhythm. Over a period of almost twenty years, it became entirely acceptable, and then expected, and finally all but mandatory for husbands to enter first the labor rooms and later the delivery rooms. In Lamaze training in the United States, the husband acted as his wife's "labor coach," a position held by the *monitrice* in the French version of the Lamaze technique (and arguably now held by the doula). The coach provided the continual emotional support that Dick-Read talked about, but was seen by ASPO as really being there to provide very specific coaching in the method, reminding the woman to pant, to take cleansing breaths between contractions, to relax her muscles. Since there was no *monitrice*, no member of the hospital staff assigned to help the laboring woman, the husband took on both roles in the American version, and so had to be trained along with the wife. This very much fit into the 1950s and early 1960s approach to marriage and "togetherness."

In essence, the method keeps the woman quiet by giving her tasks to do. Being a "good"—noncomplaining, obedient, cooperative—patient was the woman's primary job, "controlling herself and her behavior," while the doctor did his task.[36] And as is not uncommon with relatives of institutionalized people, the husbands are co-opted into doing the staff's work, moving the patient through the medical routines as smoothly as possible. In the classic Lamaze birth, Mother, coached by Father, behaves herself while Doctor delivers the baby.

You can imagine how well that went over with second-wave feminists and counterculture hippies.

8

Phase Three

The Counterculture

The Times They Are a-Changing

Early on in this book, when I was bemoaning how much worse the birth movement was faring than the food movement, I said I wanted Meryl Streep playing Ina May Gaskin, the way that she had played Julia Child. But really, the reference point for Ina May isn't Julia Child—Julia Child was too early on, grew out of a different world. The food movement counterpart to Ina May would be Alice Waters.

And here's where this book sometimes feels like a prolonged introduction—food people, meet birth people; birth people, meet food. I'm guessing most of my readers will have heard of one of these two, but quite a few won't know both.

Ina May is arguably the best-known midwife in the world. And that, folks, is my problem with this movement—most people still won't have a clue who she is. Ina May wrote *Spiritual Midwifery*, her 1975 book on her experiences "catching babies" on the Farm, a commune in Tennessee.[1] Ina May Gaskin started out studying English, then joined up with—and married—Stephen Gaskin, San Francisco's "acid guru," who lectured in the Bay Area on ecological awareness, psychedelic drugs, and other key elements of hippiedom. The weekly gathering, "Monday Night Class," eventually turned into a caravan of hippies headed to Tennessee. Ina May Gaskin was not a midwife by training or background. Rather, she fell into it, riding along in the middle of nowhere with birthing hippies. Out of her depth but finding her feet, she both made it up as she went along and learned from others: from an older family doctor, from whatever sources made themselves available, but also from the births themselves. Coming from her particular time and place, she called contractions "rushes," decorated the book of "amazing birthing tales" with hand-drawn mandalas, and asked women to be "groovy and selfless and brave" in labor and men to "be tantric with your ladies." Her book, published by the Farm, came out a bit too late to be helpful for me, and, well, a bit too hippie/spiritual/out-there for me too. More on all that later. The lesson for now is that an alternative, counterculture caravan of school buses traveled east out of the Bay Area, and, one thing following another as it does, babies got born en route. Ina May became a midwife.

Just as the caravan left the Bay Area, Alice Waters was opening Chez Panisse. She too had no particular training or background for what she was doing; she too rather made it up as she went along, learning from others, including the chef, Jeremiah Tower, she hired at the restaurant. Waters had been to France. She brought back what she learned there about taste, about food, about the sheer sensual pleasures of food. And she brought it back to 1960s California and "the revolution." While Jerry Rubin was eating bologna on white bread to express his solidarity with the masses, Waters was saying that you not only have to liberate yourself politically and sexually, but "you have to liberate all the senses."[2] One accusation always hurled at foodies is that they are elitist, not grounded in the people or a politics of social change. Issues of class, of race, of access seem to be lost. Who, after all, can afford to care about taste, the sensual nature of food "experiences"? Yet

> Chez Panisse wasn't a retreat from politics—it *was* politics, a representation of what American food could be if people weren't complacent about gassed, flavorless tomatoes and frozen TV dinners. The counterculture generated plenty of misbegotten movements and lysergically distorted belief systems that would later cause its members to feel disillusioned or embarrassed, but the fresh food movement wasn't one of them. In fact, it might well be the counterculture's greatest and most lasting triumph.[3]

That focus on "fresh" was in large part a solution to a logistical problem. Waters found that she couldn't make dishes taste exactly as they would in France: local ingredients are different. The flavors of fruits and vegetables "reflect the soil, water and air that nourish them, and Berkeley just wasn't Provence. But Waters turned that drawback into an asset by focusing on the rich variety of local produce."[4] We owe to Waters "the mantra of 'fresh, local, seasonal ingredients' now chanted by any chef or home cook of integrity."[5] In a way, Waters had a very sociological imagination, a way of understanding the local and the specific individual experience in its larger political context: "She joined fine cooking with community activism, supporting local farmers, organic food, sustainable agriculture, and other causes. Cooking is, in her view, a product of agriculture as well as a part of culture."[6]

This does not solve the tensions between the elitism of seeking individual pleasures in food (or in birth) and the larger politics of social change, but it does indicate where you might look if you want to address the politics. And this moment in the food movement did want to address the politics, did want to look past the products available and to their sources. It was not only about taste, this "countercuisine,"[7] as Warren Belasco so brilliantly named it. This food movement tried to pull together taste and sensuality with politics, a politics of consumption. In 1974 (the year I had my first home birth), for the third anniversary of Chez Panisse's opening, "Tower created individual pizzas he called panisses, topped with goat cheese and red-ripe Sonoma beefsteak tomatoes. In one stroke he'd started three enduring food trends—gourmet pizza, goat cheese, and an insistence on the finest local ingredients."[8]

I think it's oversimplifying to call gourmet pizza and local ingredients "trends" as if they were the same kind of thing. Gourmet pizza is all about taste and fun, things one creates in the kitchen to enjoy. Eating local ingredients connects to a much larger politics, to issues of environmental concerns, politics of agriculture, ultimately to the relationships between producers and consumers. Towers wanted nice pizzas. I wanted a nice birth. But we were also dealing with the politics of our time, whether it be the power of the medical establishment or the power of the agricultural industry. On the one hand it's selfish and petty and elitist; on the other it's a call for a rather significant social change.

This tension is a long-standing problem in the food movement. In 1906, when Upton Sinclair wrote *The Jungle* and showed so graphically the horrors of the meat industry, the vile treatment of animals and workers, most of the response was about protecting the consumers.[9] Or, as Sinclair said of the newly enacted Pure Food and Drug Act, "I aimed at the public's heart and by accident I hit it in the stomach."

Meat eating is both the clearest and the most complicated space to address this tension between individual elitism and social movements. All the strands come together: ethics, health, taste, world hunger, climate change, you name it, it's all there in the decision to eat or not to eat meat. This is such a fraught issue for people in my world. I'd best start with full disclosure: I am not a vegetarian. I did stop eating beef about twenty-five or so years ago, when I was working on issues of new reproductive technology and could not help but see how entwined the development of human and cattle reproductive services were. Some things were tested out on cattle before they were released to women; but some things seemed to be tested out on women before they moved to the cattle industry. A year or so of reading about repro-tech, and I could not face a chuck steak or a hamburger. I substituted pork in all the beef recipes and kept on cooking. I stopped eating pork on a particular day in 1999 and at a particular place: I was standing at the Brooklyn Museum, looking at the Saatchi show *Sensation*, which had garnered so much political attention, and watched Damien Hirst's Lucite-boxed, split pig slide open and closed. I stood there, transfixed, for about ten minutes, and that finished pork. Lamb, goat, they dropped off around then for me too. I cannot justify this, I cannot explain it in morally meaningful language, but there you are: I stopped eating mammals. I use milk products from goats and cows; I cannot justify that one either. I moved to free-range eggs, to organic, better-treated cow's milk, and (sometimes) more expensive free-range poultry. But outside each of the supermarkets I've shopped in over the years, there have been homeless people—just one or two, regulars, as it were—who stand there begging. I've gotten to know them, which means nothing, I guess, thinking about it as I write—I recognize them, they me, a dollar changes hands. I've stood in front of the organic chicken or turkey, looked at the sometimes twelve or so dollars difference this will cost for cooking dinner tonight, thought of the person outside the store, and just been totally stymied.

I do not want to write myself out of eating poultry. I do not want to give up Chinese roast duck, sausage sauces, all that would leave my kitchen and my life. There is not a lot of logic here. One could have the same crisis facing the seven-grain bread and the loaf of packaged white; the apples in the cheap section and the ones isolated over there in organic produce. Meat, though, raised the questions for more people earlier, made them think about the relationship between eating and what went into it, in terms of labor, toil, pain, and life itself. Isaac Bashevis

Singer was a vegetarian. When asked whether it was "for his health," he replied, "No, for the health of the chicken."

The politics of meat eating goes beyond the health of either of them. That is the point that Frances Moore Lappé, another Berkeley counter-cuisine person, made in her book *Diet for a Small Planet*.[10] Published in 1971, it became a surprise—shock would be more like it—best seller.[11] Lappé went beyond individual food choices to look at the global issues. Just one year after the first Earth Day, she was offering a connection between individual kitchens and the ecology movement. The argument is that we are using enormous amounts of grain to grow animals we then eat. Eat the grain itself, and we could feed the planet. And we were learning too that the badly fed cattle, artificially plumped up, held under awful conditions, also required massive doses of antibiotics, which we then ate in their meat. By now the idea of an ecological solution is enough of a truth to have become self-evident; in 1971, not so much. Along with the new interest in Buddhism and its vegetarianism, the part of the sixties that really happened in the seventies made tofu a rising star.

It did not, sad to say, end world hunger. (And another social movement shot to hell.) Whatever grain was saved in becoming vegetarian, or by using assorted recipes from Lappé or other 1960s classics like *The Tassajara Bread Book*[12] or later *The Moosewood Cookbook*[13]—somehow that grain did not get shipped off to feed the world. People concentrated, too much for Lappé, on the taste, sensuality, and personal health advantages of the food; not enough on the larger politics. Vegetarian cooking got to be fun, trendy, its own kind of upscale. It is the argument that Warren Belasco persuasively makes, pointing out that

> Frances Moore Lappé eventually left her own foundation, Food First, to make political change more clearly her primary focus: tellingly, the word "diet" did not appear in the name of her new organization, The Small Planet Institute. . . . Food was a handy way of gaining attraction but also proved to be something of a distraction from the wider concerns of the activists. . . . Systematic change does not flow automatically from eating better food.[14]

A food movement that focuses only on the food, on what we eat, is not going to make large-scale social change.

This is perhaps the aspect of the food movement that didn't do all that much better than the birth movement, for all of its better press. Food got better, but maybe not so much the rest of the world; the rest of the values of the counterculture got lost as the gourmet pizza and the goat cheese part flourished. How did we get to a place where it really is possible that the hand-raised cow or pig or goat on the table has had better treatment than the guy who sweeps the rented hall we served it in tonight, better than the "illegal" cooks out in the back of some of the restaurants? It's not just meat, of course. I think back to my own neo-hippie kitchen, when I used to mail-order Starbucks coffee before they brought their shops to me. That dark roast, oh that was so delicious, a whole new moment in coffee. And the education they gave me on "fair trade" and the conditions of coffee-growing countries—"Specialty coffee wasn't just delicious; it was righteous and cool."[15] Now I find anti-Starbucks petitions popping up in my lefty-organization e-mails. And Ben and Jerry's! Closer to home than those West Coast guys, right nearby in Vermont, hippies selling ice cream, natural ingredients, local dairies, pretax profits tithed to charities: "While Ben & Jerry's tactics sometimes came off as cloyingly self-congratulatory, the notion of a 'halo effect,' of being nourished morally by doing business with a socially conscious company, proved to be a powerful marketing idea in the gourmet world."[16] And now Ben & Jerry's is owned by Unilever. I'm trying to find some comfort or humor in that being a Dutch multinational, but it's not really helping. Values somehow come to matter for how well they sell. (Another social movement shot to hell.)

But is it that dismal? Are we as consumers only interested in what goes in our mouths? In her memoir, *Eating My Words*, Mimi Sheraton wrote, "I remain convinced that there are more people interested in knowing where to buy the best bagel than about the latest act of political or corporate corruption, primarily because they personally can do something about the bagel but feel powerless against the Enrons of the world."[17] What does it mean to "do something" about that bagel? Is it just finding the best-tasting one? Isn't also about finding bagels that you can feel okay about eating, that do not seem to add to the evils of the world with every bite? Of course we can make fun of that; one of the cartoons framed in my kitchen shows a customer in a diner looking up at a chalkboard menu that includes a column "Ethical Issues Related to

This Item." But the food movement—food as a social movement—made people think about those issues.

There was of course another movement going on in that same time that was pointing out how seemingly small and personal things were connected to a larger politics. The personal is political. Alice Waters, you may have noticed—or you may have *not* noticed[18]—is a woman.

Feminism

That same year that Alice Waters was finding the joys of fresh local ingredients and Ina May was setting forth, a group of women on the other coast were making feminist history: the Boston Women's Health Book Collective, which came to be known as the *Our Bodies, Ourselves* collective. Their book was first published professionally in 1971,[19] but (archival research in my bookshelf reveals) forty- and fifty-cent copies were being printed in 1970. *Our Bodies, Ourselves* is the bible, the founding text, of one kind of feminism. It was created by a collective of women, "a course by and for women," as it was subtitled. This is a kind of feminism that isn't about women moving "up" into the positions men held, but of women taking back our own bodies, lives, selves, knowledge. That is an interesting tension in feminist thinking, between women "moving up" to be like men, versus reclaiming the territory we were already in, and it can be seen in the food movement as clearly as in the birth movement.

The same year that Julia Child stepped onto the national stage, so did Betty Friedan, a connection Laura Shapiro pointed out in her biography of Julia Child.[20] It's more than a random coincidence of time. *The Feminine Mystique*[21] and *The French Chef* were addressing the same problem, coming at it from two different sides. Our post–World War II industrial capitalism was trying to make middle-class women into mindless consumers. They wanted us to take our education, take our skills and our sophistication, and go out and buy tastefully. As I write that, my fingers kept editing back and forth between "women" and "us." That was one of the first victories I found in the feminist movement in academia—we did not have to distance ourselves as scholars from ourselves as women, we could use "us" and "we" when we meant women. We could be scholars and academics *as* women, not in spite of being women. We went too far with that sometimes, put all kinds of women with all kinds of issues and interests and needs into the same "we," too often took the privileges of class and of whiteness and failed to see that not all women were to be consumers—some were to go fry the chicken we would pick up as takeout; some would sew the clothing we would carefully choose; some would clean our tastefully appointed kitchens. While poor women and women of color still struggled to get food on the table, for middle-class women, the pressure was on to go home and "arrange" things—salads on plates, schedules, shopping lists and all.

Betty Friedan rejected that. So too, though, did Julia Child. Friedan's approach, rejecting the kitchen, rejecting "traditional" womanly virtues and skills, came to be what Americans think of as feminism. Child's approach, treating that traditional work with respect, shows up in a countervoice to Friedan's liberal feminism. She didn't reduce the woman to the task, never called women "housewives." Some call the kind of thing Child was doing a more radical feminism; some call it a cultural feminism. It is a voice that says, No, women need not be like men, achieve all that men achieve in men's worlds. Rather, we should value what goes on in women's worlds, respect and appreciate women's culture, women's ways of knowing and ways of being. We don't have to slam the kitchen door as we leave—we can learn to appreciate what goes on in there.

This is a tension that runs all through the birth and the food movements: how we deal with difference. In food, we can say it is all a culturally constructed difference, that there is nothing about the bodies of women that puts them in the kitchen. In birth, we don't have that option. We have to confront that which is in fact different about women's bodies. So do we reject what medical science tells us about those bodies, and create our own knowledge, or do we ourselves become the obstetricians and gynecologists who make the knowledge? Do we reject the food scientists and nutritionists and snobby food experts who tell us what healthy food and what gourmet food ought to be, or do we become those scientists and experts ourselves? Whose knowledge will we accept as legitimate?

Women have, of course, done both. We have reclaimed the lost knowledge of our foremothers and we have moved into the top positions in the food and the birth worlds both. Of course—as with law, government, science, arts—our presence at the top is still just over token levels.

There are women at the top of these worlds, but relatively few and far between the higher up you go.

Reclaiming lost knowledge, and lost foremothers, is a pretty standard women's studies 101 task: look for the missing women. Take whatever bit of history is on offer, and ask where were the women. Someone will show up, some missing foremother, unrecognized, underappreciated, discarded just because she was a woman, but performing like a Mozart prodigy because she was one before her little brother took it all over; co-authoring the great man's texts while going largely unnoticed; out there, lost there somewhere, doing work "just as good as" men's. But there's another women's studies approach: look at those women who were doing mindless, meaningless "women's work" and start asking, Who said it was mindless? For whom is it meaningless? In this tack, we look at the work that women do and unpack it, see how much thought and intelligence and actual work there is in that. Food studies has brought us a number of such projects.

The foremost one in sociology is the work of Marjorie L. DeVault. *Feeding the Family: The Social Organization of Caring as Gendered Work*[22] unpacked what went on in that work, made the invisible work of nurturance visible: "The skills involved in feeding a family are skills of planning and coordination; the work, increasingly, is invisible work."[23] Other feminist researchers had looked at cooking, but folded it into the larger category of "housework." There is the aptly titled *Never Done: A History of American Housework* by Susan Strasser, which shows us how the work of women became increasingly transformed into market commodities, outsourced.[24] And there is the lovely work of Ann Oakley, whose research for *The Sociology of Housework* showed that cooking was "potentially the most enjoyable" of housework activity. "It presents a challenge; it can be an art."[25] That perception of creative potential, she points out, is influenced by media presentations, by the advertising discussed earlier. "They say it can be creative, but is it, in practice? . . . Limitations of time (and money) act as brakes on the enjoyment of cooking."[26]

What DeVault did was go past simply acknowledging those limitations, and look at how women maneuvered around them. DeVault shows us how shopping, or "provisioning," makes family: "Shopping for food can be seen as a complex, artful activity that supports the production of meaningful patterns of household life by negotiating connections between household and market."[27] Feeding the family is one of the ways we make family: "Feeding the family is work that makes use of food to organize people and activities. It is work that negotiates a balance between the sociability of group life and the concern for individuality that we have come to associate with modern family life."[28] Next time you stand there in a supermarket or your local greenmarket, deciding if the mushrooms can be used as a sauce so that the kid who hates mushrooms will still eat the main course, and if the spinach can be folded into the tomato sauce so your partner gets those greens he never eats enough of, and if the whole thing can be on the table by the time day care closes— well, think about that. Individuality maintained within collectivity, food organizing people—this may be invisible work, but it is not mindless and it is not meaningless.

That, however, was not the dominant feminist voice. That dominant voice told us to get the hell out of that kitchen and do not look back. One of the more delightful, poignant, and public discussions of that tension is in the introduction to Arlene Voski Avakian's edited collection *Through the Kitchen Window: Women Writers Explore the Intimate Meanings of Food and Cooking.*[29] Avakian invited a host of feminist writers, scholars, academics, poets, and others to contribute food stories and recipes. Ruth Hubbard, a biologist at Harvard who was, I should probably mention, an important mentor to me and much cited in a book I did on the human genome project, declined to participate. Never one to mince her words (which made her a great mentor for me), she wrote, "To tell you the truth, I was irritated at the idea of collecting a set of feminist writings about women and food, including recipes. Haven't we had enough of women being viewed through the kitchen window. . . . I don't find a feminist linking of *Kinder, Küche, Kirche* much more inviting than a standard one."[30] I guess that's where Avakian got her title. She wasn't surprised by Hubbard's response: "I had been expecting criticism for a book on women and food. Because cooking has been conceptualized as part of our oppression, 'liberation' has often meant freedom from being connected to food."[31] Avakian defends her work just the way I've been defending mine in this project: "Cooking is something that was and continues to be imposed on women, but it is also an activity that can be a creative part of our daily lives. As such, the work of cooking is more complex than mere victimization. . . . By reclaiming cooking we ensure that we are not throwing the spaghetti out with the boiling water."[32]

It gets more complicated. While some women were walking out of the kitchen, men were walking in. The post–World War II rise of a new food culture had brought men, as chefs but also as food writers, into the world of food, and sometimes right into the kitchen via the back door from the barbecue. James Beard's second book was on grilling; *Cook It Outdoors* proudly proclaimed in its jacket copy, "It is a man's book written by a man."[33] "It's very important that Jim was a man," says Barbara Kafka. "That's how he made a difference. Historically, you had cookbooks and cookery writing by two groups of people, women and chefs. And, as in so many things, Jim was a crossover person."[34]

In those same years of the post–World War II era, Craig Claiborne wanted to write about food for the *New York Times*, and approached the food editor. "Don't get your hopes up," she advised him. "A man as a food editor . . ."[35] But Claiborne was hired, and food writing changed in America: "His hiring by the *Times*, Ephron says, was an amazing moment, a symbolic moment—the whole way the old food section was reinvented for the upper-middle-class reader."[36] And then, by the feminist 1970s, "It was a perverse measure of Claiborne's achievements that, nearly twenty years after he had to pester Jan Nickerson about the legitimacy of his candidacy, as a man, to be the paper's food editor, now the *Times* management had decided that only men were worthy of the position."[37] Mimi Sheraton, now one of our best-known food critics, had a hard time, as a woman, breaking in.

As much fun as it is for me to cook for my graduate students, to bring them into my home and serve them and visit, it took quite the revolution to make that thinkable. In the 1970s, when I was being fired for being pregnant and clearly not "serious" about my career (fired by a woman department chair, it's worth noting), there were really two kinds of women: those who cooked and cleaned and had babies, and those who had careers. Women like Mimi Sheraton and the new women trying to become chefs were bridging those gaps. By the 1980s my men students were as likely to be cooking—and more likely to be bragging about it—than my women students. And by those 1980s, there was a new baby boom among feminist women: I'd been the oldest pregnant woman I knew when I had my first baby at twenty-six; I was the youngest I knew when I had the second at thirty-three. The delayed childbearers, the second-wave feminist generation of mothers, had arrived.

A Bite before We Move On: Tofu

Let's make something with tofu, shall we? Maybe a tofu burrito? Chipotle's just added that to its menu. Like cold cereal and like meatloaf, tofu's apparently got some staying power, but it truly is of its moment. And its moment is right there in the 1970s counterculture. Tofu has its roots in Asia, was probably first produced in China, though the word itself is Japanese. In the United States, through to the middle of the twentieth century, non-Asians probably encountered tofu only in excursions into Chinese restaurants. With the meat restrictions of the Second World War, there was some interest in using tofu in non-Asian recipes, even a few soy cookbooks published in the 1940s. Its Japanese name probably didn't help; the author of one of those cookbooks, Mildred Lager, called tofu "soy cheese," and that "dairy" idea continued. The non-Asian tofu producers in the United States in the early 1960s were run by Seventh-day Adventists, intriguingly enough. When meat consumption soared in the 1950s, interest in tofu dropped, but with the counterculture's new vegetarianism, and the search for less wasteful, more efficient ways of feeding the planet, tofu was suddenly everywhere—low-calorie, low-cholesterol, high-protein, bland enough to use in almost anything—the perfect food for the moment. The Farm, the commune that produced Ina May and the midwives, also developed the first soy ice cream, Ice Bean, and named its soy-producing project a "soy dairy." Dozens of tofu cookbooks came out in the 1970s and on into the 1980s. Tofu became the go-to item for taking meat or dairy-dependent recipes and turning them vegetarian in the 1970s, and later on "vegan," when that wave landed.[38]

And there you have the counterculture/countercuisine. Take something exotic, make it in a commune, talk about peace and love, the planet and vegetarianism and all that—and watch it get branded, sold, and brought into the marketplace. It's not a bad thing—it's the kind of success I only wish we'd see for the birth movement.

Raising Consciousness

The reproductive rights issue that captured the headlines of the 1970s wasn't the home-birth movement, it was *Roe v. Wade*. That Supreme Court abortion ruling said that "the abortion decision and its effectuation must be left to the medical judgment of the pregnant woman's attending physician." It didn't actually give women the right to have abortions; it gave doctors, and *only* doctors, the right to provide them. That medicalization was what made legalized abortion palatable, to the extent that it was. Medicine is itself a kind of state religion, after all, and many people felt then—and continue to feel now, when the vast majority of Americans do still support legalized abortion—who are the courts to argue with the doctors?

The doctors, like the judges, were men. Through the 1960s fewer than 10 percent of medical students were women. The numbers started to grow with second-wave feminism and the passage of Title IX of the Higher Education Act in 1972, and the Public Health Service Act of 1975, banning discrimination on the grounds of gender. More and more women moved into medicine, but in 1973, when the Supreme Court was talking about the pregnant woman's attending physician, those were almost all men.

Those of us who wanted to make midwifery care available had to argue that birth did not require a physician. No, that sounds wrong. That is what we had to say, I suppose, but what we meant was that birth did not belong in the same box as medical procedures. Saying that it didn't require a physician is like saying, "Oh, birth's so easy, you don't need medical training!" And that is indeed the path we had to go down, normalizing birth, demedicalizing it, but sadly at the same time, deskilling what we understood midwifery to be.

We could—and many feminists did—make the same argument about abortion. Women provided each other with abortion care "throughout all of human history." Learning how to do abortions was a political act. As the sociologist and women's health activist Pauline Bart reminded us, "They can't legislate away skills!" If we know how to do our own abortions, to help each other by providing abortions woman-to-woman, abortions will always be available to us. Looking back on all that has happened and has failed to happen in making abortion available to women who need it, that might have been a good way to go. But it wasn't; abortion remained medicalized. Abortion fit neatly into the liberal feminist model, the idea that women could live their lives as men live theirs, get equal pay for equal work, have control over our lives, and the right to avoid or postpone motherhood while we went to medical school or law school.

Abortion went with liberal feminism; birth veered off to the radical feminism, the Julia Child, celebrate-the-kitchen end of things. The Boston Women's Health Book Collective did some bridge building. In those early, prepublication, newsprint copies of *Our Bodies, Ourselves*, the chapter on birth is mostly about "prepared childbirth," with a sentence about how home birth ought to be an option. It was 1970, 1971, and there were no books around on home birth in America, and none cited in the bibliography. Lester Hazell did the first academic work I know of on the home-birth movement, an anthropology master's thesis entitled "Ethnography of Home Birth in the San Francisco Bay Area" in 1974, and included it in her second printing of *Commonsense Childbirth*,[39] just in time for me, and with an endorsement by the collective on its cover. And it was a year later, with my son Daniel crawling up and down the steps at an open meeting of the Boston Women's Health Book Collective at Harvard, that I first learned about the new midwifery movement.

It may be hard to understand now, but back in the 1970s having a baby felt like some kind of caving in, a sellout of feminist ideals. For me, it certainly felt that way when I was let go from my teaching position at Brooklyn College by the woman chair of the department because I was "obviously not serious" about my career. (I am repeating myself, I know that—I'm still angry.) We didn't have the phrase "pregnancy discrimination" at the time. When I tried to explain how crushing that experience was, the husband of one of my study group members said I should just get over it, I'd finish my dissertation and get a job, it was no big deal. I asked him to think about how he would feel if he had been in an accident, lost the use of his legs, suddenly was in a wheelchair, and then got fired from his job. My identity was at stake here. I wanted to be me still, to be pregnant, to be a mother, but still to be me. That struggle to maintain a feminist identity, an identity as a budding scholar, a doctoral student, while pregnant and as a mother was so much like the struggle people with disabilities have had; for feminists and for academics, motherhood was a kind of stigma, a spoiled identity.[40]

My article on my home birth was published in *Ms. Magazine* in 1976[41]
Ms. Magazine was founded in 1971 by Gloria Steinem and Letty Cottin
Pogrebin as an insert in *New York* magazine, and was on its own by
January 1972. One of its first editions had an article about women who
had abortions, published while it was still illegal. It felt like a kind of
vindication when they published my article. The line they pulled out on
the first page, the one in that big print magazine articles use, was "I don't
want my consciousness raised on the delivery table." It was one of the
best sentences I have ever written. I once heard someone quote it on an
elevator at a conference and I almost burst with joy. In the text, I went
on to say, "I'm a feminist, and I'm pregnant. That shouldn't be contra-
dictory. There has to be a way of having a baby with dignity and joy—as
a feminist, not in spite of being a feminist."[42] I read Karmel, I read the
(then) newer work on "prepared childbirth," and saw then what I see
now: "I gather that if you're a very good girl and you show how cooperative you're being, then probably the nurses won't strap your hands down.
If you're very polite and rational with your doctor, then maybe you won't
be anesthetized when you don't want it."[43]

That's what brought some of us to the home-birth movement. But
there were other voices being heard. While I sat with my pregnant belly
in an abortion clinic with a beloved friend terminating her unwanted
pregnancy, and while I'd talked a member of the Jane Collective into
doing a home birth, Ina May was singing a different song. The conclud-
ing section of the 1975 edition of *Spiritual Midwifery*, the absolute final
page of text, shows an image of a fetus labeled "the baby at eleven weeks"
and says, "Don't have an abortion. You can come to the Farm and we'll
deliver your baby and take care of it, and if you ever decide you want it
back, you can have it."[44] Home birth resonated with "traditional" values
too, not just feminists and hippies. Amish communities have been big
supporters of midwifery, and there's a whole collection of home-birth,
home-school, Christian traditionalists. The spiritual glorification of
motherhood that Dick-Read wrote about appealed to a lot of very traditional people, and home was a far better place to have a natural birth
than hospitals ever were.

It was a strange, strange community that we brought together in the
home-birth movement. I remember walking into a lunch room at a
meeting of the Midwives Alliance of North America sometime in the

1980s and looking at the interest groups that were gathered at round tables to discuss their concerns: Amish women with their traditional costumes, the hippies with their tie-dye costumes, the lesbian separatists in their flannel. I loved it, still do. All the feminist tensions that existed in the world of food were there—and more!—in the world of birth. It's what single-issue politics can sometimes accomplish. You want to serve them all goat-cheese, locally sourced pizza. There's a lot that we will never agree on, but this matters to us.

Bringing Back the Midwife

If Phase One was bringing in anesthesia and thus the doctor, and Phase Two to move out the anesthesia, Phase Three is about moving the doctor back out again, and bringing back the midwife. Writing about this phase is going to be hard—I'm my own data here. When I write about the history of second-wave feminist movements around childbirth, I'm writing about myself too. That *Ms. Magazine* article was my first publication. When I read books on the history of childbirth, I find myself cited in the discussions of the home-birth movement and midwifery politics. So I sit here, aging, reflecting on a movement that I threw myself into in my youth. And the mistakes as well as the (very minor) successes of that movement—those are my mistakes as well. I'm going to fall into the vocabulary of the movement, and I'll forget to do it ironically—I'll talk about "empowering" women and really mean it. Forgive me, bear with me as I wrestle with my disappointment.

Having studied midwifery issues for almost forty years, I have quite the collection of midwifery T-shirts, including one from the first Midwives Alliance of North America (MANA) meeting, T-shirts from organizations long defunct, shirts with women and babies and moons and stars. But my favorite is the first one I ever got. Between the words "The Midwives" on top and "Daughters of Time" on the bottom is a drawing of two women, clearly intended to be midwives, striding forth. One is from the nineteenth century, wearing a shawl, long skirt, and high-button shoes, hair knotted in back. The other, younger and taller, has long, loose hair, an open-necked shirt with rolled-up sleeves, a wristwatch, sandals, and bell-bottoms. Midwives of the 1970s are now as much a part of our history as are midwives of the 1870s.

The midwife of the 1970s was aspiring toward her midwifery; it was a goal, an ideal. She could not, as her sister/foremother of the previous century could, take midwifery for granted. For an earlier midwife, the practice of midwifery was important, valued, and respected, but also a part of ordinary life. Of course there were midwives, and of course what midwives did was practice midwifery. Because midwifery was so deeply damaged, so all but completely destroyed in the United States in the years that separate the two midwives on my T-shirt, it could no longer be taken for granted. Midwifery came to be something more than the people who practice it—it came to be something of an ideal, a goal, a model to which one could aspire. The distinction arose between midwifery as an occupation or a practice, as something one does, and midwifery as a model.

My feminist obstetrician, Marcia Storch, understood and agreed in principle with my right to birth as I saw fit, in the location of my choosing. In fact, in actual practice, she was clueless. When the baby was born and I was reaching up to take him, the doctor passed the child back over her shoulder to where she presumably expected a nurse to materialize. My mother—standing in the right place—was the first to hold my newly born son. And then, as if there was someone else waiting for the space I occupied and we had to move on quickly, she reached in and extracted my placenta. That hurts, is remarkably intrusive and downright dangerous, but was standard procedure in hospitals at the time, processing women through as efficiently as possible, keeping the schedule rolling. Home birth, I saw—from the vantage point of my rocking chair with my feet up on the kitchen chairs serving as makeshift stirrups that she had brought in—was very different from hospital birth, not only for the birthing woman but also for the women attending. I chose this topic to research for my dissertation as a graduate student in sociology. Living in New York City, I tracked down and interviewed all the people I could find who were attending home births. All were nurse-midwives. Most were white, but a few were Caribbean-born and -trained, bringing the still-living remnants of midwifery practice with them. Some had gone through regular nurse's training and then moved on to hospital-based midwifery before doing home births; some, the immigrants and one who started as "lay" midwives in California, had been trained and worked as midwives before becoming nurse-midwives.

I observed a few births, but it was less what the midwives were doing that interested me and more how they were thinking about what they were doing. Their knowledge, their understanding, their way of thinking about birth intrigued me. How do people know what they know? That's a basic question in sociology, and it was the one that captured my attention. My key insight was seeing that there are different models underlying practice, different ways of thinking about birth that resulted in different ways of practicing. Ways of thinking, ideology, and concepts underlie ways of practicing, of behaving and doing. I read the obstetrics literature, and I read the literature of the developing home-birth movement—newsletters, conference reports, Ina May Gaskin's *Spiritual Midwifery*—what little there was out there on home birth. I started comparing the way people think about birth at home and the way they think about it in the hospital. It was the difference between the two places that first caught my attention.

Most of the midwives I was interviewing were in a way just like the feminist obstetrician who delivered my baby. They had the best of intentions, but they were really out of their element in the home. They didn't know what to think much of the time. They were confused about what they were doing and seeing. I worked with a study group at the time in which we read each other's dissertation work. Continually talking about these different midwifery paths, I had a hard time articulating the differences between home and hospital birth.

One day my friend and colleague Eileen Moran came back to my house the day after a study group meeting. She sat down with me in my office and drew two circles on a piece of paper. The one on the left, she said, is the way doctors think about birth—the way midwives are taught about birth in their hospital training. The circle on the other side of the paper, the home-birth approach, represents the Caribbean-trained midwives, the lay midwives in California, and what Ina May's spiritual midwifery is about. And here in the middle, trying to find their way, are these midwives you're interviewing.

That was exactly right. Those were the midwives, as I quickly came to call them, "in transition," that most painful, intense, hard part of labor right before you make clear and obvious progress. Those midwives were right there, that part where you don't know if you'll ever pull through, that part where you are vulnerable and scared and working very, very hard.

It wasn't really about "home" or "hospital." A midwife could bring the hospital way of thinking into the home with her, as my obstetrician had. And a midwife could bring the home way of thinking into the hospital. Many of those midwives would tell me stories of doing home births one day and then doing hospital births the next, trying to take what they had learned at home and apply it in the hospital. "Midwifery" was a way of thinking to which most of these nurse-midwives were aspiring. I started to call these different approaches "medical" and "midwifery," rather than hospital and home.

Like many graduate students of the time, I was heavily influenced by the work Thomas Kuhn had done in his book *The Structure of Scientific Revolutions*, in which he introduced the idea of a paradigm shift.[45] Science, Kuhn pointed out, doesn't proceed at an even pace. Data are collected and analyzed and collected and analyzed. And then there comes a moment when the data no longer seem to fit the old analysis, and a "scientific revolution," a "paradigm shift," lurches the science ahead to a new place. Kuhn gave a simple example from a psychology experiment. Subjects were asked to identify playing cards flashed on a screen. Most were from a standard deck, but some were made anomalous—a red six of spades or a black four of hearts. Something interesting happens when you show people these cards. At first they "normalize them." They identify a black heart as a regular red heart or see it as a spade. After a while, though, subjects begin to hesitate. More and more hesitation is shown, until they switch over and come to see a black heart as a black heart, and a red spade as a red spade. Kuhn said science works like that too. "Novelty emerges only with difficulty, manifested by resistance against a background provided by expectation."

But medicine and midwifery aren't sciences. They are clinical practices. Science has as its goal the production of knowledge. Medicine and midwifery are geared to the provision of services, to the improvement of outcome. Clinical practice may claim to be the application of science, but it cannot really work that way. It is the nature of scientific work to expose inconsistencies, to show the flaws in the old paradigm. Clinical practice, on the other hand, is not about generating data; it's about treating people. There are no control groups in clinical practice; once something is accepted as a treatment, it is offered. It works or it doesn't work, but the situations in which treatments are offered—the real world—are far too complex for us to consistently learn anything about the treatment. A treatment may seem to have worked, but maybe the condition would have cleared up without the treatment, maybe it only cleared up in spite of the treatment, maybe it wasn't the condition diagnosed anyway. Maybe the patient never really followed the treatment. Who knows?

Not only is clinical work not organized to produce new knowledge, but one could argue that it is really designed to avoid the production of knowledge. If the data you see—what is actually happening in the patient before your eyes—do not conform to the model of the illness, the practitioner is expected to reconsider the patient. For example, medical texts offer both the theoretical effectiveness of a contraceptive, how it is supposed to work, and also its "use-effectiveness," how well it actually works in practice. If a contraceptive doesn't work the way it is supposed to, the problem lies with the user, not with the contraceptive and certainly not with the science.

While I found the story Kuhn was telling extraordinarily useful, I didn't want to adopt his vocabulary. If science works with paradigms, what could I say clinical practice works with? "Models" are what I came up with. Models serve much the same purpose for the clinical practitioner as paradigms serve for the scientist: they attract groups of adherents; they become focal points for social organization as well as the organization of knowledge. And while paradigms are open-ended enough to leave all sorts of problems for the scientist to solve, models are useful to provide guidelines for practice. Both make work possible. Kuhn looked at paradigm shifts and scientific revolutions; I saw shifts in models and clinical revolutions.

What makes a clinical revolution? If, unlike science, clinical practice is not designed to produce new knowledge, where does new knowledge come from?

Where does knowledge come from in the first place? We learn from each other. We are taught by one another to think. Models or paradigms or whatever you want to call them give us the picture we have in our heads, against which we look at the world. We hold up what we know to be true and judge what is before us according to that. If the model tells me what a normal labor is like, then what is this labor I am seeing when compared with that? Longer? Shorter? Stronger? Weaker?

Or take something very simple: We have learned what a newborn baby should look like. There is a model, an ideal type—not ideal in the sense of being the "Gerber baby," but ideal as in paradigmatic, the essence of new babyhood—having the necessary and essential characteristics that mark it as a new baby. Given that model, we can look at any new baby and ask whether it varies, and how. In the direction of pathology? Is the head too big? Too small? Are the limbs proportional? How is the muscle tone? Compared with what? Compared with what you know is "normal," compared with the model you have in your head of what a baby's muscle tone should be at birth.

So where do models come from and how are they developed? We are accustomed to thinking that we know what we know from what we have observed, but it is just as true that how we practice sets up what we can observe—what is observable in the first place. If every new baby you ever saw was born from a deeply anesthetized mother, what would you know about normal muscle tone in a newborn?

That was the type of problem, if less dramatic, that was confronting the midwives in transition—these hospital-trained nurse-midwives doing home births for the first time. Their models did not apply. So how could they know what was normal? Clinical practice in hospitals was structured to avoid the production of just the knowledge they now needed. Want to know how long a placenta can take to separate from the uterine wall and still be healthy? You will never find out if all placentas are removed within fifteen minutes of the birth, as is done in hospital delivery rooms. Want to know whether you are looking at a "second stage arrest," a pathological condition, or a normal "rest period" for a woman who has had a difficult labor, before she begins the work of pushing forth the baby? If you always and immediately treat any cessation of contractions after full dilation as second stage arrest and rush to pull the baby out, as they do in hospitals, you will never observe the rest period or its resolution.

Examples such as these flowed forth in those early years of the late 1970s and 1980s as midwives confronted the limits of hospital-based knowledge for home-based practice.

Setting—place, location—counts. The differences between medical and midwifery models of birth are not just about attitudes, not even just a set of guidelines for practice. Different bodies of knowledge are produced in different settings. It's true when you take what you learned in a restaurant kitchen and try to produce it at home, and even more true if you try to take anything learned in a factory kitchen and try to bring it home. The knowledge does not transfer readily. The most important thing, I now know, about the third phase of the childbirth movement in America was the attempt to bring birth back home, and the accompanying rebirth of midwifery.

The Importance of Place

It is not just a matter of moving from place to place as we examine birth under different circumstances. Under different systems of care we are not just doing the same thing in a different place. Different places give us different meanings, and those make birth a different event. Teeth, tongue, jaw, intestines are all pretty much the same thing the world over, but the meaning of a meal could not be more different as we move from a famine in a country under siege to a food court in a suburban US mall, from a Passover seder to a fast-food lunch, from a high tea to a steakhouse. So it is with childbirth: the social and cultural variation overwhelms the physical sameness.

Institutionalization—any institutionalization—disempowers, drains power from the birthing woman and gives it to the institution itself, as it homogenizes the experience. The late Annemiek Cuppen, an extraordinarily fine midwife in the Netherlands, shared the following illustrative story. She had attended a birth in which the woman planned to give birth in the hospital. While the Netherlands has a 30 percent home birth rate, midwives do attend births in both places. Annemiek Cuppen came first to the woman's home for the early labor. As she came in the door she was greeted by the woman, who told her husband to go and get the midwife a cup of coffee, sent her children and mother-in-law scurrying on errands, and generally kind of bossed people around and remained the center of her home. And then came the move to the hospital, a move chosen, remember, by the woman herself. As they entered the hospital room, the woman sat herself quietly on the edge of the bed. With a new demeanor now, no longer at home and in charge, she looked up at Annemiek, and asked deferentially, "Uh, excuse me, do you think it would be okay if maybe we opened the window, please?"

It is not only at this individual level that an institution drains power from women. Once institutionalization is inevitable for birth, once all births move as they have essentially done in the United States, out of the home and to a specialized site, that site, the institution itself, comes to seem necessary. And once it seems necessary, it seems causal, as if the birth itself depends on the institution. That is how it is now in much of the world where home birth is not so much unavailable as unthinkable. Most Americans cannot imagine home birth.

That is one reason that maternity homes or birth centers are often suggested as a compromise for places like the United States that have lost their home-birth traditions. Even if there is absolutely nothing that makes a particular birth center any safer than a home birth, people who are now several generations removed from home birth can accept the possibility of a maternity home or birth center. Just going there will somehow make birth safe and possible in a way that simply staying in one's bedroom will not. Because to trust the home as a place for birth is to fundamentally trust the woman to give birth and the midwife to know how to help her—and that is the fundamental trust that most of the world that we now live in has lost. The power that is the birthing woman's has been drained from her and given to the institution in which she is placed.

The differences between the models of birth care developed by obstetrics and by the home-birth movement and midwifery are based both on underlying ideology and on political necessity. Physicians control birth in hospitals because it is done in their territory, under their expertise. That control over their work space is what makes them "professional." As the senior professionals around, they obviously control all the other workers, including midwives and doulas, along with nurses, orderlies, and aides. But they also control the patients. The medical management of birth means the management of birthing women. To control or manage a situation is to control and manage individuals.

The Overstated Understated

The alternative to physician and institutional control of childbirth is childbirth outside medical institutions, outside the medical model. In this alternative, birth is an activity that women *do*. The woman may need some help, but the help is, for the most part, in the form of teaching her how to do for herself. The word "deliver" exemplifies the medical model: it is a service delivered. The word "birthing" clarifies the midwifery model: birthing, like swimming, singing, and dancing, is something people do, not have done for them. A lot of us at that time used the word "catching" for what midwives did. Ronnie Lichtman, a key figure in American midwifery education, has suggested a better way to talk about what midwives do: they don't "catch," and they don't "deliver." One term is far too passive; the other too active. What they do, she says, is "guide" a birth.[46] But back in the 1970s midwives were downplaying their role, using their words to give the power of birth back to the birthing woman. Home-birth midwives struggled to redefine birth, but also to define their *own* role, what they did at a birth. Nancy Mills was a direct-entry midwife in the 1970s, not a nurse, but a midwife who began by helping a friend during labor. By the time she had attended over six hundred births, she had come to see her role at birth as this:

> I see myself going in and being a helper, being an attendant. Sometimes I play with the kids, or I do some cooking. Sometimes I sit with the woman. Sometimes I help the husband assist the woman. Some families need more help than others, but it is easy to go in and see where you are needed and how you can fill that role.[47]

The birth is not made to fit the routine, but the attendant to fit the birth. The birth is something the mother does by herself, but "it is important for that woman to be able to look at you, to know you are there, to hold your hand, to be reassured. I know it helps when I say to a woman, 'I know how you feel. I know it's harder than you thought it was going to be, but you can do it.'"[48]

What did midwives actually do when they got to a birth at home? I'm going to draw on my own late 1970s research,[49] and share what the midwives showed and told me about how they were practicing in New York. They came in, said hello, introduced themselves to anyone they didn't know. Just as any guest in a home would do. And in that entry, in that way of entering the home, they made the statement that they were not there to "do" the birth. One midwife, when asked what she does when she first gets to a birth, said, "Nothing, first. Which is very important, because they expect me to do something, like I'm supposed to do something. But they're doing it already and that's what we're going to be doing, so I find it very important to just come in and sit down."

This approach was intended as a radical departure from the medical model, in which the entry of the doctor signifies the start of the performance, or the admission of the woman to the hospital signifies the official start of the labor. Judy Luce, a Vermont midwife who had been practicing for over twenty-five years when I spoke to her in the 1980s, liked to show people a birth film made in Australia. In this film, the woman is seated on a big lounge chair, and casually brushes away the midwife's hand. The camera watches as slowly, without any touching, the vagina bulges and the baby emerges. It reminds her, she said, that whatever midwives are doing or not doing with their hands and their skills, it is women who give birth.

Which is not to say that midwives don't have and use their skills. This is something that we all, midwives and social scientists and activists of that home-birth movement, played down way too much in the interests of empowering the birthing women. Now I think we *are* ready to talk about the artisanal work and the craft of midwifery, to learn from the foodies that the words "natural" and "skilled" can be used in the same sentence. We know that wine will ferment on its own, but that doesn't mean the vintner brings nothing to it; yeast will make flour mixtures rise, but a baker can make it worth eating.

But back then, when we were trying to understand the differences between the medical model and the midwifery model of birth, we focused only on the ways that midwives "supported" women, ways they "backed off," not the ways they reached in and helped. They did vaginal exams during labor, but not on a clocked schedule. On a more regular basis, they listened for fetal heart tones. The role we valued was someone to keep a check on the physical changes, and not to interfere with personal interactions. Often that meant that the midwife had to "support the support person," providing reassurance not only to the woman but to her support people, that labor is progressing normally, and occasionally offering advice on how to give support. People are often not fully prepared for just how painful labor can be, or how needful the laboring woman may become. The midwife provides reassurances that her condition, however distressing, is normal, and suggests positive ways of coping. And she provides appropriate interventions—sometimes breaking the bag of waters, for example, when that is what is needed to help a labor progress. We may not have talked about it, but midwifery care was never about "not intervening," but about intervening intelligently, thoughtfully, and skillfully.

Unlike the typical American hospital of the 1970s, there were of course no changes in room (labor to delivery room) for the second stage of labor, but there is usually a marked change in the ambience. The end of active labor (transition), as the woman reaches full dilation, is usually quite painful for the mother and difficult for the support person. The pushing stage is usually exciting, climactic. The mother may be semi-sitting at the edge of or on a bed, braced by her support person, or she may be squatting, lying on her side, on a chair, or on her hands and knees, depending on her comfort and the suggestions of the midwife. The mother is in no way physically restrained. Sometimes the midwife encourages the woman to reach down, to push the baby out into her own hands. Sometimes the midwife's hand skills are needed—to unwrap the cord from the baby's neck, to ease a stuck baby through a tight space— again, it's the intelligent, thoughtful, and skillful use of interventions that marks midwifery care. After the baby emerges, into either the mother's hands or the midwife's, the mother draws the baby up to her. As one of the home-birth midwives I interviewed in the 1970s said, "There are at least thirty seconds of both mother and baby looking at each other and going, 'Who are you?' Then everybody usually starts climbing all over the baby and we usually back off at that point, just back off a bit and keep an eye on the placenta, what's going on."

That ability to "back off" was raised almost to an art by some midwives. One said that she never lets herself call out, "It's a boy" or "It's a girl," because "All of her life a woman will remember the sound of those words, and she should hear them in a voice she loves."

After a few minutes the midwife will either cut the cord herself or help the father (or, less commonly, the mother or someone else) do it. The baby will be wrapped in warm blankets and given back to the mother to put to the breast. Suckling usually stimulates uterine contractions, and the mother will hand the baby to someone else while she expels the placenta. After checking the placenta and showing it to the mother if she is interested in seeing it, as most women are, the midwife will check the mother for tears and for excessive bleeding. In the unlikely event of a tear or an episiotomy, the midwife will do the repair with a local anesthetic. If all is well, the mother might get up and bathe or shower while other people dress the baby and weigh it.

Midwives stay for some hours after birth, depending on the needs of the family and the condition of the mother and baby. Many families celebrate the birth with the traditional glass of champagne, some with birthday cake. People are frequently ready for a meal, and a party atmosphere may prevail. At other births the family may just want to sleep. The midwife eventually bids good-bye; as one said, "My aim is that when I leave that family feels they birthed it. I was there and I helped, but they did it . . . so that in their whole recollection of the experience I will be very minimal. That's my goal and that's my aim." That role and that goal are very different from the role of the doctor in a hospital birth—in Shaw's words, "the director and the star."[50]

So that's what that movement was about—every second-wave feminist idea you ever heard of, all about ending patriarchal control, ending dependence on men, and empowering women. You can see the enormous appeal it had to many high-achieving white women. We were confident of our own worth, very aware—"conscious" would be the word of the day—that we had a right to respect, and power was like a new muscle we were just starting to flex. I am woman, hear me roar indeed!

9

The Risky Business of Life

I began this tale of two movements bemoaning the state of my move-ment, the birth movement, compared to how well the food movement has done. And for sure, that food movement has done really, really well. Everybody talks about cooking. Carbs and calories, gluten and vitamins come up in conversation. It is common knowledge that processed equals bad; organic equals good. Whole-wheat and seven-grain breads out-number white breads on supermarket shelves. There's even whole-wheat and gluten-free matzoh for Passover. And yup, my friend Eileen Moran checked it for me, and there are indeed gluten-free Communion wafers.

And yet everybody also knows that in some countries, like the United States, rates of type 2 diabetes are at epidemic levels, obesity is a prob-lem everywhere from nursery schools to nursing homes, while children are starving in all the countries—including parts of ours—you'd expect them to be starving. Race and class disparities in diet-related diseases are stark. And for the first time in US history, life expectancy is declin-ing, again with dramatic race and class differences, and diet is under-stood to be a factor.

My movement, meanwhile, is maybe not doing so badly. The Ameri-can College of Obstetrics and Gynecology occasionally stumbles on the obvious: you can let a woman who has had an epidural take a bit lon-ger to push her baby out. The cesarean rate is too high, having topped a third. (A third! One-third of American babies are born surgically!) Canadian obstetricians have decided they really ought to at least know and teach how to do a vaginal breech birth.[1] Some OBs just released yet another study that not only does waiting a minute before you clamp the cord get the baby's blood into the baby's body where it belongs, but the mother can actually be holding the baby while you wait for the cord to stop pulsing.[2] American midwives are at least starting to talk to each other across their great divide between the nurse-midwives, with their nursing degrees and hospital-based education, and all the other midwives struggling for state recognition. The home birth rate just about reached 1 percent in the United States.[3] And PBS is showing the British series *Call the Midwife* and it's kind of almost practically a hit. How bad could things be?

Okay, pardon my adolescent sarcasm, but my movement's not doing so great. And neither is the food movement. And if the truth be told, the world is going to hell in a handbasket.

Social movements are inherently hopeful—all those people splashing together, believing that they can make waves, they can make change. Up to now this book has looked at what worked, and how it worked, how changes in food and in birth connected to the larger changes in (mostly American) Western society over the last century. But we're well into another century now, and struggling on many fronts to move forward. I explored what food and birth looked like in an age of science, an age of consumer culture, and an age of counterculture. Where are we now?

The legacies of each of those three waves of social movements are still with us. Birth and food are unquestionably scientized. It is impossible for people to think about their own bodies without the language and images of science. Can you think about your heart without understanding it as pumping? A donut without thinking about its calories? The moment of conception without an image of a sperm entering an egg? These are all relatively new ideas, new "facts" brought to us by science, taken in, internalized and made part of ourselves, part of how we see the world and our own bodies. We have that science, but we have also "softened" it with the values of that second wave, in which ideas about consumer society, about living nicely, made it palatable, sometimes romanticized, sometimes stylized. Extra calories are treats we share; children's books show happy eggs and competitive racing sperm. The workings of the third phase's movement are harder—for me!—to really evaluate. We're still here, after all. In some ways the legacy of feminism is clearly a success: there are women obstetricians, coming to outnumber the men. Yet in some ways not so much: they "lean in," hire other women to make dinners, watch the kids, as they take on the values and working ways, along with the hospital-produced knowledge, of the men obstetricians.

But more important than those social movements in shaping our contemporary world is the larger social system in which they are embedded, out of which they grew. Early on in this book, when I first introduced these two social movements, I spoke about them as "meaning-seeking" movements. We live in a world in which it sometimes feels that meaning is slipping away, that we know, as they say, "the cost of everything and the value of nothing." More and more of our lives are bar coded, systematized, controlled by forces outside our control and not in our interests. Of course people inherently live in a world controlled by things beyond them: I could be struck by lightning, drowned in flash-flooding, lose people I love to an earthquake.

It is not just those "acts of God" that threaten and control us. What you can feed your kids is more determined by international corporations than it is by the weather—and the weather itself, we are coming to understand, is also being shaped by those corporations. That child you love so much is a statistic. That child's odds are determined by things beyond your control that are not God's doing. The odds of surviving birth and infancy, of graduating from high school, of being shot, of having any of a long list of diseases—those things are better predicted by your zip code than pretty much anything else. Being able to talk about these nightmares in terms of their odds is itself noteworthy.

One way of categorizing our contemporary approach to the world is that we live now in a "risk society." The term goes back a bit, but still seems to capture something profound in how we understand the world, and absolutely resonates in both the kitchen and the birthroom. We understand our life in terms of the risks that we confront: environmental risks, lifestyle risks. Life is a series of risks to be managed and minimized as best we can. But we are also at a time of enormous class awareness. Risks are not the same for everyone, but raced, gendered, and—very importantly—classed. I do like the relatively new use of the word "disparity" for naming the unimaginable, enormous, and growing gap between the haves and the have-nots within our shores. There is a disparity here indeed, and it evokes the word "despair," which is what I am really feeling. This disparity grows and grows, and its consequences are dying before us, even as we turn our eyes away. We have more income disparity—or as I prefer to think of it, income despair-ity—than we've had since the turn of the last century, the age of the robber barons and the end of the global slave trade.

Risk is going to be a key issue in thinking about pregnancy, birth, and food, and will be a dominant theme in the rest of this book. I'm going to talk about what risk means, how ideas about risk permeate our understandings of how we birth and how we eat. My focus in the rest of this book is more clearly on birth. The food movement is pretty well launched, and I am hoping to build on what it has accomplished to make people think a bit differently about birth.

Income despairity is a harder thing to tackle in this book. Its influence is everywhere but harder to nail down. We are living in what is called a postindustrial society, but the only thing we're really "post" is the industry, the making-things part. We are still very much organized around the ideas of industrial management, with corporate rather than individual or guild control. We operate in a system of corporate management: we fight corporatized education, corporate food, corporate "health care" or, more accurately, corporate medicine. That income disparity means that the experiences of corporate control are different for people at the bottom and people at the top—within the United States, across the globe, in medical services and in food provision. We all face corporate power, but we face it from different places, with indeed very different risks involved.

Do this thought experiment: Your child desperately needs something. There is some object or service that you know, truly know, would make a world of difference for your child. If you're a billionaire, just go buy it. Otherwise, you find yourself on the phone, advocating in one or another system: maybe the school system, maybe your insurance system. Just saying that the child needs this thing is not going to work. You need to be strategic,[4] you need to make your argument in terms of their categories of need and service. Find the right diagnostic category and you may be able to make this work. We've all been there. Caregivers are there all the time. People who are spending their lives taking care of others who need care, be they elderly failing parents or disabled friends or family, they can all tell you that often they find they spend as much time filling out forms, trying to get the needs into the language of the system as they do actually taking care of the person.

It's a kind of crazy communication, not a real conversation between people who understand each other and are trying to work something out, but a strategy session, working with sets of rules so hyperrationalized and rigid they often seem parodies of themselves. In my family we still joke about the pediatrician translating "diaper rash" into

Latin so that the insurance company would cover the visit. The baby was clearly hurting and we didn't know how to fix it ourselves. But it's not really a laughing matter: real people with real needs are waiting, and with a lot more than diaper rash. How much time have we all spent comforting each other, taking care of someone, meeting their needs while carefully translating those needs into whatever it takes to get the systems moving. It's as if you are living in two worlds, speaking two languages, one real and connected and caring and loving, holding tight as if just your presence will make this all right; and the other strategic and manipulative and designed to match a set of forms.

There have been lots of attempts to find a way to talk about the two very different worlds we live in—one world that is about our own personal, irreplaceable self, a world in which we and the others in our life are not interchangeable parts but unique individuals; and the other world, in which we really are all interchangeable, replaceable parts, occupying statuses and roles and jobs and positions but not really any special place in anyone's heart. When I teach undergraduate intro sociology, and I am trying to explain the idea as it is expressed in the language of "primary groups" and "secondary groups," I sometimes focus on the issue of interchangeability. If on my way home from class that afternoon I get hit by a truck, there had better be a substitute professor in that room within a week. You can be a bit freaked, sure, and it'd be rather nice if someone in the class was a bit sad, but that's about it. It's not going to cost you the semester's credit; the class will go on. But if you get home and your father says, "Sorry, your mother got hit by a car yesterday. Here's the new one, she'll have dinner on the table soon," that is *so* not okay. He may indeed eventually bring in a new woman to be his wife, your stepmother, but she is never the "replacement" for the other. That person is gone. The relationships within your family—good or bad—are primary relationships, and those in the classroom—again, good or bad—are secondary.

Over and over again sociologists and others have tried to talk about this, struggled with the language and the concepts of private and public worlds, the system and the lifeworld, sometimes separating out specifically the world of family from the world of work, and sometimes gendering those—women's worlds and men's worlds. That public world, that "system," as Habermas calls it, is the world in which the market, the state, and their bureaucracies rule.[5] The other world, the "lifeworld," as he calls it, is the private, intimate, personal world. And it's hard to find an institution that better represents the "system" than an American hospital, with its rigid rules, regulations, and protocols.[6] We'd like to think that all those rules are there to protect patients. But we know they are also there to protect the workers, the system itself. Follow the rules, and no matter what happens, you—the worker and the institution—will be safe. Break a rule because it genuinely looks to be in the best interests of a patient, and if things go wrong anyway, you are sunk, with no hope in a malpractice suit.

The sociologist George Ritzer wrote about the "McDonaldization" of society,[7] how more and more parts of life are being run like fast-food restaurants, using the principles of rationalization: efficiency, calculability, predictability, and control. The person—customer or burger flipper, laboring woman or nurse—becomes part of the machinery. It's not without some advantages. The surgeon and author Atul Gawande has written rather favorably of the industrialization of birth.[8] All those variables, all those maneuvers, all the different ways babies can be placed and labors can move forward: it's too complicated to teach, too much to manage in the system. Substitute the simple, replicable, efficient cesarean section.

Gawande points out that medicine is less efficient, less organized, less good at incorporating new practices than is the Cheesecake Factory chain of restaurants. Anyone who's ever tried to get any kind of customer service out of a hospital would have to agree. He thinks that perhaps chains like the Cheesecake Factory offer a good model, that more routinization and rationalization would bring us better medical care. It's true if you are doing a highly routinized procedure, like a knee replacement or a cesarean section. It is less true if you are talking about a labor.

But obstetric discourse entered into the common vernacular, and the obstetric gaze is now "common sense." Birth is commonly understood as essentially a medical, surgical-like event, not all that different from a knee replacement, and medicine as a profession—more accurately as a stakeholder—has co-opted the language of choice. Much as soda sellers in the United States have done, they are arguing for the consumer choice that resulted after decades of aggressive sales. People want hospital births, they even sometimes (though considerably less rarely than popular media report) want cesarean sections. Soda manufacturers rely on the language of choice to subvert public health measures to limit sales of unhealthy products. Obstetricians do much the same.[9]

And so the birthing woman enters the hospital and she leaves the personal, the lifeworld behind—or brings in one or two people who can try to connect her to that reality, maybe a doula who can try to translate between her real needs and the system categories that might get those needs met. But in that institution she is one of a long line of laboring women, completely replaceable. And each of those workers is replaceable for her; the people engaged in intimate activities, touching her, moving her, looking at her—they are on shifts, replaced with each shift change. Birth, this most intimate of activities, is colonized, moved out of the world of the family and personal caring relationships, and into the system. She and the baby get tagged, matching little wristbands so that these interchangeable parts don't get confused, the wrong baby going home with the wrong mother. It's something we joke about in our culture, a response to that niggling little fear that it does sometimes happen, that in the system we really are all interchangeable and replaceable.

If that system really worked to provide the best possible care, it might be worth it, might be worth turning our lives and our births over to it. But over and over we see that—in birth as in food—industrialization is less in the interests of the consumers or the providers, and more in the interests of those who own those systems. Doctors used to really own that, were in "private" practice, controlled their work settings. That is less and less true today, as they too are replaceable parts in the machine.

A birth movement now is no longer about wresting power out of the hands of doctors. It is about deindustrializing birth, just as the food movement is focusing on deindustrializing our food. It is a movement occurring in a systematized, industrialized world, a world in which we try to make personal meaning in our lives, seek safety and security, want health and comfort for ourselves and our children, and are constantly being made aware of the risks we face, and our very unequal positions within that system. We are at a moment where the powers-that-be demand of the powerless enormous individual control, restraint, and individual management of risks, all but sing a discourse of personal responsibility; but it is in a world in which most of us have pretty much no control over the larger risks we face. Small wonder some of us are eager to retreat to the kitchen and to the birthroom, as places to seek hope and personal control.

Risk Society

If you simply Google "risk and pregnancy," you get over 42 million hits. Try "risk and birth," and you get over 41 million—undoubtedly with some overlap. So no question, pregnancy and birth are understood as having risks, creating risks, being risky business indeed. But not the riskiest of businesses. Google "risk and food," and you get more than two and a half times as many hits—over 109 million.

That doesn't feel right somehow. Pregnancy and birth are always and everywhere in our world understood as risky; food not so much. A woman announces an early pregnancy and we know the risks of Down syndrome, neural tube defects, miscarriage, multiples, prematurity, postmaturity, even stillbirth. Some of us actually could start citing those numbers off the top of our heads—Down syndrome risks by age, miscarriage by month of gestation, and more. It's not just medical personnel who know those numbers. Women of childbearing age have had many of those drilled into their heads, and anyone who has had a baby has had to sign off on knowing some of those things. And we all, as members of contemporary societies, know factors that increase risk in pregnancy and in birth. Drinking, smoking, illicit drug use, being too young or too old, birthing in an unacceptable location—all come to mind. And then there are the structural stressors, the race and class issues that we know affect pregnancy outcome, pregnancy risk. There are ever more risks, many of them foods, actually. Tuna, spinach, coffee, oysters, a glass of wine, bleu cheese, even potatoes have all come and not quite gone as risks in the last quarter century or so.

Outside pregnancy, food risks feel less immediate for most Americans. The nutritional problems of Americans, even poor Americans, are not often frank starvation, or deficiency diseases. We are not looking at rickets, at beriberi, at scurvy. Too many Americans struggle with what is called "food insecurity," not being confident they can get the next meal on the table. I teach at the City University of New York, a public institution, and the students—and for that matter, the adjunct faculty—have a high percentage (as high as one is likely to find among colleges, bordering on 40 percent among our students now[10]) of food-insecure people. Experiencing food insecurity is different from looking at a meal and feeling fear, having a heightened awareness of the long- and short-term risks of the meal in front of you. One could say that food insecurity is to fear of food as infertility is to fear of birth. From the position of those without food security, just as from the position of the "desperate infertile," the risks of the meal or the risks of the birth are not the problem. Food insecurity and infertility are both linked to poverty and race in America.

How do Americans think about the risks that are there in the food? I nibble some snacks as I write, sip some tea—are you worrying for me? Wishing me luck with that? Thinking about the odds of food poisoning? Insecticide exposure? The long-term risks of diabetes, joint pain, heart troubles, cancers that might be flowing forth from the snack choices I am making?

And what about those snack choices? Do they not carry much of the same moral weight that pregnancy choices make? If I tell you it's green tea and carrots, or if I tell you it's a honey chai latte and multigrain crackers with organic almond butter, or if I tell you it's a family-sized bag of Doritos and a Big Gulp Coke—do I not create different images of myself as a risk-taking or risk-sparing person, even as a more or less "good" and responsible person? The risks we perceive and the risks we take are judged, by ourselves and by others.

This is what it means to live in a "risk society."[11] Ulrich Beck, a German sociologist, introduced that term in the 1980s; it was very quickly taken up, and now, among sociologists, is a kind of truism. At a recent orals exam I looked at the very long section on "risk society" and wondered out loud why it seems so very British—of course not all, but a lot of the scholars who have worked on this issue are British. Another sociologist on the committee, David Brotherton, explained it to me: the British turn to privatization under Thatcher made heavy use of actuarial principles. So everything, not just the usual life insurance tables, turned to actuarial science. The principle is the same as those life insurance tables: it's not just that we are all going to die, but that we can all look at a table and keep tossing in variables (smoke? overweight? family history of this and that?) and start figuring out our risks of dying now, soon. Want to know the odds of recidivism among various kinds of prisoners under varying conditions? The odds of completing school among various kinds of students under varying conditions? The odds of almost anything in the public order?

And so we can—and we do, in the United States as in the United Kingdom and all across Europe, all of us in this organized, managed, corporatized world, all of us living in this risk society—look at birth, or dinner, and think about the risks involved.

It is reasonable to talk about how recent this language of risk is in pregnancy and in birth, but the language of danger, that which we are in risk of, has long been an accepted part of birth.[12] It is not news that a woman could die, that a baby could die, that either could be hurt. That's why we have had midwives, people who are aware of the dangers and know something about how to avoid or resolve them. Calling it "risk" is adding the numbers—sure, there are dangers, but precisely what are the odds? And so it is with food: yes, there are risks to eating a diet that makes you fat. But precisely how many years on average does it take off your life? Thinking in terms of risk lets you say crazy things like that— precisely, on average. Being X pounds overweight takes Y years off the lifespan of the average Z-aged woman. Sentences like that are part of our world now.

It is of course not only the long-range food dangers that we worry about; any given meal could kill someone. Food handling and food choices to avoid danger are among the oldest of our human skills, right up there with midwifery if perhaps less specialized—pick that mushroom, not this one; those berries not these; you can eat that meat rare but cook this meat till the center's no longer red. That there are dangers in pregnancy and in birth, dangers in our food, and that they can be avoided or overcome—this is not news.

Dangers, disasters even, could happen in the best and healthiest of pregnancies and births, to the most careful of eaters, can happen in hospital operating rooms and in professional kitchens. The difference between food and birth is that now there is no such thing as a healthy pregnancy or birth. Birth, as the obstetricians are fond of pointing out, can be normal or healthy only in retrospect, only after the event. There still is an understanding of such a thing as a healthy meal and even a healthy diet, but no longer, it seems to me, a healthy pregnancy. The best you can hope for is a low-risk pregnancy.

The Pregnant Canary in the Mine . . .

If there could be such a thing as a pregnant canary, that's what we had in the coal mine of medicalization. How can we turn life into a problem of medical management, the body into a site of screening and diagnosis at all times for all purposes? The answer is, Let's start with how it was done for pregnant bodies, and go from there. Surveillance medicine was, it would seem, born out of pregnancy management.[13] It was early in the medicalization process, the first of life's stages to be effectively turned over to surveillance medicine. According to Kristen Hallgrimsdottir and Bryan Eric Benner, historians of birth, the context was three forces coming together: the growth of obstetrics and its grab for professional dominance; the growth of first-wave feminism with its appropriation of science; and the rise of eugenics, our first science of population management. And what have we now?

A fully realized professional dominance came—and went, as the principles of medicalization were so deeply internalized that the doctor is no longer necessary. People view their own bodies with the medical gaze now, use basic screening tools themselves, and turn to practitioners for advanced screening and diagnostic services. Think you're pregnant? Go buy a test. Worried about your cholesterol levels? Want to test with an over-the-counter tester or want to go to a lab or to a physician's office? The key thing is that you cannot know yourself whether you are pregnant or whether you are healthy. Being late for the first time in your life, feeling your breasts tender in a new way—all that means is that you should go get tested. Test says no? Try again! Keep testing until the test says what you know to be true. Because you cannot really know, until you have tested. That is the internalized medical gaze. In the early days, the doctor did not trust the woman to know her own body. Now the women do not trust themselves either.

And this now goes way beyond pregnancy. Think you are healthy? How would you know? Your cholesterol could be too high, polyps growing silently in your colon, tiny lumps too small to feel with your hand growing in your breasts, your groin, a shadow on . . . well, almost anything. Get tested! Why are you sitting here reading this? Something could be growing stealthily in you right now, something that could kill you! Or something that could be a pregnancy. Either way, how could you know without testing? Professional dominance won, and surpassed itself, so that it is now not the doctor's authority, but medicalized authority, internalized within, that dominates.

Eugenics as a word is, of course, entirely out of favor. As a concept and a practice, however . . . well, take a look at the new genetics, at prenatal and newborn screening, at the push to have healthy babies. And more basically, look at the ways that the field of public health has moved from an environmentalist approach, making the world safer for people, to a public education model, in which people need to make themselves safer in the world. That too is about population health, much as eugenics was—a good, productive society needs good and productive members. Public service announcements are all about individuals avoiding risky behaviors; ride the New York City subways and you get a rich education in individualized risk avoidance. We learn about the risks of sugary drinks and of teen pregnancy, of alcohol, of obesity, of all kinds of things we might be doing to harm ourselves. We learn not so much about the risks of environmental factors—air pollution in and out of subways, for example. No one is telling us to go breathe healthier air. What we learn is what we as individuals can do to make a healthy body for a healthy society.

And finally, we do have the universal acceptance of science as the final word, the truth, and with that, the rather absurd conflation of biomedicine with science, as if the pharmaceutical industries and health and hospital corporations are operating out of science alone. Whatever medicine offers appears to be science. How often media reports look at the medical pronouncements, even those without supportive data, and call them the "scientific" management of pregnancy or of food. And feminism? Part of what makes the medicalization of obstetrics so very acceptable to educated, egalitarian women these days is its feminization—women increasingly *are* the obstetricians, just as they are often the food scientists. What women need to bow down to in accepting medical control is not men, but science.

And what is that science? And what does it mean to bow down to it? These are two separate questions that come together forcefully for mothers. The science we have is constantly telling us the risks of this or that food in pregnancy. And we have long had a science that tells us what is the best way to feed newborn babies, though just what that way is has veered sharply between our own breastmilk and the latest formula and back to our breastmilk. But now it is increasingly so that science is informing us of risks and safety in feeding across childhood, with an enormous focus on preventing childhood obesity. That's the science part. The bowing down part is all about social control, a kind of control women have experienced as dramatically as handcuffs and imprisonment and losing custody of children, and in a more mundane way by dirty looks, unkind and unhelpful comments from strangers on the street.

Ideas about what is dangerous or risky to fetuses become seen as public health problems, issues that need management to maintain the health of the population. Mothers, pregnant women, need to be managed so that they make healthy babies. And all kinds of things get identified as risks and thus as subject to public health management: "In the late twentieth century, public health experts have identified smoking and drinking during pregnancy as significant public health problems that are harmful to the developing fetus."[14] But what are we to make of this? The data on the damage to fetuses of low levels of alcohol are, well, non-existent might be a good word. The alcohol panic has been nicely researched, and it is clear that while high levels of alcohol (alcoholic-level high), especially when combined with poor nutrition, can indeed cause what is known as fetal alcohol syndrome, there are no such data on the damage caused by low levels.[15] But what constitutes low levels? There are no answers, so a kind of decision rule was reached, or what is called a precautionary approach, advocating complete abstinence.[16] "Identifying" means labeling, and—sticking just to alcohol for the moment—any alcohol use is labeled bad maternal behavior. And yet not always. Social science researchers also show that both care providers and women themselves know that an occasional drink has not been shown to harm fetuses and in fact there is no reason to suspect it would. Not surprisingly, better-educated, higher-status women—women more like their care providers—are given a bit more leeway on this, and on occasion take such freedom for themselves. Lower-status women are not trusted, and know that they are not trusted; abstinence is asked of them.[17] There's risk, and there's class, and there's the interaction between the two. And there is gender, reinforcing both.

We see this policing most dramatically in the case of drug use during pregnancy, when on occasion actual police are brought in. While no one is advocating the use of recreational drugs in pregnancy, if the goal was to have healthier women and healthier babies, then a harm-reduction model would be in place. Instead what we see is that women rightly fear punitive responses from their "caregivers" and from the state.[18] Nine of the thirteen drug-using women interviewed in one study[19] feared that their babies would be removed from them when they were born—and they had every reason to fear. Five of them were removed. The long-lasting negative consequences of removing babies from their mothers are largely unstudied, but, as one of these women pointed out, there went her plans for breastfeeding. Obviously the least of her problems and the baby's, but interestingly at odds with other public health campaigns to encourage breastfeeding. Lower-status women know that those assigned with their care are also those from whom they are at risk. Drug use per se is a risk, but clearly so too—and maybe even more—is being identified as a drug user.

How did women, *mothers*, the people most trusted to love their children, the ones most committed to caring for children, come to be understood as the biggest risk babies face? The answer isn't with mothers or women—we haven't changed. The answer is with the ways that pregnancy has changed, the way the introduction of the fetus as a new kind of being on earth has changed our understanding of pregnancy.

The Vulnerable Fetus

It's hard to explain how profoundly pregnancy has changed, impossible for us to put that genie back in the bottle. Pregnancies are all about fetuses now, and we didn't used to have those. We had pregnancies, and then babies. Somewhere along the middle of the pregnancy we felt a movement that wasn't our own, a movement that used to be called quickening, or coming to life, and suddenly really felt that there was a baby in there. It used to be a significant moment in a pregnancy. Then when we gave birth we felt a whole new person emerge. We looked, saw our babies for the first time. Not now.

Babies enter our lives electronically now; like so many of our friends they have a screen presence in our lives before we meet face to face. The moment of quickening, the moment the baby comes to life, now happens not at a random moment in your own body, but by appointment, in an office, at a screen. This is the way that gender still structures some of our ideas about pregnancy and birth: through our ideas about the fetus. We haven't entirely gotten past the origins of Western patriarchy, the myth of Adam as the regular person and Eve the derivative, and even more directly, the myth of the seed of Abraham covering the world, the naming of children as the children of men through the bodies of women. Through the eyes of medicine, pregnancy had always been viewed as being a man's baby growing inside a woman. Believing, as my mentor Judith Lorber always reminds me, is seeing; one of the first uses of the microscope was to see the homunculus, the little person curled up inside the sperm. Given contemporary genetics, it is no longer about sperm, but it is still about precious seeds in unworthy and increasingly untrustworthy vessels.

When the fetus was seen as a product of the male's body, it followed that its presence in the female body must be an intrusion. The chapter on the fetus in the standard guidebook, *Obstetric-Gynecologic Terminology*, of 1972 was "The Fetus (Passenger)."[20] The 2001 edition of *Williams Obstetrics*, the classic obstetrics textbook in America, said, "The fetus is a demanding and efficient parasite!"[21] Looking at the way that embryonic and placental tissues produce hormones and affect the course of pregnancy, *Williams* concluded, "These are but a few examples to indicate unambiguously that the embryo-fetus, estraembryonic fetal tissues, or both, direct the orchestration of the physiological adaptations of pregnancy. The maternal organism passively responds—even at times to her own detriment."[22] The dominant organizing belief for medicine about pregnancy was that daddy plants a seed in mommy. For all of our new genetic sophistication, pregnancy was and still is seen as an adversarial relationship, in which the needs and interests of the mother-host are pitted against those of the fetus-parasite. We are well past the dominance of sperm. Babies are now half his and half hers, entirely made up of DNA, and might as well grow in the backyard—or India. Pregnancy is a holding pen, a place. Fetuses are vulnerable patients, more and more vulnerable all the time.

We have to take a brief step back now, to see where this vulnerability of the fetus came from. Until the 1960s, medicine in the United States viewed the pregnant woman as a body with an insulated, parasitic capsule growing inside it. The capsule within was seen as virtually omniscient and omnipotent, knowing exactly what it needed from its mother-host, reaching out and taking it from her—taking vitamins, minerals, protein, and energy, at her expense if necessary—while protected from all that was bad or harmful. The pregnancy in this model was almost entirely a mechanical event in the mother, who differed from the nonpregnant woman only by the presence of this thing growing inside her, and other changes of pregnancy were symptoms to be treated so that the woman could be kept as "normal" as possible. That explains the introduction of dangerous diuretics, diet pills, and other routine pregnancy care by obstetrics: they were trying to limit the effects of the pregnancy on the woman to just the mechanical growth of the uterus.

Then several things happened in a short period of time that challenged the view of the protected, insulated fetus. In 1961–1962 an unprecedented outbreak of phocomelia, a congenital malformation characterized by severe defects of the long bones, resulting in what were commonly called "flippers" (missing limbs), was observed in West Germany primarily, and throughout Europe and the world, but thanks to Frances Oldham Kelsey, a thoughtful woman at the FDA, the United States was largely spared. It was later documented that the defects were related to the use of a tranquilizing drug, thalidomide, during the thirtieth to fiftieth day of pregnancy, usually taken on prescription from obstetricians for the control of nausea during pregnancy. That at least ten thousand infants were dramatically damaged by a substance ingested by their mothers directly contradicted the earlier medical model, which believed the fetus to be insulated and protected within the womb.[23] The placenta, as a result of this experience, was no longer seen as a shield or barrier for the infant; instead, it came to be seen as what the renowned doctor Virginia Apgar called a "bloody sieve."[24]

At first, this seemed to really threaten the medical management of pregnancy, which involved using a lot of drugs of one sort or another to "treat" the many changes of pregnancy. The 1971 edition of *Williams Obstetrics* stated, "The most important practical lesson to be drawn from the experience with thalidomide is that no drug should be administered to the pregnant woman unless it is urgently indicated. This injunction applies particularly to drugs administered during the first half of pregnancy for nausea and vomiting."[25] Just a few years later, though, editors of the sixteenth edition, in 1980, substituted "in the absence of a real therapeutic indication" for "unless urgently indicated," somewhat soft-ening the statement. But in both of those editions of *Williams*, six hun-dred pages earlier, in a discussion of nausea in pregnancy, several drug recommendations are made, including one that *Williams* reported may be teratogenic (causing malformation) although "evidence is not con-vincing."[26] *Williams* had painted the thalidomide disaster as graphically as possible: a photograph of an entirely limbless baby, a formless column of flesh with a baby's head, was printed in both of those editions. On the one hand, these doctors understood the profound risks of tampering with pregnancy; on the other hand, they found—and still find—it very difficult to believe that drugs doctors prescribe could cause such prob-lems. Not twenty years after thalidomide's effects were discovered, the evidence that another drug prescribed for nausea is teratogenic had to be "convincing" enough before the editors of this basic obstetrics text-book would stop recommending it.

Shortly after the thalidomide event, there was an epidemic of Ger-man measles in the United States. These waves of German measles had been coming for a long time, and as Leslie Reagan documents in *Dan-gerous Pregnancies*, it was women, as mothers, who had figured out the relationship between this mild disease and its serious consequences for pregnancy.[27] Not surprisingly, medicine took credit, and since it was a German doctor who originally did so, and Americans can't pronounce German names, we came to know it as "German measles," and only later on as rubella.

> Without thalidomide, the German measles epidemic may have received as little public attention as it had in previous years and may have re-mained a private problem. A national epidemic of German measles af-ter thalidomide, however, hit home in a new way that the thalidomide tragedy had not. . . . Thalidomide affected few in the United States. In contrast, German measles potentially threatened every woman of child-bearing age in the country. . . . Thalidomide taught Americans what Ger-man measles might mean.[28]

It meant damaged, ruined, tragic children, all the horrible ideas about disability that came before the disability rights movement and all those that stay with us still. The specter of such tragedies legitimized "therapeutic" abortions as a maternal obligation, and maternal vigilance even more so. Fetuses were vulnerable, not protected; wombs were risky places.

More dangers were shown. While there was some acknowledgment of the hazards of radiation resulting from the Hiroshima and Nagasaki bombings and their effects on fetal development, in the early 1960s chest X-rays were still considered an important part of good early prenatal care, and X-rays were used routinely to determine fetal position, to measure the pelvis, and even to determine pregnancy itself. By the later 1960s doctors recognized that exposure to radiation in utero greatly increases the incidence of cancers in the exposed children. And then there was the DES disaster, in which diethylstilbestrol, a synthetic hormone given to some women in the 1940s and 1950s to prevent miscarriage, was found, in the 1970s, to have caused cancer in their daughters decades later. This revelation, that a baby who appeared fine may nonetheless have been profoundly damaged by a prenatal exposure, further rocked the idea of the fetus as being insulated.

But medicine never really feared tampering with the prenatal environment; if it had, it would have absolutely avoided all but lifesaving medications, radiation, and other procedures. There was, rather, some increased selectivity. For example, while radiation was used less and less frequently, sonography became widespread, along with the claim that sound waves, unlike X-rays, are not harmful. The technique became widespread long before there was, or could have been, any long-term follow-up. It is tempting to track practice after practice, technology after technology and drug after drug, year after year, as they swing in and out of favor. But what is the larger lesson here, the forest lost among all these trees? To some extent, it is that drugs prescribed and technologies used by doctors are innocent until proven guilty, that the drugs and technologies they offer are safe, or safe enough, unless proven otherwise. About one antihypertensive drug, *Williams* concluded, "There are no large epidemiological studies in early pregnancy, but its many years of use attest to its safety."[29] That standard does not apply to what *Williams* groups as "natural (herbal) remedies." For those, in spite of generations of use, they conclude, "Because it is not possible to assess the safety of various herbal remedies during pregnancy, pregnant women should be counseled to avoid these substances."[30]

Williams reports that women overestimate the risk of exposure to teratogens, and underestimate the background risk of birth defects in the general population. Its conclusion on counseling for teratogen exposure:

> With few notable exceptions, most commonly prescribed drugs and medications can be used with relative safety during pregnancy. For the few believed to be teratogenic, counseling should emphasize relative risk. All women have about a 3 percent chance of having a child with a birth defect, and although exposure to a confirmed teratogen may increase this risk, it is usually increased by only 1 or 2 percent or at most doubled or tripled.[31]

Risk is such a slippery concept. When a thirty-five-year-old woman has a three in a thousand, or 0.3 percent, risk of having a baby with Down syndrome, medical workers tell her that she is high-risk. When a drug doubles "or at most" triples the background 3 percent risk of fetal anomalies up to 6 or 9 percent, six or nine in a hundred, the counseling emphasis shifts from "high" to "relative" risk. This is quite a change from the "most important practical lesson to be drawn from the experience with thalidomide."

It seems that there has been a more widespread public than medical acceptance of the idea of the permeability of the placenta and the care that women are therefore obliged to take with what they eat and drink. Many people seem to be aware of the hazards of smoking or drinking alcohol or using caffeine, or any number of risks that show up daily in the news, and many hesitate to use any over-the-counter medications without—or even with—the recommendation of a physician. Women often find that they are more cautious than their physicians are about using medications. Doctors tend to err on the side of assuming that what they are doing is safe, or safe enough. Women, it seems, tend to err on the side of "not taking chances," to assume higher risks of teratogenicity than might actually be there, and to try very hard not to take risks with the fetus. But perhaps more striking is that the public has taken these risks to heart, and a culture of blame, distrust, and disrespect of pregnant women has "permeated the media, health education materials, law, medical attitudes, and the thinking of ordinary men and women at the end of the twentieth century."[32] People have come to worry about entrusting vulnerable fetuses to women increasingly seen as selfish and untrustworthy, less caretakers of babies within, and more like barriers to care for fetal patients.[33]

Visualizing the Fetus: Bringing Forth the New Patient

When I began looking at pregnancy care, back in the 1970s, the fetus was being thought of as a patient, but it was still quite an abstraction. No longer. When I give a talk about childbirth, sometimes I ask the audience to picture a fetus, and then "draw it" in the air with their hands. You get arms waving in the air, forming a big circle for a head with a curled-up body beneath. Then I ask them to put the pregnant woman's belly button right on that fetus. Just point where it would be. And the room is still. People have no idea where that woman's belly button would be. Of course if they were to draw the pregnant woman around the fetus, she'd be standing on her head. The fetus has been turned around to a more baby-like position. Oddly, as real as the fetus is, it's the pregnant woman that has become the abstraction. Ultrasound is a near-perfect example of an ideology made real, a set of beliefs reified with a technology. Obstetricians think of fetuses as separate patients more or less trapped within the maternal environment, and ultrasound was developed as a technology to get through that maternal barrier and show the separate fetus lying within. The separate baby becomes an entirely separated image, floating free on the screen, tethered only by the umbilical cord, like a spaceman to its ship. The woman is erased, an empty surround in which the fetus floats.

From that gray blur on the ultrasound image, a fully formed fetus is read into being. The sonographer works to construct fetal personhood, "talking about the image and encouraging the parents to see and to bond with a sentient and acting "'baby.'"[34] The irony, of course, is that this construction occurs in the very same moment the sonographer is looking for the signs and symptoms that would indicate that the fetus is not developing normally. In that case, the woman would be encouraged to consider abortion, and the "baby" would be quickly de/reconstructed as a fetus or even a "genetic mistake," an "abnormality."

But for most women, most of the time, the fetus passes its inspection, and "fetal personhood" or more accurately "babyhood" is narrated into being—with or without the participation of the mother. Some women resist: "I think we'll forget the picture. It looks like a deep sea animal," a woman says during her thirty-two-week scan. And the technician responds, "Can you see that? The foot. Little toes." And as she and her husband peer into the screen, the technician continues "tickling" the toe on the screen: "It's so cute."[35] Who could resist?

With the routine scan, done shortly before most women would feel fetal movement, the observed fetal movement on the screen is maybe not anthropomorphized; maybe "baby-ized" would be the term. Mitchell observed technicians using terms like dancing, playing, swimming, partying, or waving to describe fetal movement. A rolling fetus is "trying to get comfortable," one with an extended limb and arching back is "stretching." Not moving doesn't spare the women and her partner the process. Without movement, the fetus is described as sleeping, resting. A fetal hand near the mouth turns into "The baby is sucking his thumb," even though sonographers told Mitchell that actual thumb sucking is rarely seen. Parents, the sonographers told her, like to think that is what the baby is doing.[36]

Who knows what it is parents like to think? Sonographers, along with the rest of medicine, apparently know quite well what they should think. A racialized script exists: Some women (Black, First Nation) "never show anything," are impassive and unemotional. Other women are too emotional, giggling loudly, shedding tears, showing "excessive" joy. Both groups are punished by silence; sonographers give them only brief descriptions,[37] saving their rich descriptions that call a baby forth into being for the good mothers, the ones who respond "appropriately."

Women tend to take silence during the exam as a sign of a problem. And, for all the commercialization of the process, the pictures for sale, the souvenirs to take home and to share, ultimately searching for a problem is the reason the technology is being used. Women have reason to worry. Perhaps they ought to worry more. Informed consent has been notably lacking, and many women don't even realize what the implications of having this ultrasound could be until the sonographer is suddenly silent, seeing something unexpected on the screen.

Somewhere between tickling toes on the screen and clinical coldness, there must be a way of handling the use of this technology better. But no one seems to have found it—not Mitchell, not the other social scientists who have studied the new ultrasound diagnostic technologies in pregnancy, not the Dutch midwives I have interviewed who tried really, really hard (Rothman, 2000), and not the US and Canadian midwives who are working on it. In one generation we have truly changed pregnancy: from a time of "expecting" a baby to a time of containing a fetus. And who can resist?

Resistance to medical control comes in odd ways. It is there in women who seek home births, and it is there in women who seek every possible medical intervention and management. All are trying to manage their pregnancies and their babies in their own ways.

But all feel blamed, scrutinized, judged—and found wanting. It is in this context that we have such a profoundly bifurcated set of social expectations and potential social movements around childbirth, from elective cesarean sections to unattended home births. It's a difficult moment in which to become a mother—though I suppose they all are. But for sure, it's a difficult moment in which to create a new midwifery, a new social movement to return birth to women. Our very fetuses have been turned against us, claimed by larger industrialized forces of medicine that say they can speak in their interests and on their behalf. In *Dangerous Pregnancies*, Leslie Reagan talks about the March of Dimes campaign that grew out of all the work of all those women to find and treat and prevent the problems that came with German measles and a million other things that harm babies: a campaign of "Mommy . . . Don't."[38] They showed images of pregnant women smoking, drinking, and the voice of the fetus pleading with them to stop. It was a public health campaign that equated women with danger (drugs, alcohol, smoking), erasing the work of all those women who created the space for the March of Dimes, erasing the medical responsibility for things like thalidomide and DES, and completely ignoring the current threats to fetal well-being of all the big things—poverty, environmental toxins, and racism.

How do you create a social movement to respond to this? The very success of feminism is used against women as mothers. Abortion is the area of women's health, of reproductive health, most closely aligned with feminist activism in the public mind. All our work on birth control, on safe birth, on ending domestic violence, on education, sports for girls— all of it is made invisible. Professional women, political women, women of the world are not trusted as mothers. While women in earlier movements to change birth practices were assumed to have their babies' best interests at heart, that just isn't true anymore. It makes every attempt at creating a social movement for childbirth reform suspect.

If we cannot trust mothers to care for their babies, where can we as a society put our trust? Science steps in—bye-bye maternal instinct, hello science. But science, in the form of medicine, has its own agendas and its own concerns. It is, after all, a business—one of the biggest we have. Is there *any* industry to which we should trust our children?

Obstetrics claims to speak for the fetus. The obstetrician is the doctor to the fetus, and other branches of medicine are afraid to intervene. Feminists respond, asking for the care the women need, but often so caught up in medicalization that sometimes we too fail to see the problems in the underlying care, the risks and dangers posed by medicine itself, and end up just asking for more care, more medicine, more intervention—in pregnancy as in so much of our lives. It's not just birth. Data show that routine screening and mammography don't prevent breast cancer deaths? Feminists up in arms! How dare they take away our tests! Men do the same thing with prostate cancer screening. Data show it doesn't work? Never mind! How dare you take away our tests! An article by thoughtful, caring feminists in a bioethics journal reasonably called for pregnant women to get the same care that nonpregnant women are entitled to, to have access to medical services and not denied what they need ostensibly in the interests of the fetus.[39] Ironically, the two examples they chose to represent the supposed undertreatment of pregnant women were the case of the flu vaccine and SSRIs (routinely used to treat so very much more than severe, suicidal depression).[40] These two medical interventions are themselves being questioned for both efficacy and safety even for people who are not pregnant. Does pregnancy mean women are undertreated? Or does pregnancy sometimes spare women unnecessary and dangerous overtreatment? And so it goes with obstetric care. Data show that women and babies do better sent home shortly after the birth? How dare they! They're pushing us out of the hospital! Drive-through deliveries!

In the United States, with its profoundly unequal access to all biomedical and health services, should we be focusing on access, making sure that every woman has all the services of the most advanced hospital unit? Or should we be questioning the safety and efficacy of that care? Can we imagine asking for less? It seems so . . . un-American!

This is the moment in which some women are trying to re-create midwifery, make home birth available, create a social movement that supports women and babies in ways other than medicalizing them. But it is a hard sell in a deeply medicalized society. It is a hard sell when medicine has so brilliantly co-opted the language of feminism, selling its services as maternal choice, when so few real choices are on offer.[41]

With the introduction of the fetus as an all-but-separate player, pregnant women are constantly confronted with accusations and fears about selfishness. Is it selfish to have an epidural and expose the fetus to the risks of that so the mother can avoid pain? Or is it selfish to have a natural birth, go for a hedonistic, beautiful experience at the risk of the fetus? Is it selfish to use or to avoid what modern obstetrics has to offer? It's very hard to sort out when it is the care itself, the medical services, that may pose the risk—something we will come back to in discussions of safety. How, in sum, can you create a social movement in which birth can be reimagined, when all the forces we confront make women seem untrustworthy caretakers of those precious, thumb-sucking, waving, abandoned little fetuses in their inter-uterine outer-space environments.

Food Risk

There's a way in which fetuses are maybe the ideal person for our time: they are people who exist in the future, and increasingly, don't we all? That's what risk is about, after all, worrying about what could happen next, what future scenarios are on offer. Sometimes I wonder how deeply we are affected by being the first people to have seen the entire life span of a person moving in front of us: we can see Shirley Temple as a little girl; see her as a middle-aged woman; see her elderly self. Child actors who grew to old age on screen make a difference in what I see when I see children, don't they?

Whatever the roots of it, many would agree with the British sociologist Anthony Giddens, who says that modernity—modern society or industrial civilization—"is vastly more dynamic than any previous type of social order. It is a society . . . which unlike any preceding culture lives in the future rather than the past."[42] I don't know, I really don't know how new that is, whether other people in past times and places didn't also worry about the future, without the benefit of film or the mathematical apparatus of risk rates. But we certainly do talk and think about the future a lot, act as if a constant awareness of, and vigilance about, its risks would itself protect us somehow.

Up to now I've been a little sloppy in my use of the words "risk" and "danger." We generally are, in ordinary language. Risky things are dangerous; do something dangerous and you are taking a risk. But let's parse it a bit further; the distinction is important in the world of food. Something is dangerous when you can see the immediate bad consequences. That's a dangerous path you're walking on—I can see how you could easily trip and fall. Something is risky when the danger isn't right there in front of you, not a tangle of branches with a steep cliff that we can both see, but a long-term danger. Mountain climbing is a risky hobby because eventually you're likely to face a dangerous cliff or damage your knees.

In talking about risk and food, we need to make this distinction between immediate risks, or what we call "dangers," and what are best thought of as long-term risk, and separate both of those from the issue of food insecurity. Some Americans face ongoing worry about getting enough food. Concerns about the risks of the food itself are rather like the concerns people struggling with infertility might have about the risks of birth: that should only be their problem. For people who are not worrying about access, the risks of the food itself are less immediate. Sure, there's food poisoning, food-borne viruses that can make you feel pretty vile for a day or two, things that can even—with a lot of headlines and recalls and carrying-on—maybe even kill someone. But in a world in which you have time to be reading about food and I have the time to be writing about it, that's a pretty unlikely outcome. That is not what we really have to worry about from our food. That bag of potato chips, that hamburger, the overly sweetened fruit yogurt in its plastic container, they aren't going to make you sick now, not tonight, not this week. But someday—someday the consequences are going to catch up with you. Probably. Eventually. So yes, gotta cut down on sugar, fats, salt, absolutely. We know that. I'm working on it. But just now—please pull over at Popeye's, I love the biscuits and chicken. And just grab a pack of this, a box of that off the supermarket shelves, I'm running late.

The key books on food safety and risk are Marion Nestle, *Safe Food: The Politics of Food Safety*;[43] Anthony Winson, *The Industrial Diet: The Degradation of Food and the Struggle for Healthy Eating*;[44] and Frederick

Kaufman, *Bet the Farm: How Food Stopped Being Food*.[45] And just to make sure I truly understand whose fault this is: Michael Moss, *Salt, Sugar, Fat: How the Food Giants Hooked Us*. Nestle looks at food-borne illness, the pathogens that make you sick more-or-less now when you eat them. Mad cow and bioterrorism, E. coli and salmonella. And what about genetically modified foods? Immediate or long-term? Too soon to tell, I guess . . . seems to be okay in the short term, but why should I trust that? And that is how Nestle sums up the politics of consumer concern: distrust, dread, and outrage. Winson and Kaufman explain how food did actually stop being food, and Moss explains why we're so eagerly eating what's left.

This is a bit hard to swallow. Someone who isn't me, who doesn't love me, care about me, want anything from me but my purchases—and given the scale of the institutions involved, could really care less if I don't purchase, it won't matter—that's who is deciding what I can eat and what I had available to feed my children. And yet of course not. I had choices. I stand in the supermarket, the greenmarket, pick up my bag from the farmshare, and I choose what to eat. That tension between larger social systems and individual choices is the grand philosophical question of all time, the issue of free will. And it is the focus of the sociological imagination—how much of what is experienced as so deeply personal is actually structural. People have wrestled with that tension since at least as long as people left any written records of their thoughts. But increasingly that tension—the feeling of choice in the face of structure—has itself become part of the structure. That's what is meant by "governmentality." Not to get all Foucauldian on you, but the work of the French philosopher Michel Foucault gave us a new way of talking/thinking about power with his idea of governmentality.[46] Power isn't only from the top down—leaders and the led, bosses and the bossed. Social control consists of discipline, not only in the sense of disciplining a child with a spanking or a time-out, but discipline in the way that sociology is a discipline, a structured way of thinking. Power produces knowledge, ways of thinking, discourses, that we take in as our own, internalize, and then we don't need to be governed or disciplined, we govern and discipline ourselves.

The experience—the very real, lived experience—of choice expresses our discipline. Think again about possible food choices for me while I write this. If I went for the Coke and Doritos, one might well, in ordinary English, say that I was undisciplined, had poorly controlled behavior. I am responsible for my choices, and being given those choices is how I am being governed—by the corporations that offer me my choices, by the state and its public health education programs, by my friends and colleagues and nosy neighbors who might raise their eyebrows at the garbage going out. Think not? If your next-door neighbor had three kids and every day you saw lots of Cokes and Nesteas and Oreo packages and sugary sweet cereals and Dorito packages in her garbage . . . you wouldn't maybe raise an eyebrow? Or sigh? Internalized in the self, or subtly communicated, that's a disciplining act.

In food—as in everything in our modern world—we are given choices, lots of choices. But as I and others have written in so many contexts, we are not given any control over the circumstances in which we make those choices. One of my favorite sentences I ever wrote is "Choice is not an alternative to social control, but a mechanism for achieving it."[47] It's pretty much what Foucault's governmentality is teaching us.[48]

Go back to the cereal aisle—and seriously, next time you're in a supermarket, take a good look at that aisle, think about how you would explain that to a visitor from somewhere very different. That cereal aisle is based on discipline: I will share the understanding that breakfast is the most important meal of the day; I will subject my own body's experience and feelings, and those of my children, to this management. School starts at 8:30 or earlier, goes through to "snack time" or to lunch; our waking and sleeping and meals all have to be on this schedule. That breakfast might be the most important meal, but it won't be leisurely or familial, it's going to be on-the-go with tight schedules and eating maybe in cars or sipping coffee on the train. Cereal! Or granola bars, or one of the six kinds of apples left to be available around here, the one kind of highly standardized banana, a prepackaged very sweet yogurt with bits of fruit mixed in . . . these are my choices.

It is in this context that feeding ourselves is a kind of self-care work, a project. Jack Levinson, when he was doing a dissertation on people with developmental disability living in group homes, showed me how we are all engaged in governmentality, not just those people subject to that particular form of discipline. He pointed out how when the waiter came over too soon, before we'd finished the salad, we'd say something like

"Not yet, we're still working on that." Working on it? Eating lunch is a work project? And yet it makes total sense to talk that way. I'm working on my diet. I'm working on carb control. I'm working on lowering my cholesterol, managing my pre-pre-pre-diabetes status. Between corporate medicine and corporate food, I am a disciplined person, taking care of myself, making choices. And I do it from a position of privilege—I live in a neighborhood with well-stocked supermarkets, can afford more expensive brown rice, organic fruit, fancy granola, the time and the transportation options to get to a farmers' market. A poor mother, without those resources, living in a poor neighborhood, in what is called a "food desert," has very different choices.

And that takes us from risk to income despair-ity. Choices are different in different places in the economy and in life. For me, a woman in my sixties, a lot of long-term consequences are pretty meaningless now. As my Aunt May told Uncle Jack, "It's too late to die young." But that hypothetical neighbor of yours? With little kids, she is facing long-term consequences. But if she's poor—or just in the average income level for young single mothers these days—she may also be facing short-term dangers: not starving kids but hungry kids, kids living in a state of perpetual denial and disappointment, kids who can't have any of what they see on television, any of what is being sold to them all the time but the Coke, the Oreos. That's the affordable part of what is mass marketed, relatively speaking. She may not be able to get her children the clothes and the trips to Disneyland and the toys and the electronics they see advertised, but her kids too can have name brands of something, not only junk from the dollar store—or those name brands do sometimes show up in the dollar store. It totally satisfies the hungry kids; it's the cheapest, fastest way to make them happy. Her danger is unhappy, hungry kids. Mine is upping my chances of yet one more thing to die of if I don't die of something else first. Poverty focuses our choices for us.

Life is indeed full of risks, both short-term and long-term. Horrible stuff can happen, for sure. But what are you warned about, what are you made to worry about? Not poverty but drug use; not air pollution but a beer. Not the shocking degradation of biodiversity, the loss of nutrients in processing, but the food choices you make as individuals and even more so as mothers and parents feeding children. We are asked to worry about food-borne bacteria, reminded to wash the fruit before we put it on the table. But what's in the water? I hope you're lucky enough to live somewhere with a good, clean, safe water supply. The risks are everywhere, but our attention is consistently directed to some of them—lifestyle risks, risks of individual choice—and away from the structural components of risk produced by an increasingly unequal social world.

A Clinician and a Sociologist Walk into a Bar . . .

I think of all the irritating, tense conversations I've had and heard other social scientists have with clinicians over the years—at a meeting at the Department of Health, or at someone's kitchen table, or at a bioethics panel, or lying down next to each other on a beach. I've done them all. And over drinks or over the heads of reporters, over a cup of coffee or over the radio, we argue about choice: home birth or elective cesarean sections; drug-using pregnant women arrested for "child abuse"; the use of antidepressants by pregnant women; whatever maternity care issue is hot at the moment. I know that oftentimes, as a sociologist, if truth be told, I'm contradicting myself six ways from Sunday, and sometimes I realize that. The clinician, whatever else one can say about him/her (let's just say "her" for now), is consistent. On the one hand, the problem the sociologist is having with the clinician is that the clinician (obstetrician/midwife/neurosurgeon/internist/you-name-it) thinks that with her superior training and education, she is better equipped to make rational choices, exercise clinical authority, do what needs to be done, guide the patient to sensible, scientifically justified choices. And on the other hand, the problem the sociologist is having with the clinician is that the clinician thinks it's all about individual choice. Like the joke about the restaurant customer who complained that the food was awful and the portions were too small, the sociologist argues that there are no choices, and the choices are all the patient's to make.

How can I think my way through this? How can I, who so clearly exercise so much choice in my life, I who have gone against convention, done the unexpected, wrestled long nights with difficult choices, spent decades of my life arguing against genetic determinism, sit here and argue against individual choice? Can I claim it is an illusion—an illusion that has cost me so much pain, given me so much joy, shaped my life and how I raised my children?

On issues of pregnancy and birth, I am absolutely, passionately committed to women's choice. Even with all the historical baggage of the word "choice," I really cannot come up with a better way of framing this. Everything about pregnancy—keeping it or ending it, dedicating herself to making the pregnancy the center of her life or ignoring it as best she can, changing her diet or giving up smoking or drugs or going on as she did before, giving birth at home or in an operating room, alone or with a dozen, two dozen people there—on *all* of it, I support the woman's right to choose. Nay—more than a right. The language of rights belittles the problem. I support her moral authority to choose, the rightness of her right. It's her choice.

And yet. Does she have any real control? Can she control what really matters? As Rosalind Petchesky put it years back,[49] she makes choices, but she does not control the conditions under which she makes those choices.

It's the basic problem of the sociological imagination. How do we, on the one hand, deal with the individual troubles that plague us, worry us, take up so much of our energy, our time, and our lives; and on the other hand, understand them as part of social issues, larger structural patterns? Even on those things that really are individual choices, how can you look at an individual person making a bad choice and not hold them accountable, while at the same time understanding the larger forces that determine why at any given moment so many people are making that bad choice? Or, for that matter, any given good choice.

Choice has been used to control people—that's the issue of governmentality. Choice is a concept that is invaluable, absolutely central in marketing. Think of the recent New York City fiasco around sugary sodas. We have lots of evidence now that drinking a lot of soda is not a good thing for people. So one thing that the New York City Department of Health tried to do was to limit the size of the sodas that would be sold in single portions. No more could one buy a quart in a big cup with a straw. You'd have to buy two pints, or refill the first pint. Perhaps you heard the uproar? Within days the soda industry had ads up about protecting our "choices" from a nanny mayor. Sodas had gone from a standard seven ounces when fast-food places like McDonald's first started, to twelve, sixteen, thirty-two, sixty and more ounces, as a usual size. People always had the choice of buying six of those seven-ounce sodas at a time if they wanted to—just not in one cup with one straw, but not many people at all chose to order a tray full of regular-size sodas. It was a choice, but not standardized, normalized. And so—welcome supersize!

The city wanted to enact a limit on the size of a single portion. The choice of drinking as much soda as you wanted wasn't at issue. Nor was the choice of selling as much as the company wanted. The issue was not normalizing a quart of soda as a drink to go with lunch. The city lost. It just puts lots of ads on the subway telling us that drinking too much soda is bad for our health, while the soda industry and the fast-food industry tell us what a great deal it is. Your choice! And now lots of people choose that supersize, or feel like they are being nicely disciplined and self-controlled if they order a "regular" sixteen ounces.

Go to a physician for a checkup, and if you're overweight she'll be weighing you, talking to you about food choices and diet. At the clinical level, you will be encouraged to make better choices. At the policy level, that encouragement will be voted down if it doesn't work for the food industry.

In pregnancy it is all the more fraught. A clinician can inform a woman of all the things that she is doing that might be good or bad for her in her pregnancy, that might help or harm her baby. She should stop smoking, avoid drugs, eat well, drink moderately or not at all, exercise, yadayadayada . . . But the clinician knows, as the people in the world of public health know, epidemiologists know, sociologists know, so why doesn't *she* know that the biggest determinants of the health of that baby are done deals, most of them written in by the time the mother herself was born. Race, class, neighborhood—where that mother herself grew up, where she is living in this pregnancy—those are the biggest determinants of infant outcome.

When we talk about income despair-ity and health outcomes, if we talk about any public funding, it's for more "health" care—which around here means medical care, more services by more clinicians. Never more resources to ensure safe housing, good nutrition, safe parks and bike lanes and open sidewalks to promote physical activity. No—just more people testing her, checking her, advising her, telling how to take better care of herself and her baby, while on a larger level, as a society, a nation, we have made it quite clear we have no interest in caring for her or her baby outside that clinical encounter.

When departments of health launch public health ad campaigns about pregnancy, or really about anything these days, like the soda campaigns, they are all about telling individuals how to make better choices. I love the new anti-smoking campaigns. Make people look at a mouthful of rotted teeth every time they buy a pack of cigarettes. Cigarette smoking, at least when you first start doing it, appears to be a matter of choice. We've had many decades of pro-smoking advertising, of cultural endorsement, all pushing smoking. Last night at a comedy hour a young comedian suggested that the anti-smoking folks at least acknowledge that smoking looks cool (and that wasn't the part where he was trying to be funny). I doubt that the first person to try smoking looked cool to the people around them, but seventy years' worth of movies and advertising, and it sure does look cool to us now. So finally we are pushing back, advertising the other way, creating counter-images, and then . . . people choose.

But how does that work for pregnancy? We can and we do tell women to make better choices. We positively fetishize some of those; the anti-drinking campaign is a good example.[50] Alcohol is not great for fetuses, though honest-to-god and you'll probably not believe me, we don't have data to show that low levels of alcohol consumption pickles fetuses, damages pregnancies, does much of anything. But here we are, warning labels on everything, people pretty much demonizing a pregnant woman with a glass of wine or a beer in her hand. Or think about the campaigns about childhood obesity. Try handing your overweight kid a cookie in public. Not a whole package, not for lunch, but just one cookie when all the other kids get cookies. Trust me, you get mean looks, raised eyebrows, headshakes, and sighs. Disciplined! These were pretty damned successful public health campaigns, if you want to stop pregnant women from drinking, or make fat kids and their families miserable.

But if you want to improve maternal fetal outcome? End the "obesity epidemic"? Well, maybe not so much.

I have yet to get over a public health campaign that ran in the New York City subways back in the 1980s. If you're old enough, maybe you remember the "Guess which baby's mother . . ." series—placards of pairs of newborn footprints, one premie, one full size, and on each one, a question like "Guess which baby's mother smoked while pregnant?" or drank, or used drugs. I looked in vain for the one that said "Guess which baby's mother was born in the Bronx?" or "Guess which baby's mother isn't white?" or even "Guess which baby's mother was beaten by her husband?" But no. Every "guess" was "Guess which mother we have to blame for this!" And now, we can vilify the mother for over-stuffing her children with refined carbs and fats, for allowing them to fall prey to the advertising campaigns the food industry directs to them. If you think public health campaigns have no effect, think about the effects of advertising. It does work.

We're on the brink of some new public health campaigns. There's a heightened awareness of the relationship between what we are now calling income disparity and despair-ities in maternal infant health outcomes.

There are clear and observable links between poverty and infant mortality, and even when researchers control for poverty, there are clear links between race and infant deaths. It is not the melanin that kills, but what it means to be Black in America. Poverty and racism kill people. Each does. Together they are a disaster, killing people most especially at vulnerable junctions in their lives—like when they are being born and when they are giving birth.

I sit at tables with clinicians and public health advocates, and we acknowledge that, and try to figure out what to do about it. How should our public health campaigns address this? An earnest, sincere, hard-working (now damned with faint praise) woman sitting with me at the Department of Health said we have to tell young women this, show them that they have to take special care of themselves, make better choices! The clinicians at the table all agree: we have to educate them! And we have to put them in high-risk categories and monitor them carefully. More tests, more choices, more, more, more. More of the same. It hasn't worked yet, but we need more.

And of course they're right. If I were the clinician sitting opposite the young Black woman, damned straight I'd be checking her nervously, worrying about what's likely to go wrong. And when I am her mother, *of course* I tell her to take good care of herself, make careful choices.

But seriously? Is this the best we have to offer her? Teach everybody how to use the life preservers while we send them out on leaky ships?

The changes that we need to make are in racism (it's probably getting better) and in income inequality (it's definitely getting worse). I cannot say to the clinician, do that, make the revolution, and then get back to me on individual choices. Because clinicians face each woman each day, right now, and have to offer her more choices not fewer, expand not limit her options, recognize her rights, her dignity, her needs, her choices. And I get so angry when they do not do that, when they push "at risk" women into "high-risk" care, give them too many tests, too many high-tech interventions, take away their choices for good, peaceful, loving pregnancies and births. It angers me when people want to limit the choices of people on food stamps, making sure they make healthy choices, while at the same time we give tax credits to the corporations that advertise the junk food to them and their children, and now let those corporations and the people who profit from them donate all the money they want to in order to get officials elected who will appoint health department officers who won't get in their way. Ah, choice!

But I know that we have already gone very far in taking away that choice for women who are born Black and/or in poverty. Does everybody know that? Do the subway riders know that poverty kills babies? That racism does? If they knew that, if we showed them little coffins, would it help? Would that perhaps be the thing, one of the things, that gets America to deal with its growing income despair-ity?

The sociologist and the clinician, well, it's no joke. We lift our glasses to each other, recognize that if we're both doing our jobs right, we're probably in pretty much the same space—looking at the dead and dying babies and mothers and knowing that the solution isn't really in our hands. It requires large-scale public change, not theory and not clinical care.

Battling Industrialization

If we are looking at babies dead from the life we've created for their mothers, at little kids now developing type 2 diabetes from the diet we've created for them, how am I supposed to write about, *care* about, things like artisanal bread and home birth? This is how people in both of these movements end up being accused of being elitist, over-worrying the problems of the "worried well," and not understanding the pettiness of their concerns.

But we foodies and we birthies, we think this is not petty. We think that how we eat and how we birth actually do matter, both at the level of physically saving lives and at the level of living meaningful lives. We think that the industrialization of birth and of food, the massification and loss of individuality that has happened, the overwhelming standardization have costs at every level. We also know that while elite people can afford to worry about the lovely parts of this, the taste and creativity and joy of our meals and our births, the poor people of the earth are struggling just to get to the place where our problems lie. This has happened too often before to sit by and watch it happen again. The elite may be able to get some softening, humanizing touches, but what we are all battling is industrialization, turning our lives and our children, our most important and intimate experiences and feelings, over to actuarial tables, to risk formulas, to population control and management, to corporations that run the planet and manage us in the process.

Sitting here as an American, a person of no small privilege, and complaining about our food supply and our medical systems does sound a bit like a spoiled brat, and very much like biting the hand that feeds us. The foodies have made a bit more headway on making people aware that there are indeed problems, locally as well as globally, with the food production and distribution system, and that exporting modern agricultural systems is not the solution. Medicine, on the other hand, seems to remain the state religion around here, and to critique medical progress as being anything other than progress is a kind of heresy. For both of these, food and birth, a bit more historical context is in order.

It is true that you can't understand the present without understanding history. But it seems just as true that we can't understand our history without understanding the current context in which it is told. That stuff about history being written by the victors—in wars and battles large and small, that is very true. We look back at birth and think it was wildly dangerous, women dropping dead in childbirth all over the place till the doctors arrived on their white horses with black bags to rescue us. And that is not true.

But we also think there was a time of mass starvation, people always hungry, constant famines, until we developed our industrial systems of food production, and created cheap, easy food. And that's not true either. Fred Kaufman, whose book *Bet the Farm* I referred to earlier, says,

What seems to be progress is not always so. This point was driven home at the dawn of the Space Age, when famine was rampant, and many anthropologists who studied preindustrial societies began to argue that instead of slogging through a short, brutish life of Paleolithic poverty, so-called savage hunter-gatherers ate better than we eat, worked less than we work, slept a lot more than we sleep and spent a great deal of their time hanging out, doing nothing.[51]

Maybe it's a myth that preindustrialization meant starvation, and maybe it's a myth that it meant a bucolic garden-of-plenty. But it is quite clear that the upshot of industrialization has not been to solve the problem of hunger; we are at least as far from that as we have ever been. With all of our science and technology we created a "green revolution," Nobel Prize and all, and, as Kaufman shows us,

> Belatedly the bureaucrats realized that Green Revolution policies had favored large landholders over small landholders, prosperous peasants over penniless peasants and all that money, science, sophistication, and goodwill had actually *increased* economic inequality. The food bills of poor countries soared fivefold and sixfold, and since 2003 the overall proportion of hungry people on Earth has also been on the rise.[52]

Kaufman sums up the larger issue, and I am pretty confident the larger causes too: "Today, as half of the world heads toward obesity and the other half toward starvation, it's worth asking who, exactly, is making the money."[53] Kaufman's one of the ones who's followed the money, tried to see who is profiting and how. And that does bring us right back to risk and income despair-ity, the two issues of our time. What happens when food becomes an industrial product? Kaufman says it stops being food; it becomes a commodity. He followed the path that leads to pizza, a cheap, easy food that can be reasonably healthy, okay to serve. And once it became a commodity, once it left the world of food, evil things happened. Not from people trying to be evil, but from people dealing with food as a commodity. If the point of making pizza is to make money, the meaning of a tomato, of flour, of cheese all change. Each of the food items that make up a pizza becomes a commodity, and taste, health, culture, ecology—everything else about the food—drops off, no longer of interest or value if it doesn't work toward profit.

It took me a while to fully understand this. First it just seemed to me that industrial food is food grown big. I can cook for five people without a ruffle. I can manage to do twenty-five. It takes bigger pots, more organization, larger measures. I can imagine, in a bigger kitchen, cooking for fifty or even a hundred. My brother-in-law was in the Navy once, and told me about cooking chili for hundreds. We laughed at how you threw in not a couple of pinches of chili powder, but two cans. Using a cup of some herb in one of those pots was like just opening a jar of it in the same room at home—so small a pinch you can't measure it.

But these industrial food suppliers are talking about cooking for thousands. And then really, it isn't cooking anymore. It's processing. You start using different techniques when there are machines not people doing the task. Hand grinding is different from machine; different things happen to the food you started with. Factory cooking is not home cooking only bigger. They do things in factories you cannot do at home: extrusion cooking, explosion pressurization and instantization, using extreme temperatures and pressures, repeated wetting and drying, and in the end the starch molecules of the processed flour aren't what they would be if you cooked them over a hearth or over a stove.[54] It's not a food—it's a product.

Think about the difference between looking at a few peaches on sale at the farmers' market, or on the shelf at the supermarket, or grown off the tree in your backyard. The peaches aren't even the same. Some are bred for industrial sales; some are what happens to grow around there. But even so, you take the peaches into the kitchen and think about what they'd be good for. You could just eat them, or cut them up and serve them in a fruit platter, mix them into yogurt, put them in a pot and make some soft peach thing you could put in a pie or serve for dessert, or spice up and use as a chutney, or . . . You get the point. You could, if you are so inclined, have some fun with a pile of peaches. Compare that with deciding you can offer a new peach product in your multinational company's food line. Now you're looking for a particular kind of peach, a lot of them ready at once, all very similar in size and taste. You're hoping this product will fly, so you want something you can replicate year after year, hopefully in increasing amounts for larger and more distant markets. You're looking for peach flavor, which of course can also come out of a lab, so the taste of the peach is actually one of the least important parts of it. Oh, color too, that lovely peachy color, is also laboratory-replicable, so whatever clue to its ripeness color meant in your backyard or the supermarket shelf, that doesn't count in your factory. If a peach product is supposed to be dessert-y, then sweetness, of course. And why should the sweetness come out of the peaches? That's an expensive and unreliable source of the sweetness. Peach sweetness varies between peaches, between points in the ripening process. And so it goes. To see what I mean, pick up a package of Gummi Peach Rings (ingredients: corn syrup, sugar, K gelatin, fruit juice, citric acid, lactic acid, natural and artificial flavors, oil, carnauba wax, colors added FD&C Red #40, Yellow # 5 & #6, Blue #1.) A peach-flavored product without a peach in it.

It is very tempting for me right now to go off into a long, enraged rant about how bad our food system is. And it is, on so many levels. But this is a book that is trying to be hopeful, a book looking at the social movements that are responding to all that bad news.

As I have been writing these couple of pages, in just the last two days, the following e-mails arrived in my in-box: MomsRising.org has asked me to sign petitions to get junk food advertising out of schools. They are deservedly also rather celebrating the fact that junk foods themselves can no longer be sold in schools starting with the next school year, but apparently you can still advertise junk food. The food movement won the new standards for what can be sold and is moving on to the next battle. I just signed.

KillerCoke.org is writing to tell me that Coca Cola is co-opting the work of the corporate social responsibility movement, and offering me "detailed documentation of Coca-Cola's human rights, child welfare, and environmental abuses spanning decades and continuing today." Coca Cola, they tell me, is aggressively marketing to children even while assuring us it is not, and engaging in abusive practices toward workers around the world. This one is a purely informative e-mail about the work of these food activists, telling me about what college students in Binghamton and what lots of other groups are doing to protest in response.

The Center for Science in the Public Interest e-mailed me with the subject heading "How many more must die before the FDA acts?" to tell me, "Salt is perhaps the deadliest ingredient in our food supply, causing heart attacks, strokes, kidney disease, and other health problems. But don't blame your salt shaker: Upwards of 75 percent of the salt we consume comes built in to processed foods and restaurant foods."

And just this minute, Nation of Change e-mailed me its top stories of the week, leading with the French parliament banning GMO maize and an article suggesting that organic farming can reverse climate change.

It's only noon on Tuesday. Think of what the rest of the week will bring.

You have to be in a particular frame of mind to think of all those campaigns as good news. But to me, that's what they are: they are the proof of an active social movement. And if I introduce any of these things into conversation, people know what I'm talking about. Enough people have splashed in those waters long enough that a social movement wave has been created. The concerns so many of us now have about food are no longer our own personal problems. In the language of C. Wright Mills, that great social movement theorist, these things have moved from being personal troubles to social issues.[55] When we raise concerns about one or another aspect of our industrialized food systems, we are not accused of wanting to turn the clock back, dispense with progress, move back to some early unfathomable primitive time—all things people have said to me when I talk about replacing obstetrics with midwifery as the standard of care. They understand that deindustrializing food is not about going back but moving forward in social justice and in access.

That is what I want to accomplish with the movement for deindustrializing birth. Bringing back and respecting the skills of midwives, valuing indigenous midwifery care, as we are being asked to value indigenous agriculture, is not a step back but a step forward. As has been shown with food, industrialization has its costs, and those costs are not equally distributed. Rich people can buy their way out, be spared some of the risks; not so with the poorest countries in the world, and not so for the poorest people in the richest countries.

What I am going to do with most of the rest of this book is try to convince you of the value of my social movement, what we in the birth world are trying to accomplish with home birth and midwifery care. The problem for me is in the industrialization of birth. That is what I find so appealing—and so parallel—in the food movement. It too is addressing what happens when central parts of our lives, intimate and embodied things, move into industrial management. Weber used the term "the iron cage"[56] to describe this rationalization of life under Western industrial capitalism, a life governed by rationality, the kind of actuarial calculation that risk society traps us in. He of course couldn't yet know the half of it. Could he possibly have foreseen just how fully controlled our lives would be, how totally consumption as well as production would yield to industrial management?

The thing about being humans, about being social and smart and all that, is that we don't just live inside an iron cage, we take that cage inside ourselves, we build ourselves up along its bars. We don't have some pure internal self looking through the cage, but see ourselves through the lens that the cage gives us. We internalize. So we take that medical gaze, that "scientific" gaze, and turn it inwards. We are subject to the discipline of governmentality as Foucault showed us. We understand our own body, our own sensations, our own needs, through the lens that our cage gives us.

That's what I meant by the internalized medical gaze. You don't need a doctor to get you to see your body in terms of symptoms and signs; you now know to look for those, name them, go online and do your own initial diagnostic workup before you get to the office. We may even feel that we're now better at it than our doctors are, have more information to work with, more time to spend on the self-diagnostic process. And yet we want the same confirmation the doctor wants—the definitive tests, the science to prove what we know about our bodies.

But remember, this is not just science. This is industrialized science. The scientific findings that come down to us, the public, come through a series of filters—what research gets funded and thus which questions get asked; which findings get announced; which announcements get reported. Obviously money is in there at each step. Things that have sales potential are far more likely to be funded. One of the saddest moments of confrontation with that basic truth came for me at a UN conference on the issue of patenting genes. Many of us thought that would be a mistake, that the human genome should not be up for patenting. But a very nice young man, sincere, dark suit and tie, very serious, stood up to explain to us that we must permit this, we needed to understand how terribly important this was: If we didn't permit the patenting of human genes, there would be no incentive to cure cancer. I sat there stunned for a minute, then stood up and asked whether, if we thought really, really hard, couldn't we maybe think of other incentives for curing cancer than profit? But basically, he was right: we may want something very much indeed, but we have no path to get there without profit. If a company can make a fortune on the cure for a particular kind of cancer, it will invest in finding that cure. If not, not.

The food industry leans hard on science, justifies itself through its use of science, just as the biomedical industry does: its products are based on research, on nutrition, on science. And we learn the appropriate science to make the appropriate choices in medications and in food— which increasingly start to feel remarkably similar. Did you have enough potassium in your meals today? How much sodium did you feed your kids? How's the calcium level in their meals? And don't forget iron—you don't want anemic kids!

In that ongoing push between science and taste, we have to balance all this, choosing intelligently, governing our bodies and our diets. We don't want to go to the extremes of a meal in a pill or even some soylent-all-purpose mix. We want what we understand as food, cooked not produced, in kitchens not laboratories. We don't want to go to the extreme of medicalized food, feeding tubes or IV mixtures: we rightly understand those as last resorts, tragedies of illness, not extremes of health.

So off we go food shopping, but we take on the scientific gaze. We make our choices, and we use our understanding of how food works with the body. But that gaze is itself the product of the industry that sells us the food. Gyorgy Scrinis, an Australian philosopher in a food and nutrition program, calls it an ideology of "nutritionism," thinking about food in terms of its nutrients. The assumption, he tells us, is that "a calorie is a calorie, a vitamin a vitamin, and a protein a protein, regardless of the particular food it comes packaged in."[57] This idea of nutrients and vitamins being in our foods—added to our foods—also pretty much comes out of that cereal aisle and the food movement's work. Post introduced Sugar Crisp in 1949, which took off big-time, so in short order came Sugar Corn Pops, Sugar Frosted Flakes, Sugar Smacks, and so on.

Not until the 1970s with the work of food activists, people worried about health consequences and advertising to children, did sugar become not a sales asset but a liability.[58] The word "sugar" started to get dropped— not so much the sugar levels but the word—and other ingredients came to be highlighted. Bran! Vitamins! Fiber!

Of course there is a science of food and nutrition, and sure there are particular nutrients we truly need. That is good to know. (Pack oranges for sailors on long sea voyages, they prevent scurvy.) But that science, Scrinis shows, is co-opted by the food industry and marketing. Rather than thinking about something we could call "whole food," we focus on specific nutrients and the related testable, diagnosable body markers. It is a kind of health reductionism, Scrinis says, a biology of functionality. You eat this food for this nutrient, which does this thing for your body. It pulls food out of any other context or meaning, "at the expense of other ways of encountering food through its embedded sensual, cultural or ecological qualities."[59] "While this functionalized—and essentially medicalized—view of food and the body is not in itself new, it has significantly moved from the margins to the center of everyday food discourse and consumption practices."[60]

Thinking this way is no accident. You learned how to do it because it works really well for the food industry. It's cheap to add a nutrient. It encourages all kinds of nutritionally engineered foods: low fat, high fiber, low cal, high calcium, now with twice the iron! You can put calcium in orange juice! Who'd have thought? But the orange juice is starting to look like the cereal aisle a bit—choices galore! With and without pulp, fortified with this or that, things that were never even in orange juice, but why not? Meet more nutritional needs! A lowly orange on the tree cannot compete.

And so we feel empowered, individually shopping for the right nutrients, making good food choices, being healthy.

When I first wanted a home birth, it was the issue of control that drew me. I wanted to be in charge of myself and my surroundings, decide who had access to me and to my space. In institutions like hospitals, in which people are the objects of work, it's not just the workers who are products of their work space, who are controlled by the bureaucracy. In institutions in which people are the work product, the task is to produce particular kinds of people—hospitals produce patients, schools produce students, jails prisoners. Sometimes we want to be the product. Come, Disneyland, do your magic, make us a happy family on vacation. Have at it, McDonald's, make us a Happy Meal. And sometimes we want something else, something more personal, more authentic, more ourselves—and of course, increasingly at the high end that is being branded and marketed as well. Once again though, the higher you are in the class/race hierarchy, the easier it is to get that individualized attention. A hospital marketing to rich people advertises, "Forget everything you know about hospitals!" They will give you (you who can afford it) something nicer, better.[61])

And few institutions are more tightly hierarchical than hospitals. Where else, outside the military, do we routinely talk about people giving "orders"? One thing we know about institutions is that when they are more hierarchical, it is the people at the bottom who have the most direct contact with the product. The CEO doesn't have his hands in the mayonnaise, isn't screwing on the windshield wipers, isn't running the hemming machine. I once saw a cartoon of a huge factory labeled something-or-other Dairy, with a boardroom full of white guys in suits, looking at a picture of a cow on a wall calendar and saying, 'What's that?" Doctors have some patient contact, but far less than do the lower workers they give orders to. And the people running the hospital, making the decisions that control the doctors, have even less hands-on-patient contact. When you get to the hospital corporate headquarters, where decisions that really count are being made, well . . . Actuarial tables are more relevant than operating tables.

Of course this raises questions about all kinds of medical care, not to mention teaching and imprisonment. But I'm going to keep my scope narrow here. Maybe the only way to have brain surgery to remove a tumor in your head, or the only way to get your inflamed appendix out or whatever, is to just submit to what's on offer. If having a baby is only one more medical procedure, then so be it. But if it's not just that, if it's a different kind of event, then we can ask what are the costs of putting it into medical settings. These are the questions people are starting to ask about dying; these are the questions I am asking about birth. What is being lost when you move it into institutional settings? What is being gained when you move it back out, when you deindustrialize birth? What happens when you bring birth home?

Feeling Safe

If people's ideas—or more accurately, their feelings—about safety are not data-based, thoughtful risk assessments, then what are they about? Plenty of people will read the studies showing the safety of home birth, even dozens of studies all showing the same thing, and say, yes, well, sure, but I'd just *feel* safer in a hospital. Some things feel safe, and some things feel risky, even when we know it's not logical. One oft-discussed example is air travel. Lots of people boarding airplanes feel fear. It's a crazy situation, sitting in a metal box in the clouds, gliding down over buildings and streets and landing on those little wheels. But we know that the chances of being killed in a car accident are way greater than being killed in an airplane. Mile for mile, the trip to the airport is something like sixty times riskier than the flight. Daniel Gardner looked at what he called the "science of fear" and said that even if terrorists were hijacking and crashing one passenger jet a week in the United States, a person who took one flight a month for a year would have only a 1 in 135,000 chance of being killed in a hijacking—a trivial risk compared to the annual 1 in 6,000 chance of being killed in a car crash.[62] Hard to believe? Makes you want to jump on a flying cow, doesn't it? The shift from planes to cars after 9/11 lasted a year before plane use resumed prior levels, and an extra 2,595 people died in car accidents—about 60 percent of the total deaths from the 9/11 disaster, and six times the total number of people on board the doomed flights on 9/11. Cars are more dangerous than planes.

Some of us feel that—we get nervous in cars (yes, me, sorry)—but most people don't, especially when they are the drivers. People driving cars feel in control, and think they won't do anything to get themselves killed. Feeling in control is a powerful thing. One of my Dutch colleagues did research years back on newborn screening.[63] If you ask parents what they would do if there was a test that could tell them whether their newborn baby has a very, very tiny chance of having some terrible, could-be fatal condition, they pretty much all want the test. And if you say, as he did in his hypothetical, "What if the only testing facility is way up in the north of the Netherlands—you'd have to drive the baby for five hours to the testing center." Well then, into the car! And if you tell them further, as he did, that the chances of the baby being killed on the way to the testing center are very much higher than the chances of the baby having the condition, it changes *nothing*. They say something along the lines of, "Don't be silly—we're not going to get killed driving there. We drive all the time! We're careful. But if there's a risk that the baby could have a disease you can test for and maybe try to treat—how could we not test?" It's not rational. It's not about risk. It's about the feeling of riskiness, and the feeling of safety.

One of the things that seem to make contemporary Americans (and Dutch, and the rest of us in advanced Western-style capitalist countries, if not everyone else too) feel safe is feeling in control. And if you think back to the history of the childbirth movements, remember that what started as "natural childbirth" quickly morphed into a focus on feeling in control, or maybe just as importantly, not feeling or appearing out of control. This is something we all learn early, and women more than men—to control ourselves, behave ourselves. And think about it. When can you let your hair down, let all the control and best-behavior just slip away? Where and when can you safely lose yourself, forget about control, and just let yourself go? What makes for safe space, and how could we make birthrooms safe in that way?

Giving birth requires some loss of control, some giving up of control. People sometimes talk about the very hard physical work of giving birth in almost athletic terms, like running a marathon, and there is truth in that comparison, but there are profound differences. If a half mile from the finish line the runner says, "The hell with it, it's not worth finishing," she can stop putting one leg in front of the other. Not so with the laboring woman. Ready and willing or *not*, here comes the next contraction. So you can either give yourself up to the process, or—in that "strength of weakness" made possible by anesthesia—demand that someone else take over the birth. And that seems to be the root of the contemporary bifurcation of feminist ideas about birth. Give yourself over to the power of birth, the power of the female body, or order the services you want, and manage this like you manage everything else, stay on top of it and stay in control by thoughtful management and purchasing decisions.

Birth is a deeply embodied experience. It doesn't happen in the abstract, it happens in your gut and genitals; it's pretty centrally located and hard to ignore. To think about controlling birth makes us question what makes a person feel in control or out of control of her body. There is some larger sense in which this is an absurd question. It implies a space between the person and the body that is both impossible to conceptualize and impossible (for me) not to. The question speaks to an understanding of the body as an object under the control or management of the self. While I know there is no "self" sitting somewhere else controlling the body, I certainly feel that I am controlling the fingers that write this, that it is I who am holding my confused head in my hands as I try to figure this out. I am, myself, in here, inside this body, looking out.

This fundamental mind-body question underpins so much of our confusion and strange behavior around birth. Is the birth an activity the woman does? Something that happens to her? Something she goes through? Something done *to* her or *by* her? How you answer that sets the ground for how you make the woman feel safe. The answer has shifted across time and space, and is not the same for all women in all times. The answer reflects larger political, social, and cultural understandings of the body.

You probably don't need me to go back to Foucault to tell you that the contemporary body is disciplined, tightly controlled in all kinds of ways, and that the discipline is internalized, done through self-care, self-mastery. We control ourselves, and acknowledging that control is among our highest praises. It's perhaps particularly obvious in the issue of weight control, and especially for women. It is hard to find a woman who does not know her weight, know how much it has varied over the last few years, few weeks. We measure not just weight but calories, carbs, and measures that are reflections of that control. People are expected to know their cholesterol levels, BMI, blood pressure, sugar levels, and more and more. The body is to be in tight control, muscles doing the work that perhaps undergarments did for women in an earlier day, sculpting flesh to firmness. This has consequences of course for pregnancy, and much has been written about pregnancy and weight, perhaps best expressed in another favorite old T-shirt: "I'm not fat, I'm pregnant." But my interest here is broader than the weight management issues. Women who grow up with disciplined bodies, who learn early and powerfully to control their bodies, are not likely to be particularly adept at letting go, letting loose. It's been discussed in terms of sexuality—the inhibiting consequences of worrying about what you look like, of controlling response at all times to match the images of what women are

supposed to look like, whether those images come from fashion magazines or from pornography. But it is no less an issue in birth. Letting
go—roaring, figuratively or literally—is not what the disciplined body
has learned to do.

Part of the achievement of second-wave feminism was teaching
women to feel strong and competent and most important, in control,
owning their bodies. Whether it was about the apocryphal bra-burning,
or the real razor-tossing, we worked on accepting our bodies as ours.
Unshaven legs or armpits, silly as it seems, were a way of taking control:
It's my body! It's not here for display or objectification. How much more
significant was the growth of women's athletics, the hard-won Title IX
programs that said girls' sports activities have to be funded right along
with boys' in school. Athletics is all about discipline, a different kind of
self-discipline of the body, disciplining not to restrain but to achieve,
not to hold in but to let go. It made sense, for some of us, to think of
birth the same way. Birth is what our bodies are built to do. These hips
are wide for a reason. These breasts are not just ornaments. We can own
and use our bodies, control them, learn to give birth and feel strong and
competent and in control doing it. Good-bye high heels, hello Birkenstocks! Every silly stereotype about hippie dressing—the shoes, the loose
clothes, the wild hair—was about accepting the woman's body for the
powerful and beautiful thing it naturally is. So for my generation, us
hippies and all us 1970s feminist second-wavers, the birthplace could
be a safe space, somewhere we could roar. We could feel safer at home,
where we could be in charge, than in any institution anywhere. I reread
what I wrote in that first piece on my own decision to have a home birth,
and it was all about control: I will choose who comes in. I will choose
who touches me. I will choose how I birth. Me. I'm in charge 'cause it's
my body.

But, as keeps coming up in a discussion of childbirth, there are many
ways to feel and to be in control. Those first-wavers taught us that you
could feel in control by demanding services, hiring people to do the task
for you. That brought us the early anesthetics. We are way past that now.
Women want to be there, to be present for their births. What did last
from that "natural childbirth" movement was the idea that birth was a
beautiful thing to see and to share. Husbands especially should be standing right there, and the parents should see it happen together. The idea

of watching the birth as conferring motherhood goes into unanticipated places: adoptive parents want to be there; people hiring surrogates want to watch the baby born. And so, of course, does the birthing mother; the mirror was probably the most lasting contribution of the natural childbirth movement. For a generation of women who'd been watching their fetuses develop onscreen, watching them emerge in the mirror was a lovely thing. They didn't need to *feel* it, but they did need to *see* it. Enter the epidural—perfectly separating the mind and the body. That unending problem of childbirth, of the body, solved: the mind can watch and see the whole thing; the body can be turned over to someone else. "I could watch, not scream," says an epidural user.[64]

As Jacqueline Wolf tells us, "In a single generation, the predominate portrayal of the ideal birth had gone from an invigorating, spontaneous, full felt athletic event to a nontaxing, carefully scheduled, fully numbed, relaxing event."[65] It's still and always about control, but the meaning of control had changed: "Natural childbirth conferred control by allowing women to take charge of their labors and deliveries and be the central character. Epidural anesthesia, in contrast, conferred control by allowing laboring women to maintain their composure."[66]

The feminists of the first wave expressed their power by demanding services for their weak bodies, demanding anesthesia. The feminists of the second wave expressed their power and control by letting go, by refusing to control their powerful bodies. The post-feminists demand services and want to watch them being performed. Power in weakness, weakness in power—these are flip sides of the same coin, different ways of working with the overwhelming physicality of birth, something that just does not lend itself to control. In that, birth is, Wolf tell us, all but "un-American."[67] We feel we should be able to control things: convenience and efficiency are core values for Americans. I heard a talk by a bread baker, Jessamyn Waldman, founder of Hot Bread Kitchen, a business teaching immigrant women in New York City to be culinary workers. She said, "Bread baking is the most un–New York thing you can do. It's slow, you just have to bear with the process, there's nothing you can do to rush it. It's like you're in this three-thousand-year-old bubble."[68] She could have been a home-birth midwife talking about birth.

Lots of us would like to enter that bubble for a bit. An afternoon in the kitchen confronting the limits and wonders of yeast can be a joy.

And what's the worst that can happen? A failed bread? Go buy one and try again next week. With birth it's so different. Even for those who find that bubble tempting, who would like to engage with the body as their foremothers have done, give birth in this un–New York way, at a slower pace, it's still scary.

As important as controlling pain in childbirth was for our sense of feeling safe, increasingly so was controlling its timing. Controlling timing is partly about scheduling. I just locked in two hours on a Friday afternoon four months from now for a doctoral defense. The student and I feel that we're back on top of things, on schedule, moving along. "I just love deadlines," she tossed happily over her shoulder as she headed out of my office. She wasn't going to finish this dissertation when it gets done, she was going to finish it in time for the defense. Under control! Home safe—or so it feels. I could be hit by a bus, or she could; she could lose her mind, forget how to write, anything could happen. We know that. But it's in our calendars, all set.

Controlling timing isn't only about scheduling, it's also knowing what the timing is, what to expect. Consider the new subway countdown timers. Used to be, if you missed a train, you'd just stand there and wait for the next one, maybe five minutes. Now you look up and there's a sign that says the next train is due in five minutes. To wait five minutes is one thing. To wait a minute, and then another, and then wait a minute, and then wait another, and then think maybe you hear the train, and then— well finally! It's about time, there it is! It's the same five minutes of your life standing on a subway platform. But it's not the same experience at all. Predictability gives a feeling of control, and order, which in turn feels a lot safer.

Predictability in timing is one key to feeling safe. But other kinds of predictability also make us feel safe. If today's commute feels pretty much like yesterday's, and last week's, and the one before that, if pretty much the same trains pull in at pretty much the same time, filled up pretty much as usual, it all feels okay. If there's an odd delay, and/or a truly overcrowded car, or a really empty one—any of those things make us look up, check what's happening, make sure everything's okay. If you walk into work, or the grocery store, or the corner coffee shop, and pretty much the same people are doing pretty much the same things they always do, you feel okay, you don't even think about safety. But if it's suddenly empty, or a tight-packed crowd, or a noticeably strange group of people have stepped in, you look up, ask what's happening, want to be reassured.

That certainly works well with children; they seem to crave predictability, repetition. The same bedtime story over and over and over again (till I want to scream!), the same people, the same places, the same everything. Faith Ringgold put it perfectly: "I had a good childhood. Nothing happened."[69] A whole food industry is built on that kind of safe predictability, the comfort food that tastes just the way it is supposed to taste, just the way it always tasted. McDonald's and the other fast-food chains built their empires on that. You're at work? traveling on an interstate highway? near your kid's school? Doesn't matter. Walk into one of those places and it will be exactly the same, same food, same tastes, same systems. It's amusing to people to go to truly foreign places and see the little tiny tweaks—the Beijing McDonald's, the Dutch one, the French. Le Big Mac is the same.

Is that food safe? We are back to the distinction between immediate danger and long-term risk. What makes a birth safe? Mother and child are doing well. What makes a meal safe? No one's puking, no weird rashes, whoever ate it seems all set till the next meal. But we are not seeking just individual safe births or safe meals. We are seeking safe systems of delivery, dependably and safely delivering food and babies with good outcomes, and our outcome measures are longer-term. That's one of the problems with high rates of cesarean sections: the outcome of this particular birth may be okay, but the woman's later births have been put at greater risk. Some of the longer-term outcomes of cesarean sections and other contemporary birth practices are not well studied. What, for example, are the problems of late-in-life surgical adhesions in mothers? I watched my mother-in-law begin her decline to death with the surgery in her seventies to repair the adhesions from her cesarean forty years earlier. We are increasingly understanding that human beings are hosts and beneficiaries of a world of bacteria; what are the long-term consequences of the absence of the exposure to the vaginal flora (the healthy bacteria) for the babies? And then there are the "soft" issues, whatever psychological or emotional consequences there may be to entering motherhood or entering the world via surgery.

On food we have indeed got a good long-term picture, and no, those meals are not safe. All that processed food, all the supersizing, we know it's causing long-term health consequences at a population level, some of which show up later in life, but increasingly we're seeing the consequences earlier as diabetes and obesity start showing up in younger folk, are increasingly seen as complications of pregnancy.

But it feels safe to eat familiar food in familiar settings. In contrast, walk into some odd, very foreign restaurant where you truly do not know what is in half the things available. Some of us love it, and some of us hate it, but it is not about comfort. New foods, strange foods, push us out of our comfort zone. When someone needs calm and reassurance, we bring them the standard foods of their childhood, and now, like as not, that is something that came out of a package or out of a fast-food restaurant, Kraft macaroni and cheese or a Big Mac. Eating that way may kill you eventually, but not today. It feels safe.

It's All in the Timing

How can an industry make birth feel safe? Partly it is done with set design. The colors of cleanliness—whites and that weird hospital green—are all over surfaces that harbor far more dangerous germs than your kitchen floor, even than your bathroom floor. The benediction of the medical religion works well, too; we believe in the power of medicine to save us, to rescue us. Partly it is done with pain control—pain is scary, debilitating, makes us feel out of control—but a lot is done with the control of time, the standardization and predictability of time in labor. Women want to know how far along they are, how much farther they have to go. While we talk a lot about the history of controlling pain in labor, the other change in birth management that has occurred with medicalization was a shift in energy from managing the *pain* of labor to managing its *length*. Drugs and procedures to ease pain or to speed labor both carry risks, make birth less safe. In both of these, birth was made to feel safer but be riskier.

As obstetrics and hospitals took over birth, it became more and more meshed into the pace of work. That predictability in time is only partly done to make women feel safe. The speedup is also done to make work

predictable, because hospitals are institutional workplaces, with scheduled shifts. Unlike a restaurant, which can predict noon and dinner
rushes, labor admissions are less predictable. That itself explains the rise
of "planned inductions without medical indication," doctor and woman
happy to schedule the birth. But whether a scheduled or spontaneous
labor, once admitted, some sense of how long this is going to last is helpful for all concerned.

The standard obstetrical model of time in labor is best represented by
"Friedman's curve," a "graphicostatistical analysis" of labor, introduced
by Emanuel A. Friedman in seven separate articles between 1954 and
1959 in the major American obstetrical journal.[70] "Graphicostatistical
analysis" is a pompous name for a relatively simple idea. Friedman observed labors and computed the average length of time they took. He
broke labor into separate phases and found the average length of each
phase. He did this separately for primiparas (women having first births)
and for multiparas (women with previous births). He computed the
averages, and the statistical limits—a measure of the amount of variation. Take the example of height. If we computed heights for women,
we would measure many women, get an average, and also be able to say
how likely it was for someone to be much taller or much shorter than
average. A woman of over six feet tall is a statistical abnormality.

What Friedman did was to make a connection between *statistical*
normality and *physiological* normality. He used the language of statistics,
with its specific technical meanings, and jumped to conclusions about
physiology: "It is clear that cases where the phase-durations fall outside
of these (statistical) limits are probably abnormal in some way. . . . We
can see now how, with very little effort, we have been able to define
average labor and to describe with proper degrees of certainty the limits of normal."[71] Once the false and misleading connection is made between statistical abnormality and physiological abnormality, the door is
opened for medical treatment. *Statistically abnormal labors are medically
treated.* The medical treatments include rupturing membranes, admin-
istering hormones, and cesarean sections. Using this logic, we would say
that a woman of six feet one inch was not only unusually tall, but that we
should treat her for her "height condition."

How did this work in practice? Every labor that takes "too long" and
cannot be stimulated by hormones or by breaking the membranes will

go on to the next level of medical intervention, the cesarean section. Breaking the membranes is an induction technique that is particularly interesting in this regard. The sac in which the baby and the amniotic fluid are enclosed is easily ruptured once the cervix is partially opened. Sometimes that happens by itself early on in labor, and the waters breaking may even be the first sign of labor. But once broken, the membranes are no longer a barrier between the baby and the outside world. The *Listening to Mothers* survey reports that 55 percent of women experienced artificially ruptured membranes. (*Williams* states, "If the membranes are intact, there is a great temptation even during normal labor to perform an amniotomy [rupture them]."[72]) Once the membranes are ruptured, the chances of infection increase, more so in hospitals with frequent vaginal examinations, but in any case more than if the membranes remained intact. Once the membranes are ruptured, it is important that the labor proceed more quickly to avoid infection. Thus the intervention to speed the labor itself demands that the labor indeed be sped up.

Length of labor is not a basic, unchanging biological fact, but is subject to social and medical control. In 1968 a Dublin hospital introduced the "active management of labor" as an obstetrical approach focused on providing control over the length of labor.[73] As long as one is prepared to stop the labor with a cesarean section, one can guarantee a labor no longer than any arbitrary time limit one chooses: twelve hours seems to have become the standard figure. Even before the introduction of the Dublin-style "active management of labor," which guarantees a labor of no more than twelve hours, there has been a kind of "speedup" of hospital labors. Looking at *Williams* in its different editions, we see that the reported length of labor dropped from an average first stage of labor in first births of 12.5 hours in 1948, down to 10.5; and from 7.3 hours for second and subsequent births in 1948 down to only 5 hours by the 1980 edition.[74]

The speedup was even more dramatic for the second stage, which dropped from an average of eighty minutes for first births in 1948 to only fifty minutes for first births, and from thirty minutes in 1948 down to twenty minutes for subsequent births. Third stage is barely measurable in time, with some obstetricians practicing "routine manual removal of any placenta that has not separated spontaneously by the time they have completed delivery of the infant and care of the cord in women with conduction analgesia."[75] In 1980 *Williams* said that if the placenta has not separated within three to five minutes of the birth of the baby, manual removal of the placenta should probably be carried out,[76] and in 2001 that "manual removal of the placenta is rightfully practiced much sooner and more often than in the past."[77] And that is what my obstetrician did in my home birth—reach in and get it out fast. At home, babies are usually put to the breast, or brought up to the breast by the mother, and the suckling stimulates contractions that expel the placenta.

The rush is largely institutional: births in hospitals need to be meshed together to form an overarching institutional tempo. Predictability is important; timing matters, as staff moves from birth to birth, as women are moved from place to place. There have been many studies of the variations in interventions by time of day, time of week, even by football schedules; interventions increase when doctors are rushed, whatever the reason. Many people thought that the increased numbers of women in obstetrics would bring the c-section rates down, but no, women are yet more rushed, overburdened by their own double shifts as doctors and as mothers, and their c-section rates are even higher. One good, careful, recent study done of more than thirty-seven thousand live births in Philadelphia hospitals shows that women who give birth during the day are much more likely to have obstetric interventions than those who give birth during the "off-peak" hours of 2:00 a.m. to 8:00 a.m. Looking only at low-risk women admitted in active, non-induced labor, and excluding labors involving fetal distress or "prolonged, obstructed or abnormal labors," the researchers found that women who gave birth during peak hospital hours were 43 percent more likely to have forceps or vacuum extraction and 86 percent more likely to have drug-induced labors. They were also 10 percent more likely to have an episiotomy.[78] The institutional tempo slows down at night, and staff allow birth to take a bit longer.

But rather than feel used by this institutional management, women feel protected by it. As early as the 1950s, when Friedman was developing his curve, "*convenient* had become a national buzzword. Preplanned, highly convenient, hospitalized birth was just one of many innovations now embraced by the nation. TV dinners, remote-control television and pop-top cans were also part of the 'convenient' lineup."[79] What was true of suburban 1950s mothers with housefuls of babies and small children and commuting husbands was no less true for the overscheduled super-moms of the post-feminist era juggling demanding jobs and their one or two carefully delayed children: "the mere notion of convenience became a lifeline."[80]

Nothing in "convenience," in birth as in food, is there to increase safety. Speed and predictability are industrial values, and they moved into the kitchen and the birthroom in the interests of the systems of production, not the people being worked on. Fast food turns over product—and so money—at a good clip, and that's what makes it profitable. Hospitals move women through quickly, taking up the most expensive personnel and spaces for the least amount of time. People will stand on line for fast food, waiting their turn to get their meal quickly bundled up and turned over. The waiting time is not a problem for the producers if it is not long enough to discourage waiting, and somehow, people in fast-food places seem willing to wait on line, cars backed up in drive-through lanes, people standing behind each other in the stores, then spend more time wandering around trying to find a seat with their tray. There is the feeling of speed and efficiency, but the actual speed and efficiency are much more for the producers than the consumers. And so it is with birth—the management techniques develop in the institutions and for the institutions' benefit. As with fast food and convenience food of all kinds, some coincide with consumer interest, some not so much.

The accomplishments of modern medicine have been to compensate for the added risks of eliminating pain and shortening labor. It's a complicated balancing act. Epidurals lengthen labor. So oxytocins were used to stimulate it. But oxytocins cause very painful, strong, erratic contractions, making the epidural all the more important. Those intense contractions can cause fetal distress. A new tool, the electronic fetal monitor (developed sensibly enough out of the space industry to monitor an unreachable patient), was used to keep track of the fetus. That machine in its first incarnations required the woman to be tethered to the bed flat on her back, and so also increased pain and slowed down contractions. But the machine would tell the doctor when the fetus was distressed, heart rate changes showing up on a little paper strip. The big change was a dramatic increase in cesarean sections for fetal distress. Cesarean rates rose quickly, from something like 7 percent to over 20 percent when it first became a public issue, and to now well over 30 percent, over 50 percent in some hospitals. Recovery time—post-operative stays—are profitable, but for the women and families, time-consuming.

Electronic fetal monitoring wasn't introduced after it was shown to help infant outcome; it was introduced and brought into widespread use with virtually no research. The concept of evidence-based medicine didn't come into play in obstetrics until very recently. Tools and practices were introduced, sold—monitors aren't cheap, they need to be built and purchased—and adopted into widespread use without any research base. The cost of the tools is, as is often the case with our new electronic tools, offset by labor savings: no one has to be paid to sit with the laboring woman now. Monitors can relay the fetal information to a central station, where workers can keep track and watch for fetal distress. Research soon showed that the monitoring increased cesarean section rates without improving infant outcome, but by then it was too late: "The image of the steadfast electronic monitor guarding the perpetually imperiled fetus contributed to the view that natural childbirth was at best a naïve and at worst a reckless approach to birth."[81]

And how much difference is there between a vaginal birth and a cesarean? Once the mother is one more bystander watching the baby lifted out of her, an observer rather than the central actor, it is harder to see the difference. Is that crazy or what? I can't tell you the difference between giving birth and having major abdominal surgery? But that's what epidurals do to birth: they turn the woman into another person in the room watching what the doctor is doing. Women are encouraged to think of the epidural as giving them control over their body in labor, but just remember that with an epidural, you have to put in a catheter and a urine collection bag; control over the sensation of pain removes all other body control. And once you have all the risks of the epidural, the oxytocin, the increased fetal distress, the high rates of cesarean section—why not just skip the whole messy business, and just schedule the cesarean section in the first place? And so we have. In the Israeli surrogacy industry, state-supported and doctor-managed, the woman-as-laborer and the woman-as-birther are split into two. Both mostly want the job over with as quickly as possible, the surrogate to be done with the project; the purchaser to have the baby in her arms. Births induced at thirty-eight weeks are common.[82] And here too, in the United States, and throughout the Westernized, medicalized world of birth, labors are increasingly induced or simply bypassed in favor of planned, scheduled cesarean sections. The language of choice was brilliantly co-opted by medicine: women want cesareans, we are told, and so they should have them. The only women who actually did seem to choose cesareans were women obstetricians. It's become something of a self-fulfilling prophecy: when doctors first announced that they were doing cesareans because of maternal request, actual cases of women asking or demanding cesarean sections were few and far between. Not so now, when we actually are starting to see women ask, reasonably enough, if there's at least a one-third chance that I'm going to end up with a cesarean, why not just schedule it now and get this under control?

Industrial birth is no more about safety than is industrial bread. It's about getting out of that three-thousand-year-old bubble.

Decision Rules: Industrial Rubrics and Clinical Outcomes

When life is understood as a series of risks to be controlled, decision rules are in order. You cannot stop and fully research each and every risk, navigate afresh each moment of risk. The first decision rule I learned, as a child, was my mother's rule for cleaning the refrigerator: "When in doubt, throw it out." The risk of eating food that had gone bad was the risk to be avoided. We were poor; there was enough food insecurity that end-of-month, when the check ran out, meant special treats like noodles for dinner. But we were not so poor that the risk of not-enough-food outweighed the risk of spoiled food. This is the kind of risk balancing people do as they choose to err on the safe side. They look over their leaky boats at both sides, and see which way they are more likely to tip over. Is the illegal drug use in pregnancy the real risk? Or the state's knowledge of that use? Is it wasting food you can't afford to lose, or feeding your kids spoiled food? Is it going a week or ten days past your due date, or is it the medical induction? Is it eating highly processed food with all the extra vitamins added, or eating a few unprocessed things and not getting all the nutrients? Is it a prolonged labor or a surgical intervention to end the labor?

It is not just a matter of real risk versus perceived risk, as risk theorists (too) often describe it. This is rather an intelligent balancing of risks, weighing of risks, contextualizing of risks. People cannot eliminate risk, but they can find ways to intelligently, creatively, determinedly balance risks and come to decision rules.[83]

The risks of pregnancy drag on for months. Women are encouraged to begin risk management long before starting a pregnancy, and it continues over the full duration. Surveillance is inevitably intermittent. Women go for checkups, are observed in public and judged, disciplined, for their risk management successes and failures. It goes on all through the pregnancy. But birth takes place over a relatively short period of time, time measured in hours or at most days, not in the months and even years of pregnancy and preconception health.

Hospitals are generally understood to be at the ready to provide emergency intervention if something goes wrong, but for women who choose to birth outside those hospitals, the risks of hospitalization itself are brought front and center. In one British study, researchers found that it is not the iatrogenic concerns that the women spoke about, the risks of what is often called the "cascade of interventions" that follows medical management (leading as it so often does to surgical removal of the baby, in what is quaintly called a "Cesarean section"). The risks they addressed were risks of the hospital itself, what are called, when looking at infections, "nosocomial" risks, errors that are made when people are managed in what is essentially a factory-like setting: the risks of over-crowding; the risks of exposure to others and exposure of self.[84]

Hospital-industrialized births demand standardized care. Consider something as mundane and yet intrusive as the vaginal exam. Medical guidelines, the medical story, is that such exams are necessary to determine labor and its stages. That of course is absurd. Do you really think that an experienced midwife, someone who has attended hundreds or thousands of births, cannot tell whether a labor is established without a vaginal exam? What a midwife needs that exam for is to *document*, not to establish the labor. Those exams are not only intimate and intrusive, but for women with histories of sexual abuse especially—and that is a lot of women—they can be experienced as traumatic. For all women, raised with ideas of bodily privacy, integrity, and what used to be called modesty, such exams at a moment of vulnerable transition are problematic. Done for reasons of institutional management and control, they are one more interruption and create risks of their own. Particularly in hospital settings, vaginal exams are one more occasion for the introduction of nosocomial infection.

Managing the management thus becomes necessary in hospital settings; midwives use the vaginal exam to create the story that will be most in the woman's best interests, and occasionally in the midwives' own best interest. Midwives are thoughtful about when they measure because, for example, they are hesitant to start the clock too early. It's the same thing I found in my research on midwives decades ago: if they examined a woman and documented that she was fully dilated, she'd only have a very short period of time to push the baby out before the doctors would declare a prolonged second stage and require intervention.

If you were given forty-five minutes to repair a leaky pipe under a sink, that's it, just forty-five minutes in which to get the job done, when would you start the clock? After the tools were laid out, the junk cleared from under the sink, perhaps? And if you were being paid by the hour to repair that pipe, then when might you start the clock? Perhaps when you walked in the door? People manage timing and clocks in their own interests all of the time. Midwives are thoughtful about when they measure because they are hesitant to start the clock too early. What they are preventing, what these midwives are trying to minimize, is not the risks of a prolonged labor, but the risks of intervening in a labor medically defined as prolonged.

In hospital settings, midwives do not have the authority to use their knowledge fully in the woman's best interests. And therein lie the risks.

It is not that midwives have no clocks of their own, no ideas about time other than those medicine has established. Not letting the sun set twice on a laboring woman is a long-held understanding in many midwifery settings. It is not that midwives do not have decision rules that reflect their understandings of danger and their knowledge about ways to avoid danger. That is precisely what midwifery has been throughout time and across place: the development of a body of knowledge and skilled craftsmanship to navigate the dangers of childbirth. All of that knowledge was discounted with medicalization.

People sometimes make fun of the use of the word "natural" in the birth movement, finding it ironic that women think of birth as natural, and yet study so hard, make plans, prepare for it. Yet is there anything that is natural for which people do not prepare? Changes in the season? Hunger? Defecation? Sex? Sleep? Have you ever shopped for just the right pillow? Ever tried to move your bowels at home before you went out for the day? Ever eat food that was *not* prepared? We learn, manage, and prepare that which is natural all the time. Women are preparing themselves and using expert assistance sometimes precisely to avoid medical interventions, which themselves have become the perceived danger.

What medical dominance has done is not only take over from midwifery and women's own embodied knowledge of birth, but also deny that such knowledge ever existed or could exist. What a woman knows from knowing her body, recognizing her own pregnancy without need of a pregnancy test, feeling things are good or maybe not-good with the fetus within from changes in its movements—all that is discounted. A woman who has poked and been poked back by her baby, turned from side to side trying to negotiate a sleep position, been driven nuts by fetal hiccups—that woman is "introduced" to her baby by the delivering doctor. Her knowledge, her experience—it is as if it never existed.

Scientific or medical knowledge is real and authoritative; other knowledge is reduced to "intuition" or "spiritual knowing," made all but laughable. But when a baker adds a bit more flour because the dough is sticky, is that intuition? Or is that knowledge based on craft, skill, deep knowledge of the hands? When a violin maker rejects a piece of wood in favor of one lying next to it that looks just the same to me or to you, is that intuition? Or experience, skill, and craft? And when a leading neurosurgeon examines a dozen stroke patients who all present pretty much the same way on all of their tests and feels hopeful about some and concerned for others, is that intuition? Or knowledge based on experience, using a range of senses and information that may not be captured in the tests?

Obstetrics was late, all but laughably late, in entering the world of evidence-based care, of using science to back up practices. They did things like rupturing membranes, cutting episiotomies, manually extracting placentas—all kinds of dangerous and foolish interventions—without any scientific evidence to back it up. So I am not about to complain about their new focus on evidence-based care. Clearly it is better that practice be based on evidence than not. But evidence is population-based, it's part of an industrial actuarial model. Birth is also individual—highly, extraordinarily individual. What one woman with her body, her history, her life, and her baby feels and experiences isn't simply interchangeable with another. Clinical care needs to be artisanal, handcrafted, highly responsive to minute, hard-to-quantify differences. If you are going to set up industrial practices, you cannot possibly account for that. In any given hospital, you will need guidelines for things like how long second stage can last or when to do an episiotomy. And guidelines, suggestions based on evidence, quickly morph into protocols, actions required of clinicians. If a clinician does not follow a protocol and particularly if there is any kind of bad outcome, she has put herself at great risk, particularly in the American context, in which a liability case is one of the few ways that extra needs can be met. Clinicians are rightly frightened to use their clinical judgment. But does that give any particular woman the best possible care in her particular birth?

Can something as fluid, as varied, as complex as birth be subject to a simple set of decision rules, a rubric for management based on actuarial tables, without something precious being lost?

10

Great Expectations

A Childbirth Movement for Now

Splashing in New Waters

Different moments call for different kinds of social movements, different languages, different framings. If the chloroform of the mid- to late
nineteenth century was about weak women demanding help, and the
twilight sleep of the 1890s through 1930s about "Gibson girls" scooting
through their births unscathed (as Wolf shows us), and the natural-
childbirth and home-birth movement about strong empowered women
controlling our bodies, ourselves, where are we now? Now that we have
moved beyond second-wave feminism?

For the next couple of pages I am going to address myself primarily to
older birth activists—to people like me who are and have been part of a
birth movement for a long time. If you are new to this, what I am saying
now might not mean much, though when I presented this at a couple
of birth-related conferences over the last few years, younger midwives
came up and hugged and thanked me for finally getting it across.

Our Bodies, Ourselves, the bible of the women's self-help movement,
on the one hand, and *Spiritual Midwifery* and the very different kind
of feminism that book represented, on the other—these were crucial
moments in my generation's development. Those two books could not,
of course, have represented more different worlds and politics. It was
in that swirl of eddying waters, in which feminism, in all its complex-
ity, was but one stream, along with the civil rights movement, self-help
groups of many kinds, and a movement rejecting urbanism and calling
for a return to the land, that midwifery bobbed to the surface.

Women entering midwifery today, and women using midwives today,
are the daughters and granddaughters of my generation. The copies
of *Our Bodies, Ourselves* or of *Spiritual Midwifery* that they read most
likely belonged to their mothers, and just as likely, to their grandmoth-

ers. For those of you who are older: Try to remember how cutting-edge, forward-thinking (hip? together? with it?) your mother's, let alone your grandmother's sex and health books were to you. That's what our books look like to our granddaughters. That T-shirt from right around the start of the new midwifery movement that shows two midwives striding forth, the one dressed in colonial costume, the other in bell-bottoms with a wristwatch—I'm not sure which of them would look more dated if she walked by me today.

It only takes one generation for something new to become something ordinary. The *Chronicle of Higher Education* runs a lovely column each September, orienting the faculty to the freshmen coming in. College freshmen are eighteen years old; the world they grew up in is not the one I live in. For last year's class, for example, there has never been a country called Czechoslovakia, DNA fingerprinting has always existed, a small-size soda at McDonald's was always sixteen ounces, the post office has always been losing business, there have always been Whole Foods stores across the United States, and the starship *Enterprise* has always looked dated. And if you want to know any more about any of those things, you could always look it up on Wikipedia.

Once-astonishing changes quickly become facts of life. And so it has been with the astonishing changes in the facts of life themselves, and more mundane facts of living. For young women giving birth today, there have always been ultrasound photo sessions. Women have always made up at least a quarter of the obstetricians. Men have always been welcome at hospital births. There have always been celebrities having home births (well, at least in California). Women could always learn whether the fetus had Down syndrome and choose to abort. Everybody has always known months ahead of time whether the baby is a boy or a girl. Women always know the Apgar scores of their babies. Untrimmed pubic hair has always looked gross.

The young women coming up today, the women facing their choices about locations and attendants at birth, as well as those who are themselves becoming midwives, are facing a very different world from the one my generation did. It is a world no less complex, with politics no less challenging, but still it is very different.

Somehow in feminism we went from the urban myth of bra-burning to Madonna's corsets in one generation, and then the meat dress of Lady

Gaga in the next generation; from refusing to shave our legs to waxing our labia; and—we rightly worry—from underground midwifery to elective cesareans. Some of us fought for a legal right to suckle our babies in public places, and some still do. But a battle can drag on forever, even while new battles supersede it. We now read about the oppressive nature of "forcing" breastfeeding on women. As part of a strange North American kind of backlash, we've heard about the oppression of natural birth as an "unattainable ideal," making women feel bad about themselves, and of "breast is best" as classist, racist rhetoric.

We used to have to battle ignorance—women did not know their bodies, know what would happen to them in labor, know how they would be treated and "managed" in birth. Five hundred weeks, a *decade*, of *What to Expect*[1] on the best-seller list has surely taken care of that. Self-help moved from living rooms to chat rooms, to sponsored forums of all kinds. Now we battle "information" as much as ignorance. We have access to all the information we could use—my *phone* has more information than any 1950s family doctor ever had. The information is, as we well know, of a certain type, coming from particular sources. Concerns and issues of the early women's health movement have morphed into a host of sales campaigns by the biomedical-industrial complex. It is most assuredly not only about birth and procreative care. My generation's concern with environmental causes of breast cancer turned in less than two generations into a flurry of pink ribbons, the "kitsching" of breast cancer, and the overselling of mammography. To just step outside midwifery, and see the way that these generational changes have occurred in women's health, read Gayle Sulik's *Pink Ribbon Blues*.[2] From having to encourage women to be willing to touch and explore their own breasts in order to find cancers before they were breaking through the skin, we moved in these two generations to women in their twenties lining up for regular breast exams.

We used to think of medicalization as a process in which medical doctors claimed expertise over given areas of life. But it's no longer externalized, with the power to medicalize located in medical authorities—it's moved inwards now. We do it to ourselves. It was the different knowledge midwives and doctors had, and the very different power that they had to act on that knowledge, that interested me back in the early 1970s when I began my work in the birth movement. It is, to use a phrase

Robbie Davis Floyd used, "authoritative knowledge"[3] that midwifery is contesting, not just authorities. Doctors no longer serve as gatekeepers to medical knowledge, pontifications, or research. When information was gathered in small groups of women teaching each other, when patients met outside medical settings to help each other in a nascent self-help movement, seeking information was a form of resistance to medical authority. No longer. It is now a form of compliance. Many of the "self-help" online forums are run by the medical and pharmaceutical industries themselves. Whether it is direct-to-consumer advertising or the less direct marketing done online in patient groups, doctors—for good or for ill, and I could argue either—are no longer barriers between the medical industry and the consumer/patient.

The knowledge, the information, the "facts," have moved into our own ways of thinking, and we have become our own medical authorities, living and experiencing our bodies in medical terms. Women now keep track of their own pregnancies by weeks and test results. It's not just pregnancy, of course. Many people can tell you their cholesterol levels right off the top of their heads, know their heart rate, blood pressure, a string of numbers evaluating and mediating "health." Psychological status is medically evaluated and maintained: Sad? Or clinically depressed? Shy? Or suffering from social anxiety disorder? Scattered or ADD? Ask your doctor. Increasingly, people understand their own lived experiences in the language of biomedicine. In this world of medical management, in which every significant human experience, characteristic, emotion, strength, and failing is traced to its genetic and/or neurological "cause," how can we think about midwifery and birth?

And of course in many ways we are post-feminism in birth, which is not really handled differently from any other medical/surgical event. It is medicalization that I am concerned about, not the gender of the players. Birth no longer looks like a gendered battleground: women obstetricians are among the loudest objectors to home-birth midwifery. It's about an industry, not about the sex of the actors. As I have always said, "Scratch a doctor and you find a doctor." And now that the doctor has moved inside us, been so thoroughly internalized, most people don't know how else to begin to think about birth.

Our daughters and granddaughters are having their babies in this very different world. Young women do *not* want their elders, 1970s-style feminists, babbling—murmuring to them in labor, claiming loudly in congressional hearings—about the power of women's bodies to give birth. Not to a generation whose bodies have been medically micromanaged from infancy, not to women who have their *own* fetal ultrasound photographs in albums. These are women who, in many cases, know well their own power. They found their birth providers, they chose them, they *hired* them. Yes, there are enormous class and race/ethnic differences, but information is no longer a scarce resource, and the "powerlessness" of women is no longer the lived experience of middle-class white women. While women of my generation had to learn how powerful we truly were in the face of our feelings of powerlessness, young women today are more often far less powerful than they feel.

How do we make a childbirth movement for these women?

Making Change: What Can Fly?

First we have to convince them that there *is* a problem, that medicalized, industrialized birth management is not working in their interests, is not providing them with the best care. It is an uphill battle, a fight against a hegemonic state religion, a value system so deeply entrenched that it sounds heretical to question it. It's that cows flying at night kind of problem: argue against modern medicine and you sound crazy, lunatic-fringe crazy. The world, people seem convinced, needs more of it, not less. We think our medical system has to be expanded, made available to every last woman on the planet. Obstetrics acknowledges that all it developed all these years wasn't actually based on evidence, and that seems to pass without much of a ripple, though now it does refer to the databases to defend practice. We birthies have provided study after study, and we are called "ideological." Home birth became a kind of "moral panic" issue, something dangerous fools do who care more about their "experience" than their babies. DeLee, that famous obstetrician, said birth for babies was banging your head against a barn door, and over the years, I've come to think he had a point: birth *is* like banging your head against a wall for us birthies. We fight, we argue, we provide data, we reason, we stick to the facts—and we're dismissed as nuts, and dangerous nuts for risking our innocent babies.

Let me make this as clear as I can: Obstetrics has not provided the best of care for women or for babies. The data are there, the data are clear. But this is not about data or facts, it is about a deep ideological commitment, a belief in science, and obstetrics stole the mantle of science without doing the hard work of research. If one stops thinking about obstetric knowledge as a scientific product, and realize that it is at least as much an industrial product, the product of industrialized hospital management, the specific risks and dangers of obstetric care become apparent.

But how to see obstetrics for what it is? How to open up a sensible space for valuing the handcrafted, individualized midwifery care? Let me take a deep breath, and do what I have been arguing for in this book—learn from the food movement.

Let's start with the obvious: follow the money. If social movements are all about splashing around the edges, we have to think about which edges are available to us, where the water can be reached. Confronting profit making head-on is not going to be particularly successful in our current world. Consider these two women whom Fred Kaufman found in his work on the end of food:

Pamela Ronald is working on rice. "Rice is one of the most inexpensive, healthy, and delicious ways to feed everyone on Earth. It nourishes more people than any other food."[4] Rice is at risk from a bacteria, Xanthomonas. There have been epidemic infections over a long time; Japanese scientists were working on it in 1902. In the 1970s it assaulted rice in Africa, the Americas, and Australia. Ronald began working on genetic modification. In 1995 "Ronald had inoculated rice. Her chemistry had insured the world's supply of inexpensive healthy and delicious food."[5] For a while it looked like this would fly; the University of California–Davis and Ronald patented the gene for immunity, and Monsanto and Pioneer began to negotiate. "

But as the UC-Davis Office of Technology Transfer haggled over the terms for returning the inoculated rice genes to the International Rice Research Institute, Monsanto and Pioneer lost interest in the deal, and the commercial development of the technology stalled. Disease resistance, it turned out, did not have the same appeal for multinational food producers as it did for Ronald and UC-Davis, perhaps because Monsanto and Pioneer were already enjoying windfall profits from more lucrative agritech innovations, such as their Roundup Ready crops. . . .

Pamela Ronald may want to save the world, but her killer app has never left the greenhouse. Even though the Xanthomonas bacteria remains a threat to Asian rice supplies, Xanthomonas-resistant rice is not grown anywhere on Earth aside from the sterilized pots of locked laboratories. . . . If molecular food can't earn rent, the molecules wither on the vine.[6]

Esther van der Knaap, on the other hand, Kaufman tells us, is

a plant geneticist who has toiled for years on a problem that would never have occurred to me: the isolation and analysis of the genes that program the shape of a tomato. Her goal is neither to save tomato farmers from tomato viruses nor to create a better-tasting or a more nutritious tomato. Instead she wants to engineer a square tomato—the kind of tomato that Heinz or Unilever might prefer to the round variety, particular when it comes to packing as many as possible into square cardboard boxes. Along the way van der Knaap is also trying to unlock the secret of a long, cucumber-like tomato shape, the kind of tomato Burger King, McDonald's or Wendy's might desire so they could get more perfectly round, hamburger bun-size slices out of each individual fruit.[7]

She's probably not going to have a problem selling that one.

I've never actually seen a square tomato. Or a perfect baby. But I know, as I guess we all do by now, that they're coming. That tomato is being perfected for whom? And the baby? There are larger questions there, questions about new reproductive technologies, advanced gamete, embryo, and fetal testing, about the host of technologies that are being developed to bring us better babies. I've thought about and worked on those issues before, but for now, let's just focus on helping people give birth and getting them fed.

As people in the food world have found, improving diet and ideas about diet and food in the rich part of the world will not translate directly into better food in the poor parts of the world. That's what sent

Frances Moore Lappé away from the food world to more directly work on world poverty.

Midwives around the world are being pushed out much the same way that indigenous farmers are, their work, their tools, and their products disvalued, as corporate, Westernized methods push in. The skills and relationships that local midwives have are not recognized; they are asked only to use those relationships to bring the women into hospitals and medical care. Rather than making a few truly useful tools available to indigenous workers—whether bacteria-resistant seeds for farmers or antibiotic injections for midwives—the workers themselves are tossed aside.

If our science and our industry, if the corporate decision makers, aren't saving humanity from hunger, aren't improving maternal and infant outcome, then what are they doing? As with everything, this has to be answered at both levels, the individual and the political. At the individual level, of course there are people who really care, are really trying—in both birth and food spheres. I don't think that the people who work in the laboratories on agriculture and on food production are evil, focused on profit above all else, any more than I believe that the doctors who set the standards for birth care are evil, or out for personal gain. But somehow we have created a system in which things don't get moving out of goodness; they get moving out of profit. We don't have mechanisms to move our incentives, our deepest and truest needs and desires, to fruition.

The food movement is pushing healthy food as a cost-saving measure; eating healthier will cut down the economic burden of obesity, high blood pressure, heart disease—the many and varied consequences of eating all that cheap food. The food movement is asking us to step back from the immediate costs, and take a larger view. Of course fast food, junk food, mass-produced agriculture, and industrialized meat are cheaper than their organic, artisanal counterparts. But if instead of adding up the costs of the two alternative dinners in front of you, you add in the costs of their long-term outcomes for populations, the numbers look different. The food movement is making connections to the world of public health, asking us to think about sugar the way we thought about tobacco. It is an argument that has some traction. Certainly the sugar industry is fighting back much the way the tobacco industry did.

Because midwives are so very much less well-paid than are physicians, and because home births don't ring up hospital bills, it's been tempting to talk about home birth and midwifery as cost-saving measures. That, I imagine, more than carefully examining the data or caring deeply about birth, is what made the United Kingdom just put home birth back on the agenda as something to be encouraged. But the argument doesn't always work so well in the US privatized capitalism model, where cost saving is the opposite of revenue generating. Medical services, what is called "health care," is one of our largest industries in the United States; cutting spending is a very different thing when private corporations are making money.

On the other hand, home birth is also critiqued as being expensive. Hospital-based midwifery services, it is argued, can save even more money, combining the cost savings of the institutional management with the cost savings of the lower-paid worker. In poor areas, for poor women, hospital-based midwifery care is the choice on offer, and that itself makes midwifery care look second-rate to many of its recipients. But just as real food—actual vegetables, fruits, unprocessed grains, animals and animal products like eggs and milk—rather than a McDonald's Happy Meal or a microwavable taco ought to be the standard against which we understand nutrition, so too a midwifery-attended, personalized birth needs to be the standard against which we understand birth. Home birth is not some frivolous perk of the elite, some artisanal treat for the wealthy, but the solid foundation of birth care, the standard against which in-hospital services can be judged. Yes, it may well cost more to provide home births, and economies of scale might call for a more industrialized version of birth care. But that does not make it right, any more than outsourcing school lunches to fast-food outlets would be. It might well be cheaper to move all women to more centralized locations, plug all of them into centralized fetal monitoring systems, and eliminate all of the one-on-one personalized care of midwifery. Even with the inevitable rise in the cesarean section rate that such "care" brings us, even with increased maternal morbidity, even with modest rises in neonatal morbidity, it might well be cheaper, at least in the short run. That does not make it acceptable as a standard of care.

Midwives who are doing home births learn, and are continually reinforced in the knowledge, that birth is all the things we like to say it is—healthy, beautiful, a meaningful human moment, natural, an activity that women engage in, not a procedure done to them. Remove home birth from the experience of midwives and we end up with a situation like what we see in vast parts of the United States, where certified nurse-midwives with no home-birth experience at all reproduce cesarean section rates and other intervention rates at roughly the same level as physicians. We lose, in short, what makes midwifery the profession of midwifery, and turn it into a physician-extender, nursing-services occupation.[8]

There is a body of knowledge that is developed in home birth that can't be developed in institutional care. Women birth differently in strange places, with strange people coming and going, than they do in their own homes. We know this only because we have had practitioners move from one setting to the other, and learn it.

Even if we try to keep this to a conversation about costs, the answers are not clear. Certainly using midwives for individualized care, meeting the needs of the woman, traveling to her home and getting to know her, costs more than bringing her into a hospital, hooking her up to some monitors and dropping in at the end to catch a baby. But what brings a woman to the end of a healthy pregnancy, through to the end of a labor, opening up and birthing a healthy baby? Sometimes that is midwifery care. Midwifery care works to prevent prematurity; surely the most expensive single-ticket item in maternity care is the care of babies born too soon. Much of prematurity is preventable, as models of intensive midwifery care have shown.[9] Midwifery care brings women through labor without the kinds of interventions that lead to increased cesarean rates, which themselves bring up the cost of birth care. Midwifery care increases the breastfeeding rates, which, it can be argued, further decreases morbidity and thus costs.

It is far from obvious that home birth is a simple economic drain on obstetrical care services. But even if it were, it still doesn't make it right to move all births to institutional settings. Home birth is not and should not be a "frosting" kind of service, available to the wealthy, but needs to be widely available. Some of our most vulnerable women, and their babies, are the ones who most benefit from personalized, intensive midwifery care. Where the risks of prematurity, of infant abandonment, of psychiatric and drug-related problems are the greatest, midwifery can be the most important. Culturally appropriate, personalized, sensitive midwifery care can work for women the system routinely fails. And that may well save money. Even if the money is all you care about.

Going Where the Women Are: Working in and out of the System

The work of the midwife, like so much work in the contemporary world, is being fragmented, broken into its component parts and then sold off to other workers in the interests of efficiency. Efficiency is really another word for cost savings. In many fields of work, efficiency is just about profit, and maybe that is true in birth work as well. Whatever the goal, the fact remains that in many places, birth work is being subdivided. Midwifery work doesn't lend itself to globalization, though presumably fetal monitors could be read from anywhere in the world. You can see this fragmentation in the introduction of a host of pregnancy-intervention specialists, from dieticians to smoking cessation coaches to social workers, through to the introduction of doula care for labor itself and on into the postpartum with yet other care workers, like lactation consultants and postpartum visiting nurses and social workers. There is a complicated web of workers now that surrounds, and sometimes entraps, the birthing woman.

The gender politics used to be quite clear on this: men were the doctors, and women were the lower-level workers. It's not like that now; women have moved into obstetrics. Through the 1970s women were about 7 percent of the obstetricians; now three-fourths of OB residents are women, and women are well on their way to dominating the field. As usual, across all kinds of fields, men linger at the top, holding on to the glass ceiling, but with time, that too seems to be shifting. Women *are* the doctors. Some thought that women moving into obstetrics would magically change it. Others, myself included, thought that socialization into medicine would make women doctors indistinguishable from men, and we were right. Women obstetricians are, first and foremost, obstetricians.

The gender split dissolved, and the most dramatic and pervasive split in maternity care in the United States is between the obstetricians and the different types of midwives themselves: the certified nurse-midwives, who are recognized by both medicine and the state; and all the other kinds of midwives, women (and a very few men) who came to midwifery by any path other than nursing. The United States is unusual in that obstetrics pretty much took over birth care, not only from midwives but also from other physicians. General practitioners pretty much ceased to exist in the United States; few "family doctors" do births. Out of hospital, a mix of nurse-midwives and direct-entry midwives are providing the home births. In hospitals, obstetricians control maternity care, with—in some but not all hospitals—nurse-midwives working under their guidelines.

Try to think of analogous situations in which different occupational groups compete to perform a service around the same event, in the same setting, yet base their praxis in such radically opposed foundational ideologies. There are some instances: the juvenile court system, for example, or drug courts, began with radically different ideologies, housed within the larger legal system. In side-by-side courtrooms, you can find judges working with a strictly punitive legal model, judges working with a developmental psychology model, and judges working with a medical model. Over time, some have argued, these too become subsumed under the larger, more punitive legal system, and juvenile detention comes to look remarkably prison-like; drug court is progress, but certainly compromised.[10] In the food world, think about the relationships between cooks and nutritionists in institutional settings. Who has the power to decide what constitutes a decent meal in a hospital or a school? Who has to work under whose guidelines and rubrics?

Is this what happens to nurse-midwives? They're slotted into the system. Whatever underlying ideology, values, beliefs they bring, they are functioning—like the juvenile court judge to the regular judges—in a parallel position to the obstetricians, in a larger system. But they are not, of course, really parallel. Obstetricians retain the ultimate power, and the midwives, however professional, certified, trained, and approved, practice under the authority of the medical professionals.

This of course is one of the strongest criticisms that the direct-entry midwives offer of the certified nurse-midwives' practice: CNMs are not, never will be, cannot ever be, truly independent practitioners. They are not autonomous, but must defer to the obstetricians. OBs set the conditions of practice, from simple design of the setting to specific protocols. Nurses and CNMs may well participate in protocol committees, but no one ever has cause to question where ultimate authority rests.

The CNMs are cognizant of this; they are not blind to the controls under which they must work. They know they are caught up in a hierarchical system, and most assuredly not at the top. But at least they are *there*, as they often point out, to us, to each other, to themselves; they are "where the women are." And they can be doing amazing, awe-inspiring work.[11]

Most women, the overwhelming majority of women, are in that system, birthing in those hospitals. Many CNMs see the direct-entry, home-birth midwives as offering a kind of luxury service, the artisanal bakers of the world. It's the midwives, even more than the home-birthers, whom they see as self-indulgent, enjoying their work, free to love birth and women—but not being down in the trenches where the hard work needs to be done.

Direct-entry midwives may well think of themselves as the very paragon of the midwife, pure representations of what midwifery should be. They can be woman-centered, they can love women, offer all the nurturance in the world. But to whom? To a few select women, women concerned enough, educated enough, determined enough to seek them out. If they are not there doing that, midwifery is really gone in America; but doing it for a few women—is that enough? Round and round we go. Is it better to supply a real midwifery practice, to do birth as birth ought to be done, or is it better to reach out to as many women as possible? *Whatever* the midwives do, whichever side of the argument one falls on, it's not a satisfying situation. We cannot, in America, as we have things now, supply real midwifery care to all women. Is the better response to keep real midwifery alive, keep that flame burning, or is it to make whatever compromises need to be made to spread bits of midwifery-like care to as many women as possible? Bad choices all around, bad situations. And bad situations create bad politics. It's impressive, a statement of the dedication that all of these types of midwives feel, that they can rise above internecine bickering, get past the inevitable sniping, to express a strong sense of commonality. They do, all of them, want midwifery care for all women.

Given the common goal, of course each group has to worry about how the work of the other might interfere with achieving that end. Some certified nurse-midwives see the direct-entry midwives as unregulated wildcats, fear that their behavior, their occasional flaunting of the accepted rules of practice, will reflect poorly on all midwives. It's a kind of accusation we've all heard. In families, in ethnic groups, in race politics—people fear that the outliers will "bring us all down."

And the direct-entry midwives, for their part, also have reason to fear that the CNMs will be destructive of the larger goal. Co-option is scary. It's scary because it works. Move a few CNMs into the local hospital, let the local OB hire a couple of CNMs in her practice, and of course the direct-entry midwives lose clients, lose community support, become seen as the lunatic fringe. It is hardly surprising that the accusation the direct-entry midwives make of the CNMs, when they are at their angriest, most damning, is that the CNMs are selling out for money, prestige, job security. While a direct-entry midwife can take a perverse pride in her struggling, her comparative poverty, CNMs in hospital-based practices take home a regular salary, and that has to be noted. There are, undoubtedly, some CNMs who started as nurses and went the midwifery route the same way other nurses become nurse-anesthetists or go into surgical nursing. It's a career path upwards. Nobody goes into direct-entry midwifery for careerist reasons, and nobody would go into it for the money. They're paid peanuts, and sometimes literally. One Farm midwife told me, "I walked away from a birth one time with a bag of peanuts. That's what I was paid, and I was happy. And I mean it was a *bag* of peanuts—it was like a bushel."

There's a nobility to working for love not money, the anti-capitalist sensibility you'd expect on the Farm, the homegrown, tie-dyed aspect of it all. These are not just different occupational groups competing. These are different worldviews, different value systems. And the difference is not necessarily between the types of midwives but between the systems in which they operate. So while their attention may be drawn to each other, and their fears may be for the damage each can do the other, it is the medical-industrial system that creates the conditions under which these conflicts arise.

It's not at all unlike what artisanal food makers face. They start by being outside the system, cooking for the sheer joy and love of it, valuing the work as well as the product. And then Unilever buys out Ben & Jerry's, and are we better off having more people have access to a better product, or have we just sold out? You hold the line on some important issues. The wonderful factory that produces the brownies continues to

train unemployed people. Some standards on organic and hormone-free
last. But Unilever? Really?

Splashing Together

Too often social movements get divisive, wasting so much energy on
internal fighting that they never do seem to look up and face the shared
oppressor. It's common across social movements to find that when we
think we're splashing together, we are taken aback to see people and
movements we thought were right there with us drifting off, sometimes
angrily splitting away. Accusations of being our own worst enemies are
routinely hurled across social movement factions. It happened in the
Black civil rights movement, with a Black Power response to nonvio-
lence; in the feminist movement as the radical and socialist feminists
responded to the liberal framework of the National Organization for
Women; in the gay rights movement as those concerned with achieving a more conservative and traditional respectability are confronted
by the claims of a more radical identity movement. And so it is with
these movements: factions fight within both the world of food and the
world of birth. There are the tensions between the different groups of
birth workers: the obstetricians, the various kinds of midwives, doulas,
nurses, all those involved. But you also see these more ideological splits.

In the birth movement we can start with the point I raised earlier
about single-issue politics. Is this movement part of the larger feminist
movement, comfortably sitting side by side with abortion activism? Or
is it something else, a call for a traditional motherhood, ensconced in
a deeply gendered, often religious world?[12] Is it a truly universal feminist concern, addressing the needs of birthing women across every line
of race, class, and nationality? Or is it a middle-class white American
movement, not even seeing its own self-absorbed limitations?

I've been plagued by these questions all my years in the birth movement. It's why I can still remember, decades later, my sheer joy in seeing
the women in their varied costumes, Amish, flannel, and tie-dye, sitting at a Midwives Alliance of North America meeting figuring out how
to deal with a slow third stage. But it means even more to me when I
see the birth activists and our concerns recognized in feminist settings.
With the extraordinary attacks that have been ongoing against abor-

tion rights, it is not surprising that those issues, and to a somewhat less extent access to contraception, have come to seem more important than concerns about birth. But all are connected: if fetuses and even fertilized eggs are given a personhood that is more valued and more protected than that of the women who carry them, all pregnant women are at risk. This is the insight and work of the National Advocates for Pregnant Women (NAPW), headed by the extraordinary Lynn Paltrow. Paltrow and NAPW have worked for the rights of pregnant women to refuse particular medical interventions they did not want, from cesarean sections to life support; for the innocence of a woman accused of murdering a fetus after her own failed suicide attempt; for incarcerated women not to be shackled during their labors; for women seeking drug treatment not to lose custody of their babies.[13] Some years ago Paltrow and NAPW brought us all together—it felt like an episode of *This Is Your Life* as I saw people I knew from such very different worlds—to find our common ground. At a 2007 meeting in Atlanta, a "Summit to Ensure the Health and Humanity of Pregnant and Birthing Women," she brought into one room SisterSong (among the very first of the Black women's reproductive justice organizations), Planned Parenthood, Citizens for Midwifery, the Rebecca Project (protecting the life and liberties of people in Africa and America), Catholics for a Free Choice, and others. Over fifty organizations came together for the common purpose of advocating for the rights of pregnant and birthing women.

NAPW has been one of the organizations addressing concerns across what might seem a race divide, as the concerns of women of color, particularly African-descent women in the United States, are pitted against the rights of white women, especially white women of means. If birth becomes one more commodified shopping expedition, some women will indeed be able to buy good births, and others will be yet further removed from access to caring care. In the food movement, the term "food justice" is used to encompass and address the class and specifically racial barriers to good food. The phrase "reproductive justice" has similarly been used to focus on the racialized issues in America; NAPW has a working position paper entitled "Birth Justice as Reproductive Justice," showing the deep alignment of birth and other reproductive justice issues.[14] The many and varied social movements to improve the experience of women in pregnancy and in birth can and should be splashing together.

But we bring different histories. In America our history is always shaped by the legacy of slavery. This is the concern that Keisha Goode, in her work on African American midwives, has addressed: because of the historical disvaluing of midwifery, for Black women in America, midwifery care may still be seen as "going back," back to the years when poor Black women in the South had their midwives while wealthier or just whiter women were moved to the whites-only hospitals.[15] And so it is with the food movement too: Julie Guthman, writing about what she calls "the unbearable whiteness of Alternative food," points out that while the food activists may work hard to get urban farms and school projects that bring kids and families to grow their own food, "for African Americans, especially, putting your hands in the soil is more likely to evoke images of slave labor than a nostalgia."[16]

When you move tasks around between people who have historically been positioned in the strict hierarchy of race, class, and gender, some serious repositioning needs to be done. The same task just is not the same task when it changes hands across these social lines. Krishnendu Ray looks at how that repositioning is being done among chefs, and observes that cooking when done by people of color looks and feels like low-level, back-to-the-kitchen work, but when done by elite white men, is being made to look like elite work. "The discourse of haute cuisine and the practice of restaurant cookery overwhelmingly produce male, white international chefs, where 'international' is the opposite of domestic ethnic."[17] Ray draws analogies between the contemporary world of elite chefs and the first great transformation of American medicine, just when the midwives were being tossed aside, into a modern professional field.[18] Out go the people of color, out go the women, and in come the gentlemen. The gentlemen are not acting out of instincts and nature; they are learned and cultured. It brings us back to the point that Sherry Ortner made, on the distinction between culture and nature.[19]

And thus we risk having the movement splinter, reproductive rights losing sight of reproductive justice; feminist voices focusing on abortion and contraception and ignoring birth; midwives of color feeling isolated from the midwifery community and from their own sisters. To create a birth movement that gives women the best possible birth care, we need to recognize our histories, recognize each other, and we need to splash together.

Creating a New Current

This was a tale of two movements. I've been in one of those movements, been banging my head against the barn door of the birth world, for decades, and I thought I saw hope over there inside the barns, in the food world. And maybe now I'm feeling not so sure.

It is the best of times and it is the worst of times. People are dying of what food industrialization has brought us—on both sides of the divide. They are dying of starvation and dying of obesity, corporate-based famines and the overprocessed, oversold products of our aptly named supermarkets. And maternal mortality is a stubborn, unsolved problem from Afghanistan to Zimbabwe, displayed on charts brought to us by the World Bank, telling you something about how we can think about human suffering in today's world—via banking. These mortality rates are dropping in some places—notably not in the United States.

On the larger scale, on the really big issues, it's not looking good, folks.

But at home, on the smaller scale of "home," within our walls, and at home here in the United States, Canada, the United Kingdom, Australia, Europe—all the relatively well-off places in the world—there really is cause to hope. And that hope has potential. Money, rest assured, does not trickle down. Pour more money in at the top and it stays right there. That we must have learned by now. But a lot of other things *do* trickle down, and both of our movements are working on those things. Ideas about taste and style most assuredly do trickle right down. From the cerulean blue of a sweater, to a whole-grain bread, to a water birth, ideas about how we should live trickle directly down. I'm not talking about fashion or style just in the cheapest and silliest of ways, but in the more powerful ways, ideas about how life should be lived, how it can be lived when we are able to do things well.

Look at what the food movement has accomplished over time. White bread was fashionable, elite, the joy of whiteness everywhere, and within relatively short order the cheapest bread you could find was white bread. The tide turned, and lo and behold, in relatively short order it is offensive to offer white bread in poor schools, it starts to look suspicious to see those bags of white flour unloaded off of trucks for poor people. They deserve better! They deserve the whole grains of the elite. When it's all about blue shades of old sweaters, it probably is pointless. But if you think there are actual health consequences, if it really affects how people live in their bodies, how well their children grow—then a switch in fashion around food can have real consequences.

And in birth—run this little thought experiment in your head: If every woman who made over $200,000 a year in family income had a planned, elective cesarean section, how would a person making $75,000 feel about their lovely, natural, healthy birth? Cheated a bit? You can provide all the data we have about how much healthier and safer her natural or "physiologic" birth is, how much better the outcomes are for her and for her baby, but it won't take away that feeling of not being able to afford what rich women have. And what if every woman who made over $200,000 had a midwife and a backup midwife she'd chosen early in her pregnancy, met with regularly throughout, arrive at her home when she went into labor and stay with her until the baby was born, whether that birth ended up as a cesarean or a planned home birth? Then how would a person making $75,000 feel as she had to pack her bag and leave for the hospital in labor?

It is so easy to make fun of the elitism in our movements—artisanal this and that, handcrafted, personal attention to every detail. I can't even write about what these movements are offering at their best without sounding like ad copy. But really, what is so wrong with that? People want handcrafted and personalized care. I have a chair one of my daughters made in shop class. I won't part with it—she *made* it. As chairs go, it may not be up there with an Eames or a Thonet. But it is a Rothman! And oddly, one of my friends finds it the most comfortable of chairs. I toyed with just giving it to her, but I want it myself. So my son took all of its measurements, spoke carefully with our friend about what it was that worked so perfectly about that chair (the precise height of the seat and alignment of the back) and what adjustments would make it yet more perfect for her (another inch of depth in the seat, lighter, and with handles). And now that chair is sitting here, waiting for my friend to come get it. Can you imagine a more perfect gift? It's all about her, her needs, her wants. Given her history of back pain, and how comfortable she says that chair makes her feel, it's probably worth more to her than yet another meeting with an orthopedist and a round of pain treatments. Yet it is, after all, just a chair.

Things that are made for us, tailored for us, all about us, matter. Feeling special and loved—there is nothing wrong with that. What's wrong is that not enough people on earth get enough of that. Making a chair is beyond the skills of most people, I think. Or maybe that's another kind of industrialization and deskilling that I need to think more about. But a lot of us have made something for someone—knitted a sweater, sewn a dress, made a quilt, made something that was specially made for some person, and it made them feel special and loved. We do it often with food. Not all of us have done it, but I hope—and it's not an unreasonable hope—that every single one of you who read this has at some point in your life had some food that someone made specially for you.

The food movement is showing us that we can make food that is healthier and better for all of us—for the planet, and for all the people living on it. We can do this better. We can use our science, and our sense of taste, to make food better. The food movement, like the birth movement, is dealing with the same two lenses, science and taste, to understand and manage our bodies. They have worked to combine the two, not throwing out the science, but not losing taste, in all of its meanings, to the science. Of course there have been attempts to co-opt the food movement as well as the birth movement, to twist the science around to be used against the nonindustrial, less-profit-making ways of being and doing. But somehow that movement still goes along, producing convincing arguments, attracting people to its ideas and values. More and more people are trying to reject industrialization in their food.

Can we do it in our births? Can we collectively and individually say that this too matters, that birth is an important part of our lives, and that each woman giving birth and each baby being born deserve—and need—some care and attention that is beyond industrial rubrics? Can we splash together to create a new current, make birth better in our world today—our local worlds of communities, and in our big international world in which experienced midwives are called "traditional birth attendants" and going the way of European midwives in the past?

It means thinking differently about what birth is, even about what babies are. Babies are not products. They are relationships. They enter the world not through a hospital or even through a vagina. They enter the world as part of someone, a part that grows and starts to move and make itself felt, a part that separates out in a moment that lasts a lifetime.

What is left in our relationships in our modern postindustrial world?

A baby is the one relationship that actually does seem to be forever. We live alone now, more and more of us for more and more of our lives. Have a baby and you can expect to be living with that child till—if you're rich enough and lucky enough—it goes off to college at eighteen. Isn't eighteen years longer than the average marriage now? We lose our childhood friends, our college roommates (no, those have been removed; college students, now accustomed to their own bedrooms, no longer know how to share a room, need their own space, and colleges work to supply it).[20] But this relationship, the one with the child who grows in our bellies, this is a connection, and maybe this too will drift apart, but it is intense, it feels like the one death that really will be crushing, the one relationship most of us feel sure we will have till our last breath, the one person we will love forever, no matter what, unconditionally and eternally.

Is that just a moment of elite privilege? Is valuing motherlove and reifying it as universal a bit of sentimental foolishness on my part? Perhaps. I too have read *Death without Weeping*.[21] But I'm not convinced, not remotely convinced, that that bit of sentimentality is not a good thing. Maybe none of it matters, maybe all of life really is just about loss and fading away. But even if that really is all life is, it just does not feel that way when it starts. Each baby feels like the start of a new world, a fresh chance, the greatest love the world has ever known, all of that. And food—I savor it, enjoy it on my tongue. Does all that matter more as it matters less? As nutrients and people are more and more easily industrially produced, all the love and joy capable of being drained away, am I smarter and more sophisticated if I just nod and say yes, sure, none of it really matters? Or does it matter more as it matters less? As my eating is less and less about keeping my body alive, as my cooking is less and less about the survival of my children and loved ones, does the fact that somehow the necessary nutrients got into the bloodstream matter more or matter less than the experiences and the flavors? And as my genes can be kept rolling on in petri dishes somewhere, to be used whenever and wherever to create a new person with whichever of my genes might be helpful and without whichever ones might be hurtful, does the process matter anymore? Do we care how we get that baby? Or does it somehow matter more as it matters less, the enormity of the symbolic looming as the actual fades away?

The foodies have taught us to think about our food—to worry about the exploited labor from far away that grew it, the agricultural monopolies that alter plant genes in the interest of profit, the practices that cause unnecessary suffering in the animals whose milk, eggs, and meat we eat. They are teaching us to be more thoughtful consumers, more political consumers, to come together and find our power as consumers.

Can we do that with birth now that it too somehow moved from (re)production to consumption? Can we splash together to move from the growing world of international surrogacy in which we are encouraged to think of babies as the product of our precious seeds grown in highly disposable rented wombs, from the push to extend the medical monopoly over birth to every last corner of the world, and from right back home again where a woman is expected to joyfully receive the baby the doctor delivers to her from the gaping hole in her abdomen—can we shift the current to bring us a world in which a baby grows slowly underneath its mother's heart, is birthed in love and in a moment of strength and power? This is the movement we birthies have been working to bring about.

For both of these movements, one could say it is the best of times and it is the worst of times. It is the age of wisdom, it is the age of foolishness, it is the age of organic kale chips, it is the age of McDonald's, it is the epoch of belief, it is the epoch of incredulity, it is the moment of the unattended water birth, it is the moment of the elective cesarean section, it is the season of light, it is the season of darkness, it is the time of the rising of the star of the master chef, it is the time of ubiquitous processed corn, it is the spring of hope, it is the winter of despair.

No—let us end with the spring of hope. Take back the kitchen! Bring birth home! We can do this.

NOTES

CHAPTER 1. A TALE OF TWO SOCIAL MOVEMENTS

1 Gaskin, 1975.
2 Child, 1963–1973.
3 Rothman, 1982.
4 Dickens, 1999.
5 Dickens, 2001.
6 For an interesting discussion of the practice of consumer boycotts, see M. Friedman, 1985.
7 Johnston and Bauman, 2010.
8 Mathews and MacDorman, 2010; Sims et al., 2007; and Singh, 2010.
9 For a discussion of the tension between "democracy" and "distinction" in the food movement, see Johnston and Bauman, 2010.
10 Hogan et al., 2010; and United Nations, 2012.
11 See the work of SisterSong, International Center for Traditional Childbearing, and Commonsense Childbirth.
12 Benford and Snow, 2000; and Goffman, 1974.
13 C. Mills, 1959.
14 Zaretsky, 1976.
15 Zaretsky, 30.
16 Zaretsky, 64.
17 Zaretsky, 67.
18 *The Devil Wears Prada*, 2006.
19 A good and early discussion of this is found in Schrank, 1977.
20 Rothman, 1982, 1989; Simonds, Rothman, and Norman, 2007.
21 Shapiro, 2004, 214.
22 McEwan, 2005, 181.
23 Johnson, 2013.

CHAPTER 2. ARTISANAL WORKERS

1 Gladwell, 2011.
2 I would like to thank JoAnne Myers Cieko for sharing Scriver and Graville, 2009.
3 Morris, 2013.
4 Jaffe and Gertler, 2006.
5 *The Iron Lady*, 2011.
6 Schrader, 1987.

7 Ulrich, 1990.
8 Wolf, 2012, 31.
9 Wolf, 2012, 16.
10 Schrader, 1987, 36.
11 Kobrin, 1966, 353.
12 Donnison, 1977, 120.
13 Brocklehurst, 2011.

CHAPTER 3. NO PLACE LIKE HOME

1 Rothman, 1976.
2 Rothman, 1976.
3 Rybczynski, 1986; but also see Richter, 2015; and Worsley, 2011.
4 Rybczynski, 1986, 62n.
5 Rybczynski, 1986, 60.
6 Rybczynski, 1986, 60.
7 Rybczynski, 1986, 62.
8 Rybczynski, 1986, 72.
9 Rybczynski, 1986, 73.
10 Rybczynski, 1986, 75.
11 Rybczynski, 1986, 113.
12 Rybczynski, 1986, 109.
13 Rybczynski, 1986, 110.
14 Rybczynski, 1986, 20.
15 Rybczynski, 1986, 121.
16 Julier, 2013, 110–11.
17 Julier, 2013, 110–11.
18 Worsley, 2011, 20.
19 Tyson, 1993; and Luce, 2001.
20 Odent, 1986.
21 And I thank Jon Deutsch for introducing me to Erika, and Erika for her careful and thoughtful research.
22 Jon Deutsch, private communication.
23 T. Brown, 2011.
24 Hochschild, 2012, 224.
25 Mitford, 1963.
26 Lepore, 2012.
27 Rosofsky, 2009.
28 And I thank Jon Deutsch for yet another insightful comment.
29 Hochschild, 2012, 224.

CHAPTER 4. LIVING THE EMBODIED LIFE

1 Wolf, 2012.
2 Shiva, 2010.

3 Shiva, 2010, xi.
4 Shiva, 2010, xii.
5 Shiva, 2010, 53.
6 Winson, 2013, 150.
7 Winson, 2013, 163.
8 Winson, 2013, 156.
9 Winson, 2013, 164.
10 There is one exception: Grandma Tildy (Smath, 1979).
11 Ortner, 1974.
12 Ortner, 1974, 72.
13 Ortner, 1974.

CHAPTER 5. TWO MOVEMENTS IN THREE PHASES

1 Brack, 1976.
2 Kamp, 2006.
3 For a discussion of "recluttering" the kitchen and claiming it as a locus of family values, see Freeman, 2004.
4 Donnison, 1977, 31.
5 Donnison, 1977, 33.
6 Donnison, 1977, 34.
7 Donnison, 1977, 49.
8 *Birth of a Surgeon*, 2008.
9 Thomas Dawkes, cited in Donnison, 1977, 24.

CHAPTER 6. PHASE ONE

1 Wertz and Wertz, 1977.
2 Jutel and Goldstein, 2014; and McGann, Hutson, and Rothman, 2011.
3 A. Hughes, 2012.
4 He may only have said this in bumper stickers. See Shallit, 2005.
5 Spurgas, 2013.
6 Shapiro, 2004, 206.
7 Winson, 2013, 16.
8 Winson, 2013, 101.
9 Shapiro, 2004, 35.
10 Shapiro, 2004, 40.
11 Shapiro, 2004, 45.
12 Shapiro, 2004, 87.
13 Shapiro, 2004, 89. See also Freeman, 2004; and Reiger, 1985, on similar patterns in Australia.
14 Shapiro, 2004, 132.
15 Moss, 2013.
16 Smith, 2009, chap. 6.

17 Krishnendu Ray finds breakfast to be the first meal to be Westernized among Indian immigrants.

18 Winson, 2013, 23.

19 Smith, 2009, chap. 7.

20 Smith, 2009, 151.

21 Wolf, 2012, 14.

22 Wolf, 2012, 13.

23 Wolf, 2012, 36.

24 Brack, 1976, 20.

25 Wolf, 2012, 55.

26 Rion in Wolf, 2012, 55.

27 DeLee, 1920.

28 Wolf, personal communication.

29 Haire, 1972.

30 Brendsel, Peterson, and Mehl, 1979.

31 De Lee, 1920, 40.

32 Guttmacher, 1962.

33 Shaw, 1974.

34 Shaw, 1974, 75.

35 Shaw, 1974, 73; emphasis in original.

36 Shaw, 1974, 74.

CHAPTER 7. PHASE TWO

1 "Feeling Jim Crowish?," my youngest daughter, Victoria, the African American one, asked when I described the black, white, and red chili menu.

2 Hauck-Lawson, 1998.

3 Shapiro, 2004.

4 Shapiro, 2004, 63.

5 Shapiro, 2004, 63.

6 Shapiro, 2004, 64.

7 Reynolds, 1962.

8 My appreciation to Isabelle Lee, who did these interviews in a small study funded by the Professional Staff Congress of the City University of New York.

9 Shapiro, 2004.

10 Shapiro, 2004, 65.

11 Shapiro, 2004, 66.

12 Kamp, 2006, 20.

13 Smith, 2009, chap. 20.

14 Kamp, 2006, 40.

15 And I thank Erika Eitland for this as well.

16 Eisenberg, 2013, 225.

17 Eisenberg, 2013, 227.

18 Eisenberg, 2013, 213.

19 Eisenberg, 2013.
20 Mead, 1972.
21 Dick-Read, 1944, 2.
22 Dick-Read, 1944, 5–6.
23 Dick-Read, 1944, 19.
24 Dick-Read, 1944, 8.
25 Dick-Read, 1944, 155.
26 Karmel, 1959, 14.
27 Karmel, 1959, 24.
28 Lamaze, 1956.
29 Karmel, 1959, 95.
30 Karmel, 1959, 66.
31 Bing and Karmel, 1961; and Vellay, 1966.
32 Bing and Karmel, 1961, 33.
33 Vellay, 1966, 50.
34 Bing and Karmel, 1961, 33.
35 Chabon, 1966.
36 Lorber, 1975, 220.

CHAPTER 8. PHASE THREE

1 Gaskin, 1975.
2 Kamp, 2006, 131.
3 Kamp, 2006, 141.
4 Smith, 2009, 259.
5 Kamp, 2006, 123.
6 Smith, 2009, 261.
7 Belasco, 2012.
8 Smith, 2009, 259.
9 Sinclair, 1981.
10 Lappé, 1971.
11 Kamp, 2006, 179.
12 E. Brown, 1970.
13 Katzen, 1977.
14 Belasco, 2012.
15 Kamp, 2006, 192.
16 Kamp, 2006, 192.
17 In Kamp, 2006, 213.
18 The sociologist of cognition Evitar Zerubaval is writing about what is and is not "marked" in social life.
19 Boston Women's Health Book Collective, 1971.
20 Shapiro, 2009.
21 Friedan, 1964.
22 DeVault, 1991.

23 DeVault, 1991, 39.
24 Strasser, 1982.
25 Oakley, 1975, 58.
26 Oakley, 1975, 58.
27 DeVault, 1991, 59.
28 DeVault, 1991, 78.
29 Avakian, 1997.
30 Avakian, 1997, 3.
31 Avakian, 1997, 6.
32 Avakian, 1997, 6.
33 Kamp, 2006, 21.
34 Kamp, 2006, 21.
35 Kamp, 2006, 68.
36 Kamp, 2006, 70.
37 Kamp, 2006, 213.
38 Shurtleff and Aoyagi, 2013.
39 Hazell, 1974.
40 Goffman, 1963.
41 Rothman, 1976.
42 Rothman, 1976, 25.
43 Rothman, 1976, 28.
44 Gaskin, 1975, 375.
45 Kuhn, 1962.
46 Lichtman, 2013.
47 N. Mills, 1976, 131.
48 N. Mills, 1976, 134.
49 Rothman, 1982.
50 Shaw, 1974, 87.

CHAPTER 9. THE RISKY BUSINESS OF LIFE

1 Menticoglou, Gagnon, and Kotaska, 2009.
2 McDonald et al., 2013.
3 MacDorman, Mathews, and Declercq, 2014.
4 Habermas, 1989.
5 Habermas, 1987, 1989.
6 Tramontano, 2014.
7 Ritzer, 1996.
8 Gawande, 2006.
9 Campo, 2014.
10 Freudenberg et al., 2011.
11 Beck, 1992.
12 Hallgrimsdottir and Brenner, 2014.
13 Hallgrimsdottir and Brenner, 2014.

14 Hammer and Inglin, 2014.
15 Armstrong, 2003.
16 Hammer and Inglin, 2014.
17 Hammer and Inglin, 2014.
18 See Flavin, 2010 for fuller discussion, and see the final chapter for a discussion of the work of the National Advocates for Pregnant Women, addressing these issues in the United States.
19 Stengel, 2014.
20 E. Hughes, 1972.
21 *Williams*, 2001, 22; exclamation point theirs.
22 *Williams*, 2001, 22.
23 For more on risk, see Reagan, 2012; and for more on the history of the fetus, see Boltanski, 2013; and Weir, 2006.
24 Apgar and Beck, 1973.
25 *Williams*, 1971, 1069.
26 *Williams*, 1980, 344.
27 Reagan, 2012.
28 Reagan, 2012, 61–63.
29 *Williams*, 2001, 1024.
30 *Williams*, 2001, 1029.
31 *Williams*, 2001, 1011.
32 Reagan, 2012, 225.
33 For a fuller discussion of the political and social construction of the fetus as a new citizen, see Weir, 2006; and Boltanski, 2013.
34 Mitchell, 2001, 118.
35 Mitchell, 2001, 125.
36 Mitchell, 2001, 127.
37 Mitchell, 2001, 135.
38 Reagan, 2012, 227–29.
39 Lyerly et al., 2009.
40 Rothman and Tyson, 2010.
41 Wolf, 2012, 176–78.
42 Giddens and Pierson, 1998, 94.
43 Nestle, 2010.
44 Winson, 2013.
45 Kaufman, 2012.
46 Foucault, 2007.
47 Samerski, 2015.
48 Foucault, 2007; Bartky, 1998.
49 Petchesky, 1980.
50 Armstrong, 2003.
51 Kaufman, 2012, 111–12.
52 Kaufman, 2012, 113.

53 Kaufman, 2012, 4.

54 Winson, 2013, 56.

55 C. Mills, 1959.

56 Weber, 2001.

57 Scrinis, 2013, 41.

58 Moss, 2013.

59 Scrinis, 2013, 40.

60 Scrinis, 2013, 40.

61 Simonds, forthcoming.

62 Gardner, 2009.

63 Tijmstra, 2001.

64 Wolf, 2012, 176.

65 Wolf, 2012, 176.

66 Wolf, 2012, 177.

67 Wolf, 2012, 117.

68 Waldman, 2012.

69 Ringgold, 1997.

70 See summary in E. Friedman, 1959.

71 E. Friedman, 1959, 97.

72 *Williams*, 2001, 315.

73 For a critical review of the active management of labor as developed in Dublin,
see Wagner, n.d.

74 Rothman, 1982.

75 *Williams*, 2001, 323.

76 *Williams*, 1980, 425.

77 *Williams*, 2001.

78 Webb and Culhane, 2002.

79 Wolf, 2012, 117.

80 Wolf, 2012, 117.

81 Wolf, 2012, 186.

82 Teman, 2010.

83 Rothman, 2014.

84 Coxon, Sandall, and Fulop, 2014.

CHAPTER 10. GREAT EXPECTATIONS

1 Murkoff and Mazel, 2008.

2 Sulik, 2010.

3 Davis-Floyd, 1992.

4 Kaufman, 2012, 95.

5 Kaufman, 2012, 97.

6 Kaufman, 2012, 106.

7 Kaufman, 2012, 91.

8 For a thoughtful discussion of the problems facing nurse-midwives in contemporary practice, see Maureen May's 2014 dissertation on the standardization of epidurals in hospitals.

9 We eagerly await the publication of the results Jennie Joseph has been presenting in meetings for years.

10 Tiger, 2012.

11 Cohen, 2013.

12 Klassen, 2001.

13 Flavin, 2010.

14 Diaz-Tello and Paltrow, 2012.

15 Goode, 2014.

16 Guthman, 2011, 276.

17 Ray, forthcoming.

18 Ray, forthcoming.

19 Ortner, 1974.

20 Klinenberg, 2013.

21 Scheper-Hughes, 1992.

REFERENCES

Apgar, Virginia, and Joan Beck. 1973. *Is My Baby All Right? A Guide to Birth Defects.* New York: Pocket Books.

Aries, Philip. 1965. *Centuries of Childhood: A Social History of Family Life.* New York: Random House.

Armstrong, Elizabeth M. 2003. *Conceiving Risk, Bearing Responsibility: Fetal Alcohol Syndrome and the Diagnosis of Moral Disorder.* Baltimore: Johns Hopkins University Press.

Avakian, Arlene Voski., ed. 1997. *Through the Kitchen Window: Women Writers Explore the Intimate Meanings of Food and Culture.* Boston: Beacon.

Bartky, Sandra Lee. 1998. Foucault, Femininity, and the Modernization of Patriarchal Power. In *The Politics of Women's Bodies: Sexuality, Appearance and Behavior,* edited by Rose Weitz, 25–45. New York: Oxford University Press.

Beck, Ulrich. 1992. *Risk Society: Towards a New Modernity.* London: Sage.

Belasco, Warren. 2012. Food and Social Movements. In *Oxford Handbook of Food History,* edited by Jeffrey M. Pilcher. New York: Oxford University Press.

Benford, Robert D., and David A Snow. 2000. Framing Processes and Social Movement: An Overview and Assessment. *Annual Review of Sociology* 26:611–39.

Betty Crocker's Picture Cook Book. 1950. Minneapolis: Hungry Minds and General Mills.

Bing, Elizabeth, and Marjorie Karmel. 1961. *A Practical Training Course for the Psychoprophylactic Method of Painless Childbirth.* New York: ASPO.

Birth of a Surgeon. 2008. Directed by Karin C. Falck. *Wide Angle.* PBS.

Boltanski, Luc. 2013. *The Foetal Condition: A Sociology of Engendering and Abortion.* Malden, MA: Polity.

Boston Women's Health Book Collective. 1971. *Our Bodies, Ourselves: A Book by and for Women.* New York: Simon and Schuster.

Brack, Datha Clapper. 1976. Displaced: The Midwife by the Male Physician. *Women and Health* 1, no. 6 (November–December): 18–24.

Brendsel, Carol, Gail Peterson, and Lewis Mehl. 1979. Episiotomies: Facts, Fictions, Figures and Alternatives. In *Compulsory Hospitalization or Freedom of Choice in Childbirth?,* edited by David Stewart and Lee Stewart, 169–75. Marble Hill, MO: NAPSAC.

Bridges, Khiara. 2011. *Reproducing Race: An Ethnography of Pregnancy as a Site of Racialization.* Berkeley: University of California Press.

Brocklehurst, P. 2011. Perinatal and Maternal Outcomes by Planned Place of Birth for Healthy Women with Low Risk Pregnancies: The Birthplace in England National Prospective Cohort Study. *British Medical Journal 2011; 343:d7400*.

Brown, Edward Espe. 1970. *The Tassajara Bread Book*. Berkeley: Shambhala.

Brown, Tamara Mose. 2011. *Raising Brooklyn: Nannies, Childcare, and Caribbeans Creating Community*. New York: New York University Press.

Campo, Monica. 2014. Delivering Hegemony: Contemporary Childbirth Discourses and Obstetric Hegemony in Australia. Doctoral dissertation, La Trobe University, Bundoora Victoria, Australia.

Chabon, Irwin. 1966. *Awake and Aware: Participation in Childbirth through Psychoprophylaxis*. New York: Delacorte.

Child, Julia. 1963–1973. *The French Chef*. Television show. Boston: PBS.

Cohen, Ellen. 2013. *Laboring: Stories of a New York City Hospital Midwife*. New York: CreateSpace.

Coxon, Kristie, Jane Sandall, and Naomi J. Fulop. 2014. To What Extent Are Women Free to Choose Where to Give Birth? How Discourses of Risk, Blame and Responsibility Influence Birth Plan Decisions. *Health Risk and Society* 16, no. 1: 51–67.

Davis-Floyd, Robbie. 1992. *Birth as an American Rite of Passage*. Berkeley: University of California Press.

DeLee, Joseph B. 1920. The Prophylactic Forceps Operation. *Journal of Obstetrics and Gynecology* 1:34–44.

DeVault, Marjorie. 1991. *Feeding the Family: The Social Organization of Caring as Gendered Work*. Chicago: University of Chicago Press.

The Devil Wears Prada. 2006. Directed by David Frankel. Twentieth Century Fox.

Diaz-Tello, Farah, and Lynn Paltrow. 2012. Birth Justice as Reproductive Justice. National Advocates for Pregnant Women Working Paper. NAPW, New York.

Dickens, Charles. 1999. *A Tale of Two Cities*, Mineola, NY: Dover.

———. 2001. *Great Expectations*. Mineola, NY: Dover.

Dick-Read, Grantly. 1944. *Childbirth without Fear: The Principles and Practices of Natural Childbirth*. New York: Harper and Brothers.

Donnison, Jean. 1977. *Midwives and Medical Men: A History of Inter-Professional Social Rivalries and Women's Rights*. New York: Schocken.

Eisenberg, Ziv. 2013. The Whole Nine Months: Women, Men, and the Making of Modern Pregnancy in America. PhD dissertation, Yale University.

Ferguson, Priscilla Parkhurst, and Sharon Zukin. 1995. What's Cooking. *Theory and Society* 24, no. 2 (April): 193–99.

Flavin, Jeanne. 2010. *Our Bodies, Our Crimes: The Policing of Women's Reproduction in America*. New York: New York University Press.

Foucault, Michel. 2007. *Security, Territory, Population: Lectures at the Collège de France, 1977–78*. Basingstoke: Palgrave Macmillan.

Freeman, June. 2004. *The Making of the Modern Kitchen: A Cultural History*. New York: Berg.

Freudenberg, Nicholas, et al. 2011. *Food Insecurity at CUNY: Results from a Survey of CUNY Undergraduate Students*. Report from the Campaign for a Healthy CUNY. New York: CUNY.

Friedan, Betty. 1964. *The Feminine Mystique*. New York: Dell.

Friedman, Emanuel. 1959. Graphic Statistic Analysis of Labor. *Bulletin of the American College of Nurse Midwifery*, 94–105.

Friedman, Monroe. 1985. Consumer Boycotts in the United States, 1970–1980: Contemporary Events in Historical Perspective. *Journal of Consumer Affairs* 19, no. 1: 96–117.

Gardner, Daniel. 2009. *The Science of Fear: How the Culture of Fear Manipulates Your Brain*. New York: Plume.

Gaskin, Ina May, and the Farm Midwives. 1975. *Spiritual Midwifery*. Summertown, TN: Book Publishing Company.

Gawande, Atul. 2006. How Childbirth Went Industrial. *New Yorker*, October 9.

Giddens, Anthony, and Christopher Pierson. 1998. *Conversations with Anthony Giddens: Making Sense of Modernity*. Stanford: Stanford University Press.

Gladwell, Malcolm. 2011. *Outliers: The Story of Success*. Boston: Back Bay Books.

Goffman, Erving. 1963. *Stigma: Notes on the Management of Spoiled Identity*. New York: Prentice Hall.

———. 1974. *Frame Analysis*. Cambridge: Harvard University Press.

Goode, Keisha. 2014. Birthing, Blackness and the Body: Black Midwives and Experiential Continuities of Institutionalized Racism. Unpublished manuscript.

Guthman, Julie. 2011. If Only They Knew: The Unbearable Whiteness of Alternative Food. In *Cultivating Food Justice: Race, Class, and Sustainability*, edited by Alison Hope Alkon and Julian Agyeman, 264–81. Cambridge: Massachusetts Institute of Technology Press.

Guttmacher, Alan. 1962. *Pregnancy and Birth: A Book for Expectant Parents*. New York: New American Library.

Habermas, Jürgen. 1987. *The Theory of Communicative Action*. Vol. 2, *Lifeworld and System: A Critique of Functionalist Reason*. Boston: Beacon.

———. 1989. *Jürgen Habermas on Society and Politics: A Reader*. Edited by Steven Seidman. Boston: Beacon.

Haire, Doris. 1972. *The Cultural Warping of Childbirth*. Seattle: International Childbirth Education Association.

Hallgrimsdottir, Kristen, and Bryan Eric Benner. 2014. Knowledge Is Power: Risk and Moral Responsibility of Expectant Mothers at the Turn of the Twentieth Century. *Health, Risk and Society* 16, no. 1: 7–21.

Hammer, Raphael, and Sophie Inglin. 2014. "I Don't Think It's Risky but . . .": Pregnant Women's Risk Perceptions of Maternal Drinking and Smoking. *Health, Risk and Society* 16, no. 1: 22–35.

Hauck-Lawson, A. 1998. When Food Is the Voice: A Case Study of a Polish-American Woman. *Journal for the Study of Food and Society* 2, no. 1: 21–28.

Hazell, Lester Dessez. 1974. *Commonsense Childbirth*. Berkeley: Windhover.

Hochschild, Arlie Russell. 2012. *The Outsourced Self: Intimate Life in Market Times*. New York: Metropolitan Books, Holt.

Hogan, Margaret, et al. 2010. Maternal Mortality for 181 Countries, 1980–2008: A Systemic Analysis of Progress towards Millennium Development Goal Five. *Lancet* 375, no. 9726: 1609–23.

Hughes, Austin L. 2012. The Folly of Scientism. *New Atlantis*, Fall, 32–50.

Hughes, Edward C., ed. 1972. *Obstetric-Gynecologic Terminology*. Philadelphia: Davis.

The Iron Lady. 2011. Directed by Phyllida Lloyd.

Jaffe, JoAnn, and Michael Gertler. 2006. Victual Vicissitudes: Consumer Deskilling and the (Gendered) Transformation of Food Systems. *Agriculture and Human Values* 23: 143–62.

Johnson, Nathanael. 2013. *All Natural: A Skeptic's Quest to Discover if the Natural Approach to Diet, Childbirth, Healing and the Environment Really Keeps Us Healthier and Happier*. New York: Rodale.

Johnston, Josee, and Shyon Bauman. 2010. *Foodies: Democracy and Distinction in the Gourmet Foodscape*. New York: Routledge.

Julier, Alice P. 2013. *Eating Together: Food, Friendship, and Inequality*. Urbana: University of Illinois Press.

Jutel, Anne, and Marie Goldstein. 2014. *Putting a Name to It: Diagnosis in Contemporary Society*. Baltimore: Johns Hopkins University Press.

Kamp, David. 2006. *The United States of Arugula: The Sun-Dried, Cold-Pressed, Dark-Roasted Extra Virgin Story of the American Food Revolution*. New York: Broadway.

Karmel, Marjorie. 1959. *Thank You, Dr. Lamaze: A Mother's Experiences in Painless Childbirth*. New York: Lippincott.

Katzen, Mollie. 1977. *The Moosewood Cookbook*. New York: Ten Speed Press.

Kaufman, Frederick. 2012. *Bet the Farm: How Food Stopped Being Food*. Hoboken: Wiley and Sons.

Klassen, Pamela. 2001. *Blessed Events: Religion and Home Birth in America*. Princeton: Princeton University Press.

Klinenberg, Eric. 2013. *Going Solo: The Extraordinary Rise and Surprising Appeal of Living Alone*. New York: Penguin.

Kobrin, Frances. 1966. The American Midwife Controversy: A Crisis in Professionalization. *Bulletin on the History of Medicine* 40:350–63.

Kuhn, Thomas S. 1962. *The Structure of Scientific Revolutions*. Chicago: University of Chicago Press.

Lamaze, Fernand. 1956. *Painless Childbirth: Pyschoprophylactic Method*. Chicago: Regnery.

Lappé, Frances Moore. 1971. *Diet for a Small Planet*. New York: Ballantine.

Lepore, Jill. 2012. *The Mansion of Happiness: A History of Life and Death*. New York: Knopf.

Lichtman, Ronnie. 2013. Midwives Don't Deliver or Catch: A Humble Vocabulary Suggestion. *Journal of Midwifery and Women's Health*, 124–25.

Lorber, Judith. 1975. Good Patients and Problem Patients: Conformity and Deviance in a General Hospital. *Journal of Health and Social Behavior* 16:213–25.

Luce, Judy. 2001. Midwives at the Margins of Life: Home Birth and Home Dying. Master's thesis, Vermont College/Union Institute.

Lyerly, Anne Drapken, et al. 2009. Risk and the Pregnant Body. *Hastings Center Report* 39, no. 6: 34–42.

MacDorman, Marian, T. J. Mathews, and Eugene Declercq. 2014. Trends in Out-of-Hospital Births in the United States, 1990–2012. NCHS Data Brief, 144. National Center for Health Statistics, Hyattsville, MD, March.

Mathews, T. J., and M. MacDorman. 2010. Infant Mortality Statistics from the 2006 Period Linked Birth/Infant Death Data Set. National Center for Health Statistics, Hyattsville, MD.

May, Maureen. 2014. Turning the Board Blue: America's Epiduralized System of Birth; A Medical Ethnography. PhD dissertation, Syracuse University, New York.

McDonald, Susan J., et al. 2013. Effect of Timing of Umbilical Cord Clamping of Term Infants on Maternal and Neonatal Outcome. *Cochrane Library*, no. 7.

McEwen, Ian. 2005. *Saturday*. New York: Anchor.

McGann, P. J., David Hutson, and Barbara Katz Rothman, eds. 2011. *Sociology of Diagnosis*. Vol. 12 of *Advances in Medical Sociology*. Bingley: Emerald Group Publishing.

Mead, Margaret. 1972. *Blackberry Winter*. New York: Morrow.

Menticoglou, Savas, Robert Gagnon, and Andrew Kotaska. 2009. Vaginal Delivery and Breech Presentation. *SOGC Clinical Practice Guidelines*, no. 226 (June): 557–66.

Mills, C. Wright. 1959. *The Sociological Imagination*. New York: Oxford University Press.

Mills, Nancy. 1976. The Lay Midwife. In *Safe Alternatives in Childbirth*, edited by David Stewart and Lee Stewart, 127–41. Chapel Hill: NAPSAC.

Mitchell, Lisa M. 2001. *Baby's First Picture: Ultrasound and the Politics of Fetal Subjects*. Toronto: University of Toronto Press.

Mitford, Jessica. 1963. *The American Way of Death*. New York: Fawcett Cress.

———. 1992. *The American Way of Birth*. New York: Dutton.

Morris, Theresa. 2013. *Cut It Out: The C-Section Epidemic in America*. New York: New York University Press.

Moss, Michael. 2013. *Salt, Sugar, Fat: How the Food Giants Hooked Us*. New York: Random House.

Murkoff, Heidi, and Sharon Mazel. 2008. *What to Expect When You're Expecting*. 4th ed. New York: Workman.

Nestle, Marion. 2010. *Safe Food: The Politics of Food Safety*. Berkeley: University of California Press.

Oakley, Ann. 1975. *The Sociology of Housework*. New York: Pantheon.

Odent, Michel. 1986. *Birth Reborn*. New York: Pantheon.

Oparah, Julia Chinyere, and Alicia D. Bonaparte, eds. 2015. *Birthing Justice: Black Women, Pregnancy and Childbirth*. Boulder: Paradigm.

Ortner, Sherry. 1974. Is Female to Male as Nature Is to Culture? In *Woman, Culture, and Society*, edited by Michelle Zimbalist Rosaldo and Louise Lamphere, 67–87. Stanford: Stanford University Press.

Petchesky, Rosalind. 1980. Reproductive Freedom: Beyond a Woman's Right to Choose. *Signs: Journal of Women in Culture and Society* 5:661–85.

Ray, Krishnendu. 2004. *The Migrant's Table: Meals and Memories*. Philadelphia: Temple University Press.

———. Forthcoming. *The Ethnic Restaurateur*. New York: Bloomsbury.

Reagan, Leslie. 2012. *Dangerous Pregnancies: Mothers, Disabilities, and Abortion in Modern America*. Berkeley: University of California Press.

Reiger, Kerreen M. 1985. *The Disenchantment of the Home: Modernizing the Australian Family, 1880–1940*. Melbourne: Oxford University Press.

Reynolds, Malvina. 1962. *Little Boxes*. Columbia Records.

Richter, Amy G. 2015. *At Home in Nineteenth-Century America: A Documentary History*. New York: New York University Press.

Ringgold, Faith. 1997. Presentation at Brooklyn Friends' School's African American Night, February 28.

Ritzer, George. 1996. *The McDonaldization of Society*. Thousand Oaks: Sage.

Rosofsky, Ira. 2009. *Nasty, Brutish, and LONG: Adventures in Elder Care*. New York: Avery-Penguin.

Rothman, Barbara Katz. 1976. In Which a Sensible Woman Persuades Her Doctor, Her Family, and Her Friends to Help Her Give Birth at Home. *Ms. Magazine*, December, 25–32. Reprinted in *For Women Only*, edited by Gary Null and Barbara Seaman. New York: Seven Stories Press, 1999.

———. 1982. *In Labor: Women and Power in the Birthplace*. New York: Norton.

———. 1989. *Recreating Motherhood: Ideology and Technology in a Patriarchal Society*. New York: Norton. 2nd edition, updated and revised, New Brunswick: Rutgers University Press, 2000.

———. 2000. *Spoiling the Pregnancy: The Introduction of Prenatal Diagnosis to the Netherlands*. Bilthoven: Catharina Schrader Stichting of the Dutch Organization of Midwives (KNOV).

———. 2014. Pregnancy, Birth and Risk: An Introduction. *Health Risk and Society* 16, no. 1: 106.

Rothman, Barbara Katz, and Holliday Tyson. 2010. Letter to the editor in response to Lyerly. *Hastings Center Report* 40, no. 4: 6.

Rybczynski, Witold. 1986. *Home: A Short History of an Idea*. New York: Penguin.

Samerski, Silja. 2015. *The Decision Trap: Genetic Education and Its Social Consequences*. La Vergne: Ingram.

Scheper-Hughes, Nancy. 1992. *Death without Weeping: The Violence of Everyday Life in Brazil*. Berkeley: University of California Press.

Schrader, Catharina. 1987. *Mother and Child Were Saved: The Memoirs (1693–1740) of the Frisian Midwife Catharina Schrader*. Translated and annotated by Hilary Marland. Amsterdam: Rodopi Press.

Schrank, Jeffrey. 1977. *Snap, Crackle and Popular Taste: The Illusion of Free Choice in America*. New York: Dell.

Scrinis, Gyorgy. 2008. On the Ideology of Nutritionism. *Gastronomica* 8, no. 1: 39–48.

———. 2013. *Nutritionism: The Science and Politics of Dietary Advice*. New York: Columbia University Press.

Scriver, Summer Moon, and Iris Graville. 2009. *Hands at Work: Portraits and Profiles of People Who Work with Their Hands*. Lopez Island: Heron Moon Press.

Shallit, Jeffrey. 2005. Science, Pseudoscience, and the Three Stages of Truth. https://cs.uwaterloo.ca/~shallit/Papers/stages.pdf.

Shapiro, Laura. 2004. *Something from the Oven: Reinventing Dinner in 1950s America*. New York: Viking.

———. 2009. *Julia Child: A Life*. New York: Penguin.

Shaw, Nancy Stoller. 1974. *Forced Labor: Maternity Care in the United States*. Elmsford: Pergamon Studies in Critical Sociology.

Shiva, Vandana. 2010. *Staying Alive: Women, Ecology, and Development*. New York: South End.

Shurtleff, William, and Akiko Aoyagi. 2013. *History of Tofu and Tofu Products (965 CE to 2013): Extensively Annotated Bibliography and Sourcebook*. Lafayette: Soyinfo Center. http://www.soyinfocenter.com/pdf/163/Tofu.pdf.

Simonds, Wendy. Forthcoming. *Hospital Land, USA*. New York: Routledge.

Simonds, Wendy, Barbara Katz Rothman, and Bari Meltzer Norman. 2007. *Laboring On: Birth in Transition in the United States*. New York: Routledge.

Sims, M., et al. 2007. Urban Poverty and Infant Mortality Rates. *Journal of the National Medical Association* 99, no. 4: 349–56.

Sinclair, Upton. 1981. *The Jungle*. New York: Bantam.

Singh, G. 2010. *Maternal Mortality in the United States, 1935–2007: Substantial Racial/Ethnic, Socioeconomic, and Geographic Disparities Persist*. Rockville, MD: US Department of Health and Human Services.

Smath, Jerry. 1979. *But No Elephants*. New York: Parents Magazine Press.

Smith, Andrew. 2009. *Eating History: 30 Turning Points in the Making of American Cuisine*. New York: Columbia University Press.

Spurgas, Alyson K. 2013. Interest, Arousal and Shifting Diagnoses of Female Sexual Dysfunction: Or How Women Learn about Desire. *Studies in Gender and Sexuality* 14, no. 3: 187–205.

Stengel, Camille. 2014. The Risk of Being "Too Honest": Drug Use, Stigma and Pregnancy. *Health Risk and Society* 16, no. 1: 6–50.

Strasser, Susan. 1982. *Never Done: A History of American Housework*. New York: Pantheon.

Sulik, Gayle A. 2010. *Pink Ribbon Blues: How Breast Cancer Culture Undermines Women's Health*. New York: Oxford University Press.

Teman, Elly. 2010. *Birthing a Mother: The Surrogate Body and the Pregnant Self*. Berkeley: University of California Press.

Tiger, Rebecca. 2012. *Judging Addicts: Drug Courts and Coercion in the Justice System*. New York: New York University Press.

Tijmstra, T. 2001. Het imperatieve karakter van medische technologie en de betekenis van "geanticipeerde beslssingsspijt." In *Ingebouwde normen: Medische technieken doorgelicht*, edited by Marc Berg and Annemarie Mol, 40–45. Utrecht: van der Wees.

Tramontano, Marisa. 2014. Colonization of the Birthroom: The System, Lifeworld, and Medicalization of Childbirth. Unpublished paper.

Tyson, Holliday. 1993. Witnessing, Waiting and Helping: Parallels between Palliative Care of the Dying and Midwifery Care of the Birthing. Paper presentation, Environmental Studies, York University, Toronto, Canada.

Ulrich, Laurel Thatcher. 1990. *A Midwife's Tale: The Life of Martha Ballard, Based on Her Diary, 1785–1812*. New York: Knopf.

United Nations Department of Economic and Social Affairs, Population Division, Population Estimates and Projection Section. 2012. Infant Morality Rates. World Population Prospects: 2012 Revision.

Vellay, Pierre. 1966. The Psycho-Prophylactic Method: Its Evolution, Present Situation and Prospects. *Report of the Fourth Biennial Convention, International Childbirth Education Association*. Milwaukee: ICEA.

Wagner, Marsden. N.d. The Active Management of Labor. https://www.birthinternational.com/articles/birth-intervention/56-the-active-management-of-labour.

Waldman, Jessamyn. 2012. Presentation at the Tenement Museum, February 2.

Webb, David A., and Jennifer Culhane. 2002. Hospital Variation in Episiotomy Use and the Risk of Perineal Trauma during Childbirth. *Birth* 29, no. 2: 132–36.

Weber, Max. 2001. *The Protestant Ethic and the Spirit of Capitalism*. New York: Routledge.

Weir, Lorna. 2006. *Pregnancy, Risk and Biopolitics: On the Threshold of the Living Subject*. New York: Routledge.

Wertz, Richard W., and Dorothy C. Wertz. 1977. *Lying-In: A History of Childbirth in America*. New Haven: Yale University Press.

Williams-Forson, Psyche A. 2006. *Building Houses out of Chicken Legs: Black Women, Food and Power*. Chapel Hill: University of North Carolina Press.

Williams Obstetrics, various editions:

1971. Edited by Louis M. Hellman and Jack A. Pritchard. New York: Appleton Century Crofts.

1976, 1980, 1985. Edited by Jack A. Pritchard and Paul C. McDonald. New York: Appleton Century Crofts.

1993, 1997. Edited by F. Gary Cunningham et al. New York: Appleton Century Crofts.

2001. Edited by F. Gary Cunningham et al. New York: McGraw-Hill.

Winson, Anthony. 2013. *The Industrial Diet: The Degradation of Food and the Struggle for Healthy Eating*. Toronto: UBC Press.

Wolf, Jacqueline H. 2012. *Deliver Me from Pain: Anesthesia and Birth in America*. Baltimore: Johns Hopkins University Press.

Worsley, Lucy. 2011. *If Walls Could Talk: An Intimate History of the Home*. New York: Walker.

Zaretsky, Eli. 1976. *Capitalism, the Family and Personal life*. New York: Harper and Row.

Zerubaval, Evitar. 2014. Presentation, American Sociological Association.

INDEX

abortion, 35, 160; activism, 214; legalizing, 124; medicalized, 125; therapeutic, 156

activists, 5; abortion, 214; community activism, 114; consumption, 5

adoption, 186

African Americans: food movement and, 6; infant mortality, 6; midwives, 88, 216; rights of women, 215

agribusiness, 1, 6

alcohol, 146, 150, 157, 160, 170; fetal alcohol syndrome, 151

alienation, 8, 93

alternative medicine, 75

American College of Obstetrics and Gynecology, 139

American Journal of Obstetrics and Gynecology, 89

American Society for Psychoprophylaxis in Obstetrics (ASPO), 109–11

The American Way of Birth (Mitford), 49

anesthesia, 68, 86–87, 109, 185; recovery from, 92. *See also* chloroform; epidurals

Apgar, Virginia, 154

Apgar scores, 201

Aries, Philippe, 38–39

artisanal food makers, 14, 16–17, 19, 60, 172; bakers, 212; concern with deskilling, 21–22; costs and, 207; making products available, 20; starting out and selling out, 213. *See also* bakers; chefs; food movement; midwives: artisanal workers

ASPO. *See* American Society for Psychoprophylaxis in Obstetrics

assembly lines, 8, 80

authority, 211; clinical, 167; medicalized, 150; midwives and, 197. *See also* control

Avakian, Arlene Voski, 121

babies: babyhood, 158–59; Gerber baby, 132; relationship with, 220. *See also* newborns

bakers, 20; artisanal, 121; baking bread, 67, 186–87, 198

Ball, Lucille, 103

Ballard, Martha, 27–28

barber-surgeons, 71, 74

Beard, James, 99, 122

Beck, Ulrich, 147

Belasco, Warren, 114, 116

Ben & Jerry's, 117, 213

Benner, Eric, 149

Bet the Farm (Kaufman), 173–74

Betty Crocker's Picture Cook Book, 101

Bing, Elizabeth, 109

biodiversity: food movement and, 61; loss of apple diversity, 58–60

biomedical industry, 1, 179, 202

birth: birthing rooms, 11, 20, 60; breech, 21, 28, 139; bringing home, 221; centers, 33–34, 134; control and, 183–84; convenience in, 192–93; deindustrializing, 145, 181; delivery table, 55, 91, 110, 126; industrialization of, 6, 49, 61, 144–45, 178; instincts and, 55; medicalization of, 17, 89, 102, 124; physiologic, 55, 218;

ABOUT THE AUTHOR

Barbara Katz Rothman is Professor of Sociology, Public Health, Disability Studies, and Women's Studies at the City University of New York, where she runs the Food Studies concentration. Her previous books include *In Labor, The Tentative Pregnancy, Recreating Motherhood, The Book of Life, Weaving a Family,* and *Laboring On.* She is past President of Sociologists for Women in Society and the Society for the Study of Social Problems, and current President of the Eastern Sociological Society. She is proud recipient of an award for "Midwifing the Movement" from the Midwives Alliance of North America.